Pre-Public

"You have combined the art of the comic strip here ... into a literary version of Calvin and his trusty friend, Hobbes."

"The tales of your daily battles with architects and office politics make it easier to fight one's own way through the work week, armed with the knowledge that one need only look with humor at that which seems humorless."

"The inevitable life challenges that we all face are handled with sweet poignancy in 'E-Male.'"

"...this brand of humor has a child-like innocence that is very appealing."

"...a funny, timely, unique book...quite amusing and smart."

"...impressed by the witty and entertaining correspondence between Jeff and Anthony. This could be Bill and Ted, ten years later and college educated."

"Thoroughly Entertaining."

"Very funny and creative."

"I loved reading the random thoughts/machinations of two guys. It is quite fresh."

"Great Stuff."

"The authors are likable, human 'guys' and open about their feelings and their lives. The combination is charming and fun."

"Witty writing."

"...commend you for living life to its fullest. This message surpasses all others in this book."

E-Male

Of Mouse and Men

Jeff Chacon
Anthony Reynoso

Acumen House, LLC
Denver

E-Male: Of Mouse and Men
Jeff Chacon and Anthony Reynoso

Copyright © 1999 by Jeff Chacon and Anthony Reynoso

Published by:
Acumen House, LLC
P.O. Box 12548
Denver, CO 80212-0548
303/480-9501
877/480-9501
303/480-9174 Fax
http://www.acumenhouse.com

Copyeditor:	Charol Messenger/Messenger Literary Services
Cover design:	Shaeffer Reagan Design
Cover photographs:	David Reynoso

Publisher's Cataloging-in-Publication
(Provided by Quality Books, Inc.)

Chacon, Jeffrey.
    E-Male : of mouse and men / authors: Jeff Chacon &
Anthony Reynoso. -- 1st ed.
    p. cm.
    Preassigned LCCN: 98-86744
    ISBN: 0-9665406-4-6

    1. Young men--Correspondence. 2. Electronic mail
messages--Humor. 3. United States--Social life and
customs--20th century--Humor. 4. Male friendship. I.
Reynoso, Anthony. II. Title.

PN6131.C43 1998   816'.54'008017
                         QBI98-1060

Printed in the United States of America

10 9 8 7 6 5 4 3 2 1

Acknowledgments:

The authors would like to thank Kelly Crowther for her inspiration and feedback, Liz Svedek for her early enthusiasm, the members of Colorado Independent Publishers Association for their guidance and support, and all of the "test market audience" who so valiantly gave of their time to offer feedback. We wouldn't be here without you. We would also like to thank our families and friends.

.....for Julie and Alden

Table of Contents

Foreword:

This is the true story of two little boys who once went to the same college (Cal Poly San Luis Obispo) and worked in the same restaurant. Their names are Jeff and Anthony. In the beginning, they were bitter rivals, vying for the attentions of the lovely ladies who worked beside them in the restaurant. Naturally, these women wanted nothing to do with our heroes, but you couldn't (and still can't) convince them of that. Those were the dark days. Days of bitter feuding, back-stabbing, and petty jealousy. However, time and the rigors of cleaning salad bars have a way of forming powerful bonds, and Jeff and Anthony eventually became good friends. Their friendship was based on many things: a love of beautiful women, an almost unhealthy appreciation of beer, and a rather strong sense of humor. All of these things in various amounts provided Jeff and Anthony with many fun-filled adventures over the years. Yes, they did just about everything two friends could do, including houseboating, but there was one more lofty goal to which they aspired -- the formation of their own rock-and-roll band.

This inspired dream was the impetus behind Anthony moving to San Diego to hook up with Jeff in 1992. In San Diego, they enjoyed the rock 'n roll lifestyle: two grown men crammed into a tiny one-bedroom apartment, with Anthony occupying Jeff's sectional couch for more than a year. But even under these strained conditions (most of that strain the direct result of sleeping on a sectional couch), their friendship continued to grow and the small apartment constantly was filled with the sounds of laughter and terrible music. Unfortunately, "The Snipehunters" (sometimes known as "Calvin and the Hip Monks" and "The Rodents of Unusual Size") were a far cry from success, but, like everything else they'd gone through to this point, Jeff and Anthony came away smiling and settled in to continue life as best friends and roommates -- until 1993, that is, when things began to change. Both of the boys found girlfriends (neither of whom worked beside them in the restaurant). Anthony actually got a job; Jeff became restless and bored. So, Jeff married his girlfriend and moved to Denver, Colorado, to pursue his career, of all things. Now, the two friends were faced with the formidable task of sustaining their incredible friendship over a time zone and at least one pretty formidable mountain range.

Over the next few years, they wrote and called each other regularly, but this just wasn't the same as sitting down over a beer and talking about things. While their friendship was still very strong, it was clear that things were different and they were no longer going to be a part of each other's everyday life. Then, Jeff and Anthony both gained access to the Internet and e-mail. Since then, they have entered each other's everyday life again, using e-mail to re-establish and strengthen the bonds that were formed over the salad bar so many years ago. However, these messages that you are about to enjoy don't necessarily revolve around the weather, or how the family is doing. Instead, Jeff and Anthony have used e-mail as a way of interacting with each other on that incredible level of understanding and absurdity that only best friends seem to share.

Some background: Jeff is a 31-year-old structural engineer (which means he works for architects, making sure their buildings stand up), living in Denver, Colorado, with his wife, Julie. Jeff was raised in San Diego, California. He plays his guitar a lot and thinks that skiing is better than sex -- when the snow is nice anyway. Jeff's big dream is to become "Mister Mom," where he gets to stay home with the seven Little Jeffreys (approximately five more Little Jeffreys than Julie wants to have, but don't tell Jeff that), frying up all of that bacon that Julie brings home.

Anthony is a 31-year-old biologist (which means he is unemployed most of the time), living in San Diego. His fiancé, Alden, is living in Santa Cruz, California, pursuing a Master's degree in psychology. Anthony and Alden are set to be married this summer. Anthony, who also goes by the nickname "Duke," was born and raised in Santa Maria, California. His big dream in life is to be an actor, but he also enjoys writing, sports, cartoons, and the wonders of nature.

This is all you really need to know. The rest just sort of happens.

"A friend is one before whom I may think aloud."
                              -Ralph Waldo Emerson.

Chapter 1
In The Beginning....

Date: Jan 22
To: Duke
From: Jeff
Subject: Hellooooooo

    This is a test. This is only a test. If this were an actual e-mail, you would be receiving instructions at this time on how to successfully avoid a hangover. In the event of an actual e-mail, stay tuned for further instructions. This will not be repeated. This message will self-destruct in 60 seconds. This mission, if you choose to accept it, will be a dangerous one. *The big brown fox jumped over the lazy dog. E pluribus unum. In God we trust. The chicken came before the egg. The Sacramento Delta is a body of water, not a letter of the Greek alphabet. "Prince of Tides" was about neither princes nor tides. Discuss. Hear me now or believe me later.*

    Hey, buddy!!! Happy Monday! And happy e-mail as well. Yes, we have finally moved into the nineties. I can leave you annoying little messages that you will receive as soon as you turn on your computer every day and you can send me little spurts of your imagination as they come to you. Phallic, ain't it? I really do enjoy this e-mail thing. I can write little notes to people and never have to waste an evening on the telephone. I can say what I want to say without getting interrupted by call waiting or somebody's mother saying, "Time for bed, Brenda. You have your first day of junior high tomorrow." That is the worst.

    I think we should have a reunion of The Snipehunters on July 18th, two nights before your wedding. And, this time, can we finally name the band "Shag Rug and the Lost Contact Lenses?" Can we? Can we? Can we? Ohhh pleeeeeeeeeeease........We could do the coffee house thang, you know, as usual. And maybe this time we'll just play all night long.....You can play some rhythm guitar; Carol can play some guitar and bass; Tom can play some skins; and maybe I'll play some guitar and bass as well. You see, I am seriously looking to buy a bass right now. Sometimes, when I'm sitting at work making buildings stand up, I get these real down-and-dirty funky-ass bass lines in my head. Since Carol Bass Player Extraordinaire is not here to translate the down-and-dirty funky-ass bass lines for me, I feel that I need my own four-stringed-low-end-guitar-like instrument to explore my own funk. So, start thinking about what songs you might want to strum and sing, and I could start to study the funky-ass bass parts to those songs. And if they don't have funky-ass bass parts, we'll make them up.

    Other topics besides the funk (what else even matters?): How's the job? Treating you well, I hope. Paying you well as well, I hope. Here, I'm still not playing music with anybody on a regular basis, but I do jam with people from time to time. At my last jam session, a guy showed up and played for me that song "Sister Golden Hair Surprise" and I knew I was in trouble. Based on that experience and several others like it where The Eagles and John Denver seemed to be everybody's influences, I'm working towards playing some gigs by myself. Oh, and last weekend, I brewed my first batch of homebrew (home-made beer). It has to sit for a couple of weeks now and ferment or something, but I'm looking forward to drinking it -- and it tasting good -- or me spitting it out in disgust and realizing that I really don't know what I'm doing.

Well, that's about it for now. It's time to go fight with the wife. I'll e-mail you tomorrow with our exact flight information for our trip to Los Angeles this weekend. Until then, *sayonara,* and *buenos huevos.*

Date: Jan 23
To: Jeff
From: Anthony
Re: Helloooooooo

Boy, do I need help. I just read the line, "time for bed, Brenda" and SCHWING! The "first day of junior high" part helped though. Glad to see this e-mail thing works in one direction (kind of like sex). Yes, we are communicating via "The Net" and, thus, we can engage in some typical geek chat. "Kirk kicks Picard's ass!" "Mortal Kombat rules!" I did find your message interesting. You realize, of course, that we're turning into The Who. "Okay, we'll reunite again, but this is DEFINITELY the last time. Until we run out of money again." Yes, I think "Shag Rug" would be quite apropos, although I still prefer Bjork and Beans. The crowd will love it! Perhaps we should enlighten young, untalented Duke as to what the hell we want him to do at the "gig," so he may begin practicing. Anyway, it's good to be connected again, just like we were before the operation.

Hey, do you want to bring your tennis racquet to Los Angeles this weekend? Just a thought. Your input is always welcome. Anyway, I'll let you go now so you can go brawl with Julie. I bet she kicks your ass!

Date: Jan 24
To: Duke
From: Jeff
Subject: Tennis, anyone?

Yeah, we could play tennis this weekend. I hadn't really thought about that. Playing tennis in the smog of Los Angeles....it couldn't be any worse for me than smoking for nine years, now could it? Do you realize it's been three years since I had my last cigarette?

2

Julie busted into the e-mail and read the "Brenda" line, and then she said to me, "I don't get it." I said, "Go read it again." "I still don't get it." Finally, I had to explain it to her. I guess the female mind just doesn't go there, does it? Is this what you might call "the gender gap" hard at work?

I'll be bringing you some goodies this weekend to help you prepare for the reunion gig in July. Will you write a song for your bride?

"Alden Kidd
I'm glad you said you did
and you didn't ran and hid
even though I look like an arachnid
Alden Kidd.

Anthony Reynoso
I do, yes, I suppose so
The fourth Led Zeppelin album was called ZOSO
in the last election, I didn't voto
Anthony Reynoso."

Hahahaha. I think that covert Led Zeppelin reference really did it for me. I am really cracking up. Somebody has to make me laugh when you are not around, and it might as well be me. Is arachnid a word? Heeheeheehahaha. :-) That means I've reached total planet geekdom. I've started to use computer faces in my e-mails. "Uh, yeah, is this Dorksanonymous? When is your next meeting?" It's all over for me. Just to prove it, check these out:

:-D Jeff upon winning the lottery.
!-(Julie with a bug in her eye.
:~) Bewitched.
8-o Mr. Bill just before the house falls on him.
:>) Darren after Samantha turned him into Inspector Clouseau.
:-P Jeff upon seeing the smorgasbord of cookies that his wife just made.
:-] Frankenstein upon seeing the smorgasbord of cookies that his wife just made.
:-o Mr. Bill upon seeing the smorgasbord of cookies that *his* wife just made.
:-(Jeff upon realizing that his wife is taking those cookies to the office.
;-) The guy on the street corner who sells contraband replacement cookies to Jeff.

Anyway, this e-mail is already way too long. You'd think I have nothing better to do than to sit here at the computer, wouldn't you? See you Friday!

Date: Jan 25
To: Jeff
From: Anthony
Re: Tennis, anyone?

Jeff, my boy, how many times must I explain to you that it's not a gender gap which exists between us and our women folk -- it's a maturity gap. That gives me an idea actually. When we return from the bachelor weekend in Vegas and the women say, "Were you at a whorehouse?" we can muster all our dignity and say, "No my sweet, I was at a 'Bed and Brenda'." I will bring my racquet with me this weekend EVEN though we will be staying up late, drinking, AND I have to sleep on a floor at Julie's sister's place. Why can't you play fair? I know you've never tried, but if I hum a few bars.....I guess I need to remember that this is both Jeff and Julie's line, not just yours, so, in light of that fact, I offer Julie some advice for deciphering my e-mail messages. Julie, first think sex, then beer, then music and movies, then Elvis. If none of those works it ain't worth reading. See you guys on Friday and *vaya con huevos*.

Date: Jan 31
To: Duke
From: Jeff
Subject: Home again

O.K. I'm sitting here drinking my first bottle of homebrew, and let me tell you: it's potent stuff, and I's a bit drunk. On a weeknight. What a shame. It is pretty tasty, though. Not Wynkoop Railyard Ale (my favorite beer) tasty, but with a little work...who knows?

Well, it was a blast to see you and I would have finished you off if you hadn't intentionally broken your racquet on that metal net. When the going gets tough, the wimps break their racquets and claim, "I can't play anymore." If you can't stand the heat, stay out of the kitchen. Seriously, it was a good time. I look forward to the gig and the tennis rematch in July with much anticipation. But first, there is the little matter of Las Vegas and your bachelor weekend to concentrate on. When do you want to go? We still haven't figured that out. Early May, right? Should I just set a date and let everybody know? Are we looking at three days this time? My boss gave me a incredible review today, so I'm looking to take an extra day off if you are.

Hey, I bought a bass tonight. A yellow Fender bass -- from a kid, who is saving up to buy a car so that he can go back and forth to work. No, I didn't feel guilty. I gave him 120 bones for it. And now I am the funkiest mofo in Denver. Look out, world!

4

Date: Feb 1
To: Jeff
From: Anthony
Re: Home again

Geez, I'm sitting here going, "A bass? Why'd he buy a fish?" Early weekday mornings, what can I say? Yet another useful vehicle in your quest to lower property values in as many U.S. neighborhoods as possible. Don't feel guilty about helping one of our nation's youth in his struggle to buy a car. Now the fact that his big dream is to use it to go to work is a bit scary though.

If you couldn't put me away when I'm playing with half a racquet, how do you figure on doing it when it's not broken? This is some of the weakest smack I've ever heard. Speaking of racquets, Alden brought her tennis racquet to me over the weekend, so I'm going to try and keep this thing in one piece for a while. Yeah, enjoyed the opportunity to see you guys, too. With regards to the rest of your message, the beer sounds mighty tasty. Wish I was there to reap the fruits of your labor. As far as Vegas goes, how about the third week in May, if that works for everyone? And, yes, I'd like to go for three days if possible, but we'll have to see. Anyway, we'll talk soon. You guys take it easy and don't listen to any threats that Coors might throw at you. With that I say good night now and get low with yo' funky ass se'f. Oh, and have fun "slappin' your instrument." OUT!

Date: Feb 7
To: Duke
From: Jeff
Subject: Confessions of a Golf Junkie

Oh, boy. Here we go. As you know, I used to HATE golf. But apparently it is now becoming a political thing. Both Julie and I work with people who play; therefore, we feel that we need to learn as well. Five years ago, if a client asked me, "Do you play golf?" I would have said, "Yeah, right. What are you, some kind of demented sadistic moron?" But, today, a client said to me, "I belong to the Blahblahblah Country Club. Do you play golf?" After my initial urge to take his head and shove it up his....subsided, I calmly replied, "Why, yes, I do. I need some time to warm up, but by springtime I'll be ready to play. Why don't you call me when you want to play?" Dude, I'm sick. I mean, I'm a scum-sucking good-for-nothing butt-smooching money-grubbing yuppie now. I have become the epitome of all things I never wanted. And you know what? It ain't so bad!! I make some cash, I schmooze with the other half (the upper half), and I feel slightly better than completely unimportant. Surely you understand. Anyway, shall we plan on a round of golf in July to go with our GrudgeTennisMatch Part 2? I told my dad I'd play with him on that trip home; maybe we'll make it a foursome? I've basically screwed myself into a corner now, because I have to learn how to play and, more importantly, I have to learn to like it -- without throwing my clubs, probably without beer, and without the beercart. Oh, well. Growing up sucks, and ya know? I'm really scaring myself. What happened to the hopeful idealism of my early 20s?

Learning to play golf for political reasons sucks, kissing butt rules.

Date: Feb 8
To: Jeff
From: Anthony
Re: Confessions of a Golf Junkie

Sure, I understand. I understand why commercials for Windows 95 featured a Rolling Stones song. I understand why Peter Gabriel's new video has him laughing in a steam room with a bunch of bimbos. And I understand why Johnny Cash sings the praises of Folger's coffee on the radio. I understand all these things -- cash. Let me ask you something, if you worked with a bunch of gay dudes, would you learn how to...well, you know. DO NOT KISS ASS!! If you start kissing ass, I can't be too far behind because I base my entire life on your teachings. If you don't want to play golf, then don't. All it's really going to do is take away from your tennis game. Seriously, your arm gets all confused by the different motions. I think the part that irks me most, however, is, "It ain't so bad." To quote one of the informed philosophers of our time (Jim Rome, of course), "WHAT...IS...THAT?" Shame, shame!! This isn't like you, Jeff. Hey, wait a minute, maybe it's not you. Maybe this is Julie writing this! Maybe this is Julie's way of trying to make me think you sold out so I'll quit calling and there'll be no more talk of Vegas, beer, wom...bats, tennis, Elvis, stri...king teachers, and music. HA! It's no use, evil Wife Woman, I'm on to your little scheme. Jeffman will never sell out and justice will prevail. And, with that, I leave you by saying ass shining sucks and the real Jeff rules. OUT.

See, you got me so flustered that I almost forgot to address the rest of your message. We can play golf in July if you REALLY want to as long as we play on our own terms -- sneak a cooler in, swear, throw clubs, cheat, and terrorize old ladies with our golf cart. I wish you were here this weekend; one of the boys is having a birthday party and we're gonna let him unwrap some presents. Wink wink. Anyway, keep swingin'.

Loyal to the end,

Dukey

Date: Feb 8
To: Duke
From: Jeff
Subject: Apologies and Everything

Uhhh, sorry about that kissing butt thing, dude. *Mi esposa* got a hold of the computer and....well, you get the picture. I would never let you down by kissing some dirtbag yuppie's butt. And golf.....I'd rather have each one of my nosehairs plucked out one by one by some fat guy named Norman while watching reruns of "Star Search" and having liver and onions forced down my throat at the same time than play *that* "game." Where did she get that? Jeeez. And besides, it would wreak havoc with my tennis game.

Last weekend Julie and I finally broke down and moved into the 1960s. Yessir, we bought a dishwasher. And, now, I'm telling everybody it was because I was doing entirely too many dishes. HA! I thought you'd get a kick out of that. Me? Doing entirely too many dishes? That's like saying Kevin Costner does entirely too much acting!

I did speak to your brother about the "Male Weekend of Nurturing, Exploration, and Bonding" in that Capital of Culcha, Las Vegas, and he said the May 18th weekend sounds fine. I'll start to work my connections and see where we can stay.

Whoa -- Chris Duarte, the best guitar player alive right now, is touring again. I know this because he's coming back to the Fox Theater in Boulder in March. We saw him last summer, and he is absolutely amazing! Go see him and his group, The Chris Duarte Group (duh), and you will not be disappointed. If I had 1% of his talent, I would blow myself away.

Finally, enjoy your weekend. Julia *y yo* will be spending Saturday around the *casa*, cleaning and drinking homebrew. Sunday, we will be practicing God's sport -- skiing. Floating down humongous *montañas* faster than the speed of light is quite a good time. Although last time I was out I stumbled and did a horrific face plant. Literally. My head hit the snow like so many melons dropped from twelve stories up. So there I was, lying with my head planted into the snow. I slowly pulled my head up, surprised to be alive. A girl about ten feet away said to me, "Are you conscious?" "Uh.....maybe. Are you an angel? Is this Mount Heaven?" I slowly dusted myself off, realizing I deserved a concussion from this fall, but only end up with a mild fat lip and a headache that was quite like no other. Dull throbbing pain, with a distinct Coors Light hangover feel to it. Yuccccchhhh. Yet I will return to the slopes. I may slow down a bit to start, but I'm sure I'll return to my Speed Racer tendencies shortly. And I'm sure this story has killed any micro-desire you may have had for learning to ski. Anyway, enjoy your weekend, whatever you do. Face Plants suck, dishwashers rule. OUT.

Date: Feb 11
To: Jeff
From: Anthony
Re: Apologies and Everything

     My friend, I am having an excellent weekend if last night's NBA All-Star game is any indication. No, I'm not talking about how Air Jordan wins the MVP with no FGs, FTs, or PTs in the 4th QTR. I'm talking about Shania Twain, dressed in black leather from silky shoulders to edible ankles, singing one of the greatest songs around, "Oh Canada." So, now you want me to think about Vegas when my mind is still lost in the mountains of Canada (a.k.a. Shania Twain). I will go on record right now as saying that Shania Twain is the most gorgeous creature on the face of the earth (next to Alden, of course). You are not the only one who can kiss ass around here! Hey, I'll go check out Chris Duarte if you go see "Leaving Las Vegas." Extremely powerful movie!! Solidifies all rumors that Nicolas Cage IS "The Man." Take Julie, too, because, while the movie is very disturbing, I think it would make for great conversation. And, remember, Wednesday is Valentine's Day -- because *she'll* remember.

     Did I ever mention to you that Chandler Bing totally reminds me of you? Anyway, enjoy your trip to the slopes and don't worry about destroying what little desire I had to ski. There was none. Dishwashers DO rule and vacuum cleaners suck. OUT!

Later, eh,

Anthony

Chapter 2
Architorture and The Great One

Date: Feb 12
To: Duke
From: Jeff
Subject: Architorture

Mama, don't let your babies grow up to be architects. 'Cuz they suck. We didn't practice God's sport (skiing) this weekend, because He told us not to. So, we were hoping that He would let us go skiing next weekend. But noooooo. Instead of skiing, I'll probably have to work this weekend --because of an architect. Imagine that. Work getting in the way of religion. Anyhoo, I'm designing "Chicken and Bagel Shacks." If you haven't heard of Chicken and Bagel Shacks, you will. Courtesy of me. So, anyway, instead of a March 15th deadline to finish designing the Shacks, which was not quite reasonable in the first place, I now have a February 26th deadline, which is completely insane. All because the architect told the chicken people, "Uhh.....yeah, we can do it in that time. Sure! Insane deadlines rule!" Anyway, the point of my story is that I will not allow any of your children (or Alden's children, for that matter) to grow up to be architects. They should be something sane, like a personal injury lawyer or a sanitation expert. Besides, architects make less than engineers and, lord knows, we're underpaid. Health care, that's where the bucks are. Just ask my lovely wife. Ahh yes, the joys of marriage. I am one of those guys, much like yourself, who says "I don't mind if you make more dinero than me, Honey. In fact, I encourage you to make as much as you possibly can." Because, since we got married last May, half of what Julie makes is mine and half of my $5.00 an hour is hers. And she is sitting pretty. Due for another raise, even. Dude, she's been in her field of choice for a little over four years now, and she is making more than I'll probably see in the next ten years. And I've already been working ten years!!!! What is that? Am I griping? Certainly not. She's my wife. But all of a sudden I'm feeling dangerously underpaid. And the fact that my wife makes almost 150% of my salary is making me want to change my major. Is it too late for that? The good news is that the company I'm working for is grooming me for future ownership. Then maybe I'll catch up to my wife (yeah right!!). She'll probably be CEO of her company by then, or will have started Julie Health Care Inc., where I'll be answering the phones. Anyway, I'm not complaining. But when it comes time to decide who stays home with the Little Jeffreys, the choice will be easy. ME!! Because I'm the poor one.

Architects suck, rich women rule, OUT!!!

Date: Feb 13
To: Jeff
From: Anthony
Re: Architorture

Okay, I sense a lot of tension here. Ah, yes, my friend, I have listened to your plight and, believe me, I can empathize. Of course, health care is the way to go and, if my kid wants to be an engineer, I'll basically disown him. If he wants to be a biologist, however, I'll save him the trouble and shoot him dead on the spot. That's love. But it's obvious you had a bad day yesterday while, for the most part, I had a pretty good one. Wanna hear about it? Here it goes. Between the federal government, which is closed for repairs 90% of the time, and the state government, of the state which you spurned a few years ago, I'll be receiving nearly 1000 bones in tax returns this year; 987 to be exact. That's pretty much it as far as happiness goes. It's unfortunate that three states separate us because it sounds like you need a day of record-store browsing, guitar playing, and beer swilling with me. But since that's not to be, you'll just have to suck in your testes and deal with it. And, remember, it could be worse. Griping about inadequate sums of money is a helluva lot better than griping about none at all. Besides, it all adds up in your master scheme to someday be a house husband.

9-to-5 sucks, domestic lifestyle rules. OUT!

Date: Feb 14
To: Duke
From: Jeff
Subject: Wives and Hockey

Hey, it's almost 7:00 a.m. on a Wednesday. I worked until 9:00 last night, then watched *NYPD Blue,* like I always do. So I didn't get a chance to e-mail last night. But the real news is that Julie just informed me that she quotes Wayne Gretzky during meetings and presentations. The Great One: "I skate to where the puck is going, not to where it is." My Wife: "Ditto." I am completely and overwhelmingly impressed with her. She doesn't even like hockey. Can't stand it even. But she knows a good motivational quote when she hears one. Wow! Happy Valentine's Day, dude. I would ask you to be mine, but I'm claimed by The Great One (a.k.a. Julie).

Working SUCKS, Smart Babes we marry RULE -- like you wouldn't believe! OUT.

Date: Feb 14
To: Jeff
From: Anthony
Re: Wives and Hockey

Yeah Julie, quoting The Great One. I was wondering what happened to you this morning. It was more or less insanity at my work today. This is how the place operates: six weeks of nothing, then two weeks of insanity. Valentine's Day is pretty depressing for those of us deprived of our loved ones. What makes it worse is when some asshole says he'll be your valentine except for the fact he belongs to "The Great One." What up with that? Someone at work arranged for a florist to bring in some flowers today, so everyone was down in the lobby buying flowers for their loved ones. But I, the Grinch, who stayed on the second floor, was not. Oh well, I'll get my lovin's this weekend when Alden comes to town. We're going to the Mystery Cafe (interactive theater), then staying at some swanky hotel in Del Mar. WOO HOO!! So, listen, you guys have lots of fun today -- and tonight, "cooperating," as it were. Love ya both.

Valentine's Day sucks, Groundhog Day rules. OUT!!

Date: Feb 15
To: Duke
From: Jeff
Subject: The Great One

The Great One and I (sounds like a movie title) just got back from our *mucho favorito* local restaurant, Sabor Latino, where we scarfed on Chilean Wine, Chile Rellenos and Chilean Stir Fry. Yummmmmmmy!! And that is how our first married Valentine's Day went. Now, we're going to hit the proverbial hay.

Now, it's morning time. The Great One had a 7:00 a.m. meeting (probably to talk about those trade rumors), so she's already gone. I am sitting here wondering exactly how it can be only Thursday? I've worked so much this week that it should be Sunday. And I don't feel like going in today, obviously. I've got a 10:00 a.m. meeting with my idio....uh, architects, where I get to tell them "No!" a lot, and beat them over the head with all the questions they probably don't have any answers to, even though the project is due in ten days. That's the way architects are, trust me. They never have the answers to your questions. It's always, "Uhh....I'll get back to you. Someday." Nah, I don't mean to complain. It's not all that bad. It's really part of the business. But, someday, I -- like you someday -- will be able to stay home and take care of the little Great Ones, write e-mails all day, change diapers, play the guitar, go to the store for more formula, and.......

Architects still suck, Chilean wine RULES!!! OUT!

Date: Feb 15
To: Jeff
From: Anthony
Re: The Great One

Unlike you, I spent my Valentine's Day watching a double-header Kings-Lakers thang on TV last night. Tell The Great One I hope her hip pointer is okay and that if they trade her to the Rangers and force my boy Luc Robitaille to leave a legit Stanley Cup contender to return to "The Joke in the Smoke" (The Los Angeles Kings), I'm going to be pissed. Glad you guys had a nice time last night. Chilean wine, chile rellenos, stir fry. I'm surprised Julie's even talking to you this morning, considering the fireworks display you must've put on last night. Speaking of fireworks, I'll be heading down to the Sports Arena tonight to see the San Diego Girls (Gulls) play some team from Bakersfield. Realistically, if we can't beat an ice hockey team from Bakersfield, we suck. I mean the only time you see ice in Bakersfield is when the Coors truck overturns. Alden will be here tomorrow morning so, naturally, I can't wait for that. So, let's see, if Julie is The Great One that would mean Alden would have to be likened to a hockey legend of almost the same stature and the only one I can think of is Mark Messier. Therefore, I will dub Alden, "Mess." Truly apropos.

Bakersfield ice hockey sucks, Alden Mess rules. OUT!!

Dukester

Date: Feb 16
To: Duke
From: Jeff
Subject: Multicultural Friends....

Did you see last night's episode of *Friends*? Joey moved out!! OhmyGod. What's going to happen now? Will they ever see Joey again? Are they going to get a new Friend? Maybe they can get a Hispanic Friend. That would be cool. Maybe he can be an ex-gang member from Santa Maria, California. You should call the producers of the show, my friend. Because a Hispanic Friend would be cool. He could teach the other Friends how to say such things as *puta tu madre, chingazo, donde esta mi cerveza,* and *burrito.* Heck, they could have Spanish cooking classes. Monica could take some ideas back to her restaurant, where they would promptly give her a big fat raise because of her brilliant Spanish cooking ideas and the fact that the restaurant does better selling Mexican food than any other kind. Then Monica could open her own *burrito* stand, right across the street from the Daily Grind, where every other Friend would stop by and see her on their way to the coffee shop, which they apparently go to every day. Then maybe all of the Friends could take a trip to California and visit Chula Vista or Santa Maria, one of which is the homeland for the Hispanic Friend, where they would marvel at the sights and sounds of Hispanic America. Maybe the Hispanic Friend could get shot by an old rival who has been looking for him for a dozen years. (Mandy Patinkin, of course, would have to play the rival. "Hello, my name is Inigo Montoya. Ju keel my father. Prepare to die.") Then maybe Phoebe could fall for a Hispanic gang-banger in Chula and convert him to the Friends' lifestyle, bring him back to New York and learn his Hispanic songs on her guitar. At which point, she would record her first album, composed entirely of old Hispanic standards. It would be a smash hit, and Phoebe would tour FriendAmerica with Linda Rondstadt, selling out stadiums and arenas all over. Then Joey would come back into the scene, realize that the Hispanic Friend is taking over his old slot in the lineup, and decide that something must be done. So they would get into a huge fight (ala *West Side Friends Story*), the Hispanic Friend would get killed, Joey would get probation and move back in with Chandler, and everything would return to normal -- because there just aren't enough Hispanics on television and *that* sucks.

Working for a living sucks, Apple Jacks and Fridays RULE!!

Date: Feb 16
To: Jeff
From: Anthony
Re: Multicultural Friends...

Okay, I've finally stopped laughing long enough to reply. I think you need to cut down on the Apple Jacks, bro. My only regret is that I don't know what the hell you're talking about. For you see, I was at the Sports Arena last night watching the San Diego Gulls kill the Fresno Falcons (consensus in the stands was that the bird on their sweaters looked more like a buzzard). I like this concept of yours, but I'd add that while Monica is having great success with her Friend-ly Mexican Finger-Food place, she naturally has to "do" the Hispanic Friend, prompting Phoebe to get extremely jealous, leading to an all-out naked wrestling match in a big vat of Monica's Thick and Friendly Salsa. Better still, why not have an all-Hispanic version of the show and call it (naturally) "Amigos." You can star as Chuey, the wise-cracking *vato loco*; I'll star as Julio, the low-rider who wants to be an actor. Julie can be Raquel, the *ruca* waitress down at the Taco Bell, and Alden can be Aldiente, the half-breed *ruca* who wants to be the next Selena. We could all live in a government project down in Imperial Beach and all sorts of great Amigos could drop by and visit while we're hanging out down at the Taco Bell; Amigos such as Ugly Naked Vato, Officer Puto from Immigration, and El Stupido, the ex-gang-banger who's now a special officer with the cops "trying to get all you Amigos off the street." We could do funny things like make shadow animals using the search lights from the FBI surveillance helicopters and programming our useless burglar alarms to play "La Cucaracha." One of the constant storylines could be how you secretly love Raquel and want to "make a run for the border." Then everybody will want a "Raquel cut" (hair down except for the very front which sticks straight up in the air like she ran into a wall or something). Aye, aye, aye (think of Aldiente). Then on a very special "Amigos," Chuey would get deported and learn he's actually a descendant of an Aztec king. Will Chuey leave the "Amigos" if he can get

13

back over the border? Tune in *Miercoles noche a ocho* o'clock *y* find out. Outstanding effort on the e-mail, *amigo*. One of the best.

        Awesome e-mails rule. OUT!

Julio

Date: Feb 18
To: Duke
From: Jeff
Subject: Chucho Chacon

        The Great One and I just finished watching *Mi Familia*. So I turned to her at the end of *la película* and said, "That's what we'll name our first born, Chucho -- Chucho Chacon." Works, doesn't it? We watched *la película* at your suggestion and, let me tell you, it was a *great* movie! I honestly didn't think that Detective Bobby Simone.....er, Jimmy Smits (This raises the question: Is he Hispanic? Or does he merely play one in the movies? I never thought he was Hispanic) could pull it off, because I know him so well as the troubled cop on *NYPD Blue*. So when he came into *la película*, I kept waiting for him to spout off: "It would be in your best interest to not lawyer up but to tell us exactly what went on in there and who killed your wife." But no, he did a fantastic job with his role. That scene where he and his arranged wife discover each other while they're naked is intense. I was a little pissed off when his wife died and he went back to being an idiot, but it was a great movie and anything with Esai Morales is worth checking out. I liked it. It had a little anti-establishment attitude, a little sex, a lot of emotion, a great cast, and some great humor. A must see, and a movie that I may need to own, and I don't buy too many movies.

        Well, have a bitchin' week. I'll spend my week satisfying what must be an intense worldwide desire for chicken and bagels. Because we're cranking that shit out. And, you know, I go to meetings, and they don't even bring any free bagels or chicken. What is that? I could threaten them -- "Bring food, or the beam gets it," but what's the use?

        Ooh ooh ooh -- I almost forgot. We found our Chilean wine (*Concha Y Toro*) at the liquor store -- and it's bloody cheap. It's very tasty, so we loaded up on it. I suggest you do the same, if you can. The Merlot or the Merlot blend (half Cabernet) are pretty decent. Once you see the price, you'll think they're incredible. $2.99 a bottle!!! Can you get cheaper than that? And it's good. Yeah, I know, I don't drink wine, but it's a marriage thing. *Mi esposa* drinks the stuff, so slowly I am drinking the stuff. I am becoming a wine drinker, dude. Combine that with the new mutual fund that we set up and the new washer/dryer/dishwasher thing that we have going, we're talking complete sold out Double Income No Kids Yuppies here. That's DINKY. Naw, don't worry. I still brew my own beer, write my own rebel songs, beat on opponents on the court, and fart in crowded rooms. That part of me will never change. Nor will my love for great movies.

Cheap wine rules, Mondays will always always always -- until I win the Lottery -- SUCK!!!

-Chucho y Toro

Date: Feb 19
To: Jeff
From: Anthony
Re: Chucho Chacon

Ever so enraptured by the fact that you enjoyed *Mi Familia* and even happier about the fact that you called it by its real name instead of its commercialized *gringo nombre*, "My Family." Just another case of suckin' up to "The Man." It's too bad *gringos* can't seem to grasp the power of the Mexican influence. I point out again that you can say anything to a woman in Spanish and she's yours. A certain woman from my past used to go nuts over this technique which included breathy renditions of such sweet nothings as, "La cuchara esta en la cocina" (The spoon is in the kitchen). Well, let's see, Alden and I had a great weekend which included a trip to the Mystery Cafe here in San Diego, which is, to coin a phrase, "A must." It's an interactive theater play where they feed you and make fun of you all night and, because I just happened to be sitting in very close proximity to the stage, I was dubbed "Stanley the Stud" and was pawed at by this totally gorgeous actress all night long. This was a dream come true. I mean, not only was I getting manhandled by this woman but the whole time Alden was just sitting there laughing like hell. A very entertaining show but only average food. Yesterday, we went and saw "Dead Man Walking" which is a very good but majorly intense flick. This means that I've now seen all the Oscar nominated films this year except "Sex and Sensibility" or whatever it is and there's about as much chance of me seeing that as there is of "Babe" actually winning Best Picture. Although, to be quite honest, "Babe" is a fantastic film and it wouldn't pork my rinds to see it win. As for "Dead Man," another must see, but I like "Leaving Las Vegas" better. And Penn is good but he's not fit to pour Nicolas Cage a glass of cheap Chilean wine. $2.99 huh? I normally don't drink anything under 4 bucks (per 1.5 liter), but I'll see if I can find some because of your recommendation. Anyway, I'm going to go to work now even though it's President's Day and the rest of the bloody world is off. Have a good one.

Not recognizing dead presidents sucks, movies about Mexicans rule. OUT!!

Date: Feb 21
To: Duke
From: Jeff
Subject: Chicken and Bagels....

Eet's almost over....dee whole world will be able to enjoy chicken and bagels in shacks that I created for them...with their creamy filling and luscious chocolatey coating...dey will enjoy a chicken for breakfast and be able to walk next door for a bagel for lunch, or vice-versa...can't you just see it?! I will be the king!! I will eliminate all other forms of food, including the dreaded liver and onions that nobody seems to like!! The whole world will be drooling at my feet because I give them exactly what they want -chicken and bagels!! I will rule dee world!! HAHAHAHAHAHAHAHAHAHA...............

Yes, *mi amigo*, it's almost over. But next on tap for me is a shopping center with a Starbucks, a Blockbuster, a different bagel restaurant, and a liquor store. Yep, that's me. Providing Corporate America with little shacks in which they can sell their wares. I disgust myself. I'm a Corporate America Whore at this point. But I do have one saving grace -- I don't necessarily patronize the shacks which I build. No sir. Unless, of course, they happen to be liquor stores. Happy Wednesday.

Date: Feb 21
To: Duke
From: Jeff
Subject: Naked Ironing

Jeez, I'm upstairs ironing, naked, and I realize that I forgot one thing: Corporate America Sucks, Naked Ironing RULES!!! OUT!

-Chucho

Date: Feb 21
To: Jeff
From: Anthony
Re: Naked Ironing

Gonna be one of those days I can tell. Checked the e-mail this morning and found six messages. One from Naked Ironing Man and even one from our old friend George who now lives in Colorado, if you can believe that. He says to tell you Hi and he just got a new drum set and I'll leave it at that. I don't want to be responsible for tremors in the Rockies. Speaking of the Rockies, put some clothes on. So, last night, I went for an audition for a play despite the fact that I'm already committed to play softball and can't rehearse Friday nights. But I figured what the hell? If THEY say I can't do it, I won't. I'm not going to cheat myself out of any opportunities just because I'm not sure about schedules. Anyway, the director told me afterward, "So what part do you want?" "Well, I want to be director." What the hell is that? I guess I should consider it some kind of compliment that I can do what I want, but I kinda think the director should exercise a bit more control over this sort of thing. Anyway, I'm supposed to have a call-back Thursday so, then, we'll go over schedules and such. I'd like to be able to do it since it'll get me off the streets and keep me busy, but it'll seriously cut into my writing and guitar time. What are your thoughts, Hobson? More than likely, I'd get to play a grouchy old man with a heavy Norwegian accent, so it could be fun.

Directors suck, naked sex rules. OUT!!

Moco

Date: Feb 21
To: Duke
From: Jeff
Subject: Naked Chicken Dance

Yes, I'm home early. I finally lost control and started throwing bagels at my co-workers while doing the naked chicken dance, and they told me I could "go home, try to get some professional help, take a few days to think about something else besides chicken and bagels, and look for a new job." Naw, just kidding. I finished my work a tad bit early and thought I'd leave the office before 7:00 for once in my life. Or so it seems. Anyway, I'm gonna pop open a cold one and play the Stratocaster like she's never been played before, if you know what I mean. By the way, can I have George's e-mail address? I can rock-and-roll in Greeley, nothing wrong with that.

Conflicts between softball and lesbianism, ur, thespianism suck, getting home before dark rules!!!

-Señor Pollo.

Date: Feb 22
To: Jeff
From: Anthony
Subject: Sympathy for the Bagel

Hola. Ya know, considering all your work, maybe they'll name a bagel dish after you. The Jeffrey Special. A beer batter bagel smothered in mushrooms and mashed pataters with a side of Twinkies. Or maybe the chicken place will honor you with some (what else?) Chacon Pot Pie. Oh, shit, now I've done it. Now I've given myself a craving for a chicken pot pie from the Chicken Pie Shop. Wouldn't be as good without you though and, besides, I don't know how the hell to get there. So the director finally called last night -- at 10:15. One of the trade-offs to getting to work so early in the morning is that I go to bed early as well. So when the phone rang at 10:15 it woke me from a blissful dream involving myself and the cover of the latest issue of "Rolling Stone," which featured Jennifer Aniston's buttcheeks in all of their glory. Hmmm, yummy. Check it out if you haven't already seen it. So, I'm going back tonight to read for the director again, but, honestly, I just don't know about directors who call at 10:15 at night. Truth is, the play isn't anything like I thought it'd be. With a title like *I Remember Mama* I thought for sure it was about Elvis.

I'll send you George's e-mail address. Tell him you saw it in a men's room under the heading "I like to beat things -- call me." and figured he was a drummer. Why not? He thinks he's one.

I will now go to work and continue to undermine the efforts of my lab partner. You have a good one and, if anyone gives you grief today, tell 'em they can take their chicken, put it in between a sliced sourdough bagel, top it with hand-leaf lettuce and ripe tomatoes, weigh it down with Secret Sauce, add a Coke on the side, and cram it right up their corporate butthole.

Unreasonable deadlines suck, suckin' down brew while playing your Strat rules. OUT!!

Duke

Chapter 3
Chicken, Bagels, and Ghosts Of Girlfriends Past

Date: Feb 22
To: Duke
From: Jeff
Subject: Beers, Bagels, and Babes

Dear Mr. Brando,

You may not remember me, as I am sure you hang around a different crowd now that you are famous and everything, but I used to be your roommate. San Diego, 1993. Ring a bell? I thought not. We were even in that band, "Marlon and the Meltdowns," remember? No? Anyway, the point of my letter is not to reminisce; rather to ask for a little help to the next rung on the ladder of success. You see, I, too, am an actor. Yes, I know, you never thought I'd become an actor. But once I saw the success you were having, I decided to try it myself. And now that you are famous, and you have won all those awards, I thought it wouldn't hurt to ask for a little help. Because I am not able to land the parts like you. I am not the kind of actor who has directors saying to me, "What part do you want?" And I, like Mandy Patinkin (warning: lame *Princess Bride* joke coming up), am not left-handed. So, I'll take anything you can give. I'll play the strokeable cat in the next *Godfather* movie. I'll play the Streetcar in your remake of *Streetcar Named Desire*. I'll play a pillow in *Another Last Tango in Paris*. Anything, Mr. Brando. I'll do anything. I'll shine your shoes, I'll wash your underwear, I'll lick your butt. JUST HELP ME GET INTO THE BUSINESS!

Yours Truly,
Jeffwannabe.

Architects Suck.

So, uh, how'd it go tonight? Are you a star yet? Are you nominated for any awards? Because you, my friend, are a stud muffin. And I am proud of you. A bit jealous, naturally; but, at this point, I have given up my lesb...thespianism for the renewed love of the geetar. Anyway, I hope it went well, because once you make it to Hollywood and start hanging out with the likes of Mrs. Tommy Lee, Mr. Marlon Brando and the Tweed Sisters (Shannon AND Tracy), I will write the letter above. Because I will ride your long flowing coattails to the TOP!!!!!!!!!!!

Have I mentioned lately that Architects Suck?

I received a call from Jim O'saka today. And that's exactly how my receptionist spelled it. O'saka. I didn't know he was Irish.

19

Architects. I'm in a meeting this morning, no bagels, no frickin' chicken, no sustenance of any kind. "Uh, we got some bad news, guys. Although the entire project is due on Monday, we've decided to make the building bigger and add a Trojan World (as in condoms) store to it. Can you have it on our desk Monday by noon?" Just kidding. It was pretty close, though. The project is due on Monday, and the architects are not even close to being done. I can't really finish making the world safe for bagels, chicken, and condoms until they are done. You gotta love architects. If it weren't for architects, our jobs would be so much easier. However, if it weren't for architects, we wouldn't have a job!!! So, I had a meltdown when I took their drawings back to my office, started looking at them and realized how far they are from being done. But I'll be okay, and the world will eventually have Chicken and Bagels to fill their fat little tummies.

A good point of all this: I'll turn the Chicken and Bagel Shacks over on Monday, and I'll ski Vail on Tuesday. After all, God rested on the seventh day, didn't he? And He would have skied that day, if such a thing had existed. So, I'll rest on the 15th day, or whatever it is, and do what God would have done. Ski.

You know what else? I hate having people check my shit. My boss is checking my work now to insure that a steel beam doesn't fall on some loser's head as he/she bites into a juicy morsel of chicken. I mean, it's gotta be done, but it sure does raise some anxieties in me. I guess getting fired one time really screws you up. So, I'm sitting on pins and needles, hoping that I did everything exactly right, not realizing that never happens; and I'm thinking about Chicken and Bagels at all hours of the day, going over and over and over and over the project in my head -- when I'm in the shower, when I'm laying some cable, when I'm driving to work......"Did I design that beam for the chicken load, or for the bagel load?" It sucks. And you know what? Tomorrow, everything will be just fine. There will be some comments, because bosses would look stupid if they couldn't find at least one thing wrong with some peon's work, but it'll be just fine. In fact, it'll be good. Rave reviews. But I can't see that now, because I am anxious about it. All it takes is one anal retentive butthole to tell you, "Uh, Jeff, I don't think this is going to work out. Clean out your desk by five o'saka," and you start to become anxious about these kinds of things.

Wow, that was deep.
Architects suck, Acting RULES!!!!!!!!!!!!!!!

-Paranoid

Date: Feb 23
To: Jeff
From: Anthony
Subject: You like me. You really like me!

My guess is that your boss will probably say something like, "Uh, Jeff, right here where you wrote 'fucking bagle,' you spelled bagel wrong." Architects do suck. Wasn't Mike Brady an architect? 'Nuff said. Greg was going to be an architect but decided to become Johnny Bravo. By the way, have you ever seen that cartoon? It's pretty cool.

You're going to have to read this part in your best "Godfather" voice: "Ah, yes, my friend, you have been a good man. You gotta nithe little wife, washer, dryer...but you never call me Godfatha. Neva have I once thipped a pint of your homemade beer. I'm thtill waiting to order chicken and bagelth to go. Now you come to me wanting to get into show business. 'I coulda been a contenda,' you say. I will see to it that you get into show business. But always there ith a price. And you're price is to help my cousin in hith quetht to become an architect. Think about it won't you? Now come gimme a kith..... lower...thass nithe."

Anyway, I did get the part of Uncle Chris, a 58-year old Norwegian fat guy who's always bitter. The director says she'll have to age me (I told her to lock me in a room with a bunch of architects), get me a beard (I told her I stood a better chance of parting the Red Sea), and that I'd have to fatten up. Imagine. It should work out great. There are no rehearsals Friday nights or weekends, so I can still play softball, write, and play guitar. What a happy little elf I sound like.

Hey, that "O'saka" thing is great. Who knows, maybe he *is* Irish. Maybe under that outwardly Oriental exterior flows the green blood of a true Irishman. I doubt it, though; he doesn't drink.

El Mariachi was a very cool movie but the premise of switching your guitar case with a hit man's sounds like a storyline from a *Three's Company* episode. I liked it though and I'm glad to see Robert Rodriguez can now hire some real women to star in his movies. Seen *Desperado* yet? After that, you'll definitely want a big bowl of chips and some Salma.

Architects definitely suck, Irish Orientals rule. OUT!!

Evil Uncle Chris

Date: Feb 25
To: Duke
From: Jeff
Subject: Bagels Advocate

PRESS RELEASE:

DENVER: Renowned Structural Engineer/Philanthropist/Actor/Guitar God /Green Thumb Extraordinaire/All Around Handyman Mr. Jeffrey C. Chacon, Esq., today announced that he has made the world safe for Bagel and Chicken lovers everywhere.

"Yes, yes, I realize that you all have been waiting weeks for my latest invention, but quality always takes time, don't you know." Chacon then proceeded to walk reporters and a few gathered special guests through his latest invention -- a combination Chicken Restaurant/Bagel Shop. "The idea first came to me when I was walking down La Jolla Boulevard many years ago with Muffy who, as you all know, is my beautiful wife. I was eating a MLT Sandwich on an onion bagel. That stands for Mutton, Lettuce and Tomato; and I like it when the mutton is real lean.....Anyway, some young punk surfer dude was chasing his bikini-clad girlfriend down the boardwalk there and, in his hand, was a chicken leg. Being that he was a punk, he was eating the chicken leg, not one of the truly juicy and tasty parts such as the breast or the gizzard.

"As he approached Muffy and me, he tripped and fell on a rock or something and the chicken leg went 'splat' right onto my bagel sandwich. I was quite taken aback. I started to throw my MLT away when a voice from the ground, which turned out to be the surfer dude, said to me 'uhh.... huhuh....you gonna eat that, dude?' I said, 'Of course not, you idiot. What do you take me for, some kind of commoner like yourself?' I threw the ruined MLT into the trash and prepared to take my wife and go home. The dude grabbed the MLT with the chicken residue on it out of the trash and started to eat it. 'Hey, dude, this tastes great,' he said. 'You really gotta try this!!! Come on, dude!!!'

"I could not get rid of the scoundrel. As he followed me up the street, begging me to try this weird combination of bagel and chicken, I finally said 'All right,' just to get rid of him. And here we are today, and soon the whole world will know the unique taste that is chicken and bagels. I would like to thank that guy and maybe send him a small token of....oh, never mind."

Chacon's Bagel and Chicken Shacks are slated to be built in every neighborhood, on every block, in America. "I personally guarantee the structural safety of every one of the Shacks," said Chacon. "We're going to eliminate McMeat's, Burger Hut, and all those other beef-based fast food joints. Soon America will live, breathe, and eat chicken and bagels!!!!" Thousands cheered him as he ended his speech and began taking orders for chicken and bagels at the first store, right here in Denver.

Hey, dude. We engineers really get no glory, so I'll give myself some in a fantasy sequence. What the hell, right? And, yes, this morning at 11:00 a.m. your time, it will be all over. The world doesn't have any idea what is going to be coming down the line. I take my drawings to the architect, they put them on a CD ROM, issue them all over the country, and just like that -- Chicken and Bagels for everybody. Don't you just love the capitalist corporate America?

Soooo, let me get this straight. You're a 58-year-old Norwegian fat guy? Talk about a reach. You're not old, you're not fat, you're not Norwegian. But I don't doubt that you can pull it off. In fact, I think you'd do pretty well with the part. I could get you a few Chicken and Bagel type projects to work on so that you can really age like you should. Working with architects for just a few minutes a day will take years off of your life!! And show it, too!! Hell, I look like Grandpa Simpson right about now...

Whoa. It's bedtime for me. I gotta get some rest for tomorrow's final push toward an American Chicken and Bagel Future. Pretty darned exciting, if you ask me. Have a wonderful Monday, won't you? And call me when you've got that Norwegian accent down. I have no idea what one even is supposed to sound like.

No glory sucks, parts with accents rule!!!! OUT.

-Visionary

Date: 26 Feb
To: Jeff
From: Anthony
Subject: Rebuttal

PRESS RELEASE:

DENVER: Jeff Chacon, noted chicken and bagel magnate, was arrested earlier today after a seven hour stand-off with a SWAT team. Details are sketchy at this time, but early reports indicate that Chacon walked into a Burger Hut and began making loud and obnoxious comments about the structural ineptness of the building. When asked by management to leave, Chacon brandished a very tightly rolled set of blueprints, asked "do fries come with that shake?" and knocked the manager unconscious. He then locked the manager, crew, and twelve patrons in a meat locker. The SWAT team was called to the scene when it was discovered that Chacon had taken hostages and was threatening to replace all the beef in the establishment with ground chicken and the buns with bagels.

"The guy was completely mental," said a police spokesman as he noshed on a double-burger with cheese. "He kept saying, 'You'll thank me for this someday.' Poor guy. I understand he was a structural engineer, so you can see why he did it."

The SWAT team used tear gas to bring out the suspect after he turned on the PA system and started playing Sheryl Crow's new CD *Days of Whine and Roses* at full volume. "We were willing to forget the whole thing up until that point," the police spokesman added; "but he'll get the chair for this." Speculation as to Chacon's actions centers on the fact that his chain of restaurants, "Bird in a Bagel," laid an egg. The suspect's wife pleaded for leniency. "All he ever wanted to do was bring you healthy food in a safe environment. Is that so bad?" Apparently, it is.

Hey, I've heard good things about the new Muppet flick. Might have to take Alden next week when I go see her for her B-day. That would be cool to someday star in a Muppet movie. Maybe "Muppet Man of La Mancha" or "The Muppet Mark of Zorro." How about some Muppet porn? Miss Piggy starring in "The Other White Meat." Okay, let me speak for all the ungrateful when I say congratulations for finishing the infamous "Chicken and Bagel Caper." Now, go have a double cheeseburger on me.

-Dan Rather

Date: Feb 27
To: Duke
From: Jeff
Subject: Nada and Then Some.

Hola, bandido. The Great One and I slept in this morning (mostly because she hasn't been feeling well) and we'll probably go in a bit late, because it has been snowing all night, which always makes for a fun commute across town to *la oficina.* Driving in the snow is a tedious project at best.

Hey, a quick question as I'm listening to the radio: When the hell did Sting become "alternative?" Especially now. I mean, I can't tell the difference between him and Michael Bolton.

Blasts from the past Department: (1) I was enjoying that same Muppet flick the other night when a thought occurred to me: Miss Piggy reminds me quite a bit of our old friend Samantha. No disrespect intended towards Samantha; quite the contrary. Miss Piggy is quite a class act. She and Samantha have many of the same mannerisms and expressions, and they do look slightly alike. (2) I was walking through the grocery store the other day when I saw this Patty lookalike standing near me looking at the same vegetables I was looking at. So I, being the brave soul that I am, turned around and ran over to another aisle, where I stood and enjoyed the magazines. The Lookalike soon showed up there, too. Dude, she followed me all over the grocery store! I kid you not! Every frickin' time I turned around, there she was. I was SCARED. So I paid my bill, got in my truck, and took side streets all the way home, all the while watching my rear view for a Suburban (isn't that what she drives?) that might be following me. Fortunately, I lost her. Whooooo. It was a bit of a nightmare in the daytime.

Time to go be ironic and iron some clothes and figure out how to get to work in this lousy weather. Have a bitchin Tuesday, won't you?

Ghosts of Ex-Girlfriends Suck, A Good Snowstorm RULES!!! OUT.

-Señor Barracho.

Date: 27 Feb
To: Jeff
From: Anthony
Subject: REACTION

The only thing Sting is an alternative to is Sominex. But this doesn't surprise me. He's made one lame attempt at a jazz album and gets a Grammy nomination. *Sting: Man of Many Facets.* Hope The Great One is feeling better today. My sympathies with regards to driving in the snow, but even more sympathy for having to shovel it. Then again, you knew the job was dangerous when you took it.

In regards to your Blasts from the Past Department, I can see you flying through the backstreets of Denver screaming, "They're baaaaack!" Yes, I fear you are right, Samantha and Miss Piggy could've been separated at birth. The only other celebrity lookalike I can think of to that extent is my old roommate (a.k.a. Naked Idiot Man) and Michael Stipe. By the way, I fear that REM is developing the "U2 disease," clinically known as "Myopia of the Press Clippings" syndrome.

You know, I don't know why this didn't register the first time you wrote it but you do an awful lot of ironing these days. Geez, you buy a house, you buy a dishwasher, you iron your own clothes. You, my friend, have "come down from the trees" so to speak. You have evolved into a domesticated man, forever shaking off the lifestyle of the "hunter and gatherer." Don't get me wrong, this is not a bad thing; I was just curious as to how long it would take. But it's good to see you settling in while retaining that "cutting edge" mentality you've always had. Ironically enough (ha ha), I too ironed clothes last night while the Lakers bludgeoned the N.Y. Dicks. So good luck with the daily commute and tell The Great One to get better real soon so she can shovel the driveway.

Sting sucks, a good snowstorm 1000 miles from where I live rules.

Señor Cucaracha

Date: Feb 27
To: Duke
From: Jeff
Subject: Omnipotent Technicolor

Every time I watch *NYPD Blue*, I realize that the life of a structural engineer is an easy one. Get up early, go to the office, make a few architects miserable (or, more often than not, vice versa), clean up, go home. Not like a cop. There was this dude on the show tonight who decapitated another dude. And this dude was psycho, talking about the "omnipotent technicolor" or some shit, and the cops had to sit there and listen quietly, all the while not being able to say what they were thinking, namely "You are one crazy psycho loser, you know that? They oughta cut your *cajones* off, shove them down your throat, and then throw you into a cage filled with wild dogs who haven't been fed in years." So, every Tuesday night, I appreciate my quiet little life that much more .

I also notice one thing as I go through life: There is a vast difference in the talent levels of shows like *NYPD Blue* and, oh, *Beverly Hills 90210*. First of all, the acting on *90210*, at least the few times I've forced myself to sit through it, is horrific. The acting on *Blue* is incredible. If I were acting in Hollywood, I would not be able to call myself an "actor" if I were on *90210*. However, if my agent ever called and asked if I would like to play a psycho on *Blue,* I would respond with a hearty, "Hell yes!!" They get the best psychos on that show. The dude tonight was ranting and raving, soft and loud, intense, and just plain loony. I would like to have that part, and be able to play it just as well. So, my lesb...uh, thespian friend, I tell you this: when you give up on this biology sham and go to where your real talents are, namely acting, I had better never see you on a lame show like *90210,* because I will have lost respect for you at that point. I also think the highest respect from me will come only when you guest star on *The Simpsons.* And you can't be just a voice. You must be a character. "Duke, the porn star." "Duke, the Chippendale's Dancer." "Duke, the most incredible golfer in the whole wide world." Gag!!!! Or, they could characterize you. "Duke, the Duke."

Well, *amigo*, it's time for me to go see how The Great One is doing. I think she's feeling better. Have a nice day, won't you? I'll be busy wreaking as much havoc as humanly possible on the world of architecture. Speaking of which, Thursday is Free Skiing Day at Copper Mountain (a local ski resort), so a buddy and I were thinking about going. Then I got a call from my local butthead Chicken and Bagel Shack architect, who said, "Uh, Mr. Chacon? Yeah, we need you to come to a meeting on Thursday because we want to change part of the structure of this building." I tried and tried to get out of it, but no. I have to go to a stoooopid meeting that will involve me for about *cinco minutos*, instead of practicing God's Sport. For free. What a rip. Maybe I oughta go to the meeting and start spouting off about how the "Omnipotent Technicolor is coming to get us all," huh? That would get me out of the meeting early.

Architects continue to Suck, NYPD Blue Rules!!!!

-La Vida Facil

Chapter 4
Lovable and Squishy Psychos

Date: Feb 28
To: Jeff
From: Anthony
Subject: Sunny Side Up

I would love to concur with you about the acting on *NYPD Blue,* but, truth be told, I've never seen the show. However, I've seen the cast members in other projects, so I know the talent level is extremely high. Problem is, dude, you and I could never play psychos because we're too fuckin' lovable and squishy. And the one time I did get to play a psycho I was a lovable and squishy psycho. As for the talent base on *90210*.....boy, my mind just went completely blank. I guess that pretty much sums it up. But if they did offer me a part on that show I might take it just because that show actually may need a lovable, squishy psycho. Other than Tori, of course. And, yes, my ultimate dream is to one day be an animated character. If we had kept the band together, maybe we could've been the next big act to play at Moe's:

"Hi, are you Moe?"

"Yeah, that's me. I'm Moe from Moe's Tavern."

"We're the Snipehunters. We're the band."

"Oh, yeah. Hey I love that song 'Sunny Side Up'."

"That's 'Shiny Side Out'."

"Ah, who cares. You're ripping off the Replacements anyway. Listen, luxury accommodations are waiting for you guys right through that door. And don't use all the toilet paper."

"Uh, Moe, there's a drunk throwing up in the dressing room."

(A voice from the distance) "Hee-ey, it's the Snipehunters of Unusual Size. BUUURRRPP!"

Well, slap a stamp on my ass and mail me to Heaven. Today our receptionist came in and brought me a box of...ready?...BUSINESS CARDS!! They've got my name on them and everything. Excuse me, I think I'm going to cry. Never mind the fact that I have nothing to do with them (I am engaged after all), but I now have business cards and voice mail...I'M A *REAL* BOY!!

Anyway, sorry to hear that you can't go "godsporting" for free tomorrow. Chicken architects do suck the life right out of a person, don't they? But cheer up, into everyone's life a little snow must fall and, when it does, you can continue to godsport. Have a capital day and I'll rap it down to you later. Tell The Great One to please hurry up and get better.

Sick Great Ones suck, business cards rule. OUT!!

Happy Boy

Date: Feb 29
To: Duke
From: Jeff
Subject: Coolia

If Coolio had a wife, would he name her Coolia? And would their kids be Cooliotos? Cooliatos?

Grammy summary, at least the little bit that I saw: Alison Krauss beat out Alden's understudy for female album of the year? What is that? I mean, Shania Twain is everywhere. Every time I turn on my tube, there she is. On the *Grammies*. On Letterman. Hell, I'm surprised she hasn't been on the cover of *Rolling Stone* with her butt cheeks showing. You wouldn't mind that, I'm sure. But back to the *Grammies*, at least the little bit that I saw. Dwight Yoakam rules. The Mavericks are a close second. They played with Flaco Jimenez on the accordion. And both Dwight and the Maverick/Jimenez team blow Shania (not what you are thinking, read on:) off the stage. Sorry, dude. I'm just not impressed with her voice. She's a babe, sure, but that only counts for so much. Show me a woman with voice and a big pair of.....vocal chords (yeah, that's it) and I'll show you Baberaham Lincoln. Of course, my Great One only sings in the shower; but, man, you should hear her. If The Great One weren't so shy, I would encourage her to take up singing.

Happy Leap Day. And I ask you: Why the hell do we have to work on a day that doesn't exist 75% of the years? I hereby support any presidential candidate who runs on the platform that Leap Day will be a national holiday and, if it falls on a Saturday or Sunday, we'll get Friday or Monday as the holiday. Perot would understand. Of course, to top it all off, I have to go to a frickin' chicken and bagel meeting instead of Free Skiing. At least I'll be nice and cranky when I walk into the meeting: "Uh, Jeff, we'd like to..." "NO!!"

I guess it's time for me to get into the shower and get ready for the day that doesn't really exist. Sure Happy It's Thursday!!!

Free Skiing on Days That I Have To Go To Meetings SUCKS, The Great One RULES!

-Leap Jeff

Date: Feb 29
To: Jeff
From: Anthony
Subject: Leap Day

A few of my own thoughts regarding last night's *Grammies*:
Separated at Birth...
Alanis Morrissette...and Carol Bass Player Extraordinaire Olsen?
Coolio...and Beetlejuice?

28

You seem to be suffering from overexposure to Shania. This I fail to understand. How can you be suffering from overexposure to The Queen of the Universe? Face it, buddy, this may be the most perfect-looking woman to ever grace the face of Planet Earth, Planet Reebok, The Daily Planet, whatever. As for her voice, did she sing last night? My apologies, but I often shut down my other senses besides sight when I see her, because I'm convinced that if I channel all my energy to my eyes I'll be able to develop X-ray vision. Not that I'd have to have very powerful X-rays since she never wears anything and God bless her for it! Yes, Dwight Yoakam does rule. I didn't get to see Flaco but I know the Mavericks are good. Speaking of bad singing in a live situation, I love "Kiss From A Rose," but I don't think Seal sounded good at all. I actually thought Alanis sounded great because she was singing and not whining at the top of her lungs.

Concur on your Leap Day idea! As a matter of fact, since you brought it up, why don't you run for President? Hell, on that platform alone you'd get my vote (and yes, I'm registered this year, so don't go there).

Spent yesterday afternoon trying to learn some of my lines for the upcoming production. The lines are short but they come quickly and they have to be done with a lot of energy and a Norwegian accent which still sounds highly Italian to me. Not only that, but every once in a while I can still hear myself slipping into my *Tony Montana* voice. "Why don' jou try sticking jour head up jour ass, see iff it fiss."

Anyway, time for me to get to the real work at hand. Kick some chicken architectural ass in your meeting, and godsport like a fiend this weekend. Talk to you tomorrow.

Myopia sucks, Shania rules. OUT!!

The Future Mr. Twain

Date: Mar 1
To: Duke
From: Jeff
Subject: Boats Fall Down Go Boom

I just gotta tell you: *Sergeant Pepper's Lonely Hearts Club Band* is easily by far and away the worst movie ever made. Got that? The worst movie ever made. Unless, of course, you want to spend two useless hours of your life watching the Bee Gees and Peter Frampton slaughter one Beatles song after another in a movie with a plot that is, at best, ridiculous. The best part of the movie was Earth, Wind and Fire, probably because they were on screen for the shortest amount of time. It was that bad. Do you remember the few times the Snipehunters played (and I use that term loosely) "Birthday?" We were better than this movie. By about 100 times.

Anyway, that's enough of my bad movie review. We all knew it would be bad, after all. On to bigger and better things. Did I tell you about

29

the guy who a few weeks ago on a Friday afternoon asked to speak with my "supervisor?" Here's the run through: This guy, we'll call him Mr. Butthead, wanted to lease his building to "Boats etcetera" or some shit like that, but he has a wood floor. So, naturally, he called me to come out and take a look and see if his floor will support some bigass boats. So, I went to see Butthead's building and I came back to the office to think it over. I decided that the boats would make the floor fall down go boom, and that ain't good. Anyway, trying to fully understand the situation, I got into a discussion with this idio...uh, guy on the phone about the weight of the boats. He told me the rear axle weight of a boat trailer fully loaded is 3000 pounds, and the rear axle of a boat has a tire at each end. So, I said, "That's 1500 pounds per tire. Right, sir?" And this asswipe went BALLISTIC on me. Because, no, contrary to popular belief, that does not equal 1500 pounds per tire. It equals some other shit, I don't even remember what. Some "Omnipotent Technicolor" or something. So, I tried to talk this guy through the fact that 1+1=2, but he didn't get it. So, he asked me, "Is there a supervisor or someone there I can talk to, because I am getting frustrated with you." I replied, after a moment of thought, "Yeah, dipshit, there are actually two supervisors, but they are both gone right now. I'll have them call you Monday morning." It was kinda funny, in a demented sort of way, because I never had somebody ask to speak to my supervisor before. My boss talked to this Mr. Butthead guy eventually, and I'm essentially off of the hook, because this guy thinks I'm an idiot when actually I'm right, duh, 1 + 1 does equal 2. At least don't have to talk to him anymore. That makes me happy, because I was about ready to let this guy have it over the phone. Remember that scene from *Fast Times at Ridgemont High* where Brad tells the customer "I'm going to kick one hundred percent of your ass!!"? That was me.

Man, I have been cranky all week. Don't you hate those kind of weeks? Cranky every single day. Ready to snap at any given moment. Probably because I worked both days and Friday night last weekend and I have been unable to practice my religion in a few weeks. Skiing, of course. We'll have to address this issue soon, although The Great One is probably not feeling well enough to go this weekend. Maybe I'll work some this weekend and go Monday. That would be cool. Then again, if I win the Lotto on Saturday, I'll ski the entire month of March, taking time to check and write some e-mails, of course.

That's about it for me on a Friday. Time to get into the shower and yes, find something to iron. Have an excellent weekend.

Fridays always rule, Speaking to my supervisor sucks.

-The Crankmeister.

Date: Mar 1
To: Jeff
From: Anthony
Subject: A World Gone Bats

Hola, mijo. You are right, I've checked three different calculators and they all say 1+1=2. You fuckin' genius you. Yes, SGT. PEPPER may be the worst movie to date, but there may be a viable contender waiting in the wings (Do this in your best "nasally Hollywood reporter" voice): Word has it around Tinseltown that hunky Val Kilmer has flown away from the next "Batman" movie, thereby leaving the role of the Caped Cutey open to some of Hollywood's other leading beefcake. Sources say that pouty David *X-Files* Duchovny was up for the role but that the extra money needed to restyle the cowl to cover his nose would've pushed the picture over budget. Over budget? That's no reason to halt production, is it Mr. Costner? Holy Honker David, you're out. The leading candidate to be the Big Bat is rumored to be that dashing doc of the *ER*, George Clooney. One has to wonder, though, where they'll get the money needed to restyle the cowl so that the ears comb forward. Clooney is used to working with bats. In his last (unfortunately, this term only implies chronologically) movie, *Dusk To Dawn*, Clooney played one of the high-strung Gecko brothers who went down to Mexico and met up with molten Mexican *muchacha* Salma Hayek and her bad band of bat-didos. With Clooney as Batman, Chris O'Donnell as Robin, perky Alicia Silverstone as Batgirl, and villains Uma Thurman as Poison Ivy and Arnold Schwar...z...ah, you know who I'm talking about as Mr. Freeze, maybe we'll all luck out and there'll be another talking pig movie that year. This is Babwa Wawa and I am OUT!!

Yep, apparently, Val figured, "Hey, shit, I've starred opposite Pacino and DeNiro. I'm Doc Holliday. I don't need this shit. Besides, has anyone seen Michael Keaton since he flew the belfry?"

Having someone ask to speak to your super isn't so bad, if you are the super. Some lady did that once when I was managing a restaurant in Santa Maria. She waddled in on a day when prices increased and was upset that I didn't give her feed at the old price, so she asked to speak to my manager, at which point I said, "Yes, ma'am," spun around in a circle, and said, "Can I help you?" Basically, I told her, "I am the manager, and you don't get no stinking discount. OUT!!"

Please to not be cranky my friend. Count your blessings. Jou got a byootiful woman. Jou gotta chob, mein. Jou gotta leel Cyberspace fren. Jou got it all. Every dog hass hees day. On second thought, if that's the case, call it your day and go bite someone in the ass. Have a great weekend and I'll type to you soon.

Val Kilmer rules, George Clooney sucks. OUT!!

Babwa

Date: Mar 3
To: Duke
From: Jeff
Subject: The Return of The Ski Bum.

Now, this here's a story 'bout a man named Jeff
poor engineer trying to keep the world fed
one day he was out makin' chicken and bagel shacks
up from his mind came an architect attack
Chicken that is
Bagels too
Impossible deadlines

Next thing you know old Jeff's a burned out engineer
Kinfolk said, "Jeff, get away from there."
Jeff said, "O.K." and "before I jump from this ledge,
I'll be loading up the truck and going to Breckenridge."
Skiing, that is
White Gold
Colorado Tea

Aah, yes. While the rest of the world toils over such things as where to build all the Chicken and Bagel shacks I designed, I will be practicing my religion this morning -- floating down mountains on a pair of fiberglass contraptions, looking much like Baryshnikov in a ballet. Yes, I am going skiing! Finally! Skiing on a weekday is truly one of the top five things to live for, at least in my book. And today is that day. I'll get up at dawn with The Great One, send her off to work, pack my backpack full of granola bars and sunblock, and head up the highway to the great beyond. I'll be the first one on the mountain, which is really a thing of beauty. Standing there, no tracks before me, just me against the mountain. Nothing else matters at that point. Not chicken, not bagels. I'll ski alone all day, with no lift lines. I'll stop when my legs demand it. I'll eat when my stomach commands it. It's a beautiful thing. I know you can't truly relate, dude; but think of really really *really* good sex. That's about the extent of it for me. And when I get home, say around two or three o'clock (skiing alone on a week day means no lift lines, which in turn means a quicker leg burnout, which in turn means I get home early), I'll lay in a warm bathtub for an hour, letting the soothing bubble bath surround and comfort my worn out body. Aah, yes............

I've officially signed up for the Spring Tennis Ladder at the Denver Tennis Center. This means I can go out and get my butt whooped on a regular basis. I did sign up for the lowest rung, though, so I figure the butt whoopings won't be as bad as they could be. I'll let you know how it goes, because play starts this weekend. I fully expect to get beat on pretty good, but at the same time I fully expect to get better.

32

I took a bottle of my homebrew to my local homebrew supply place today and asked the guy to taste it. I told him I needed more kick and flavor to my beer. I also told him that when I open my beer, I want lots of chicks in bikinis to appear, kind of like those Miller commercials. He said he couldn't help me with that, but he did give me some advice. So, tonight, I made beer #2, and I added some hops and amber yeast to it to give it more kick. Nothing like your house smelling like a brewery, I tell you. The beer should be ready in 3 or 4 weeks, I'll let you know how it is. I'm really shooting to make a decent "Bachelor Party Brew" for you in May that I can bring to Las Vegas and we can enjoy as we discuss "men and their feelings in the 1990s." Yeah, that's it.

Well, *amigo*, that's about it for me. Think of me tomorrow as you are inventing the cure for the common cold, and I'll think of you as I glide down mountains of pure white powder. Skiing wood. Oh yeah.

Mondays suck, but Skiing on Mondays RULES!!!!

-Peek a boo.

Date: Mar 4
To: Jeff
From: Anthony
Subject: Return of the Tennis Bum

Well now it's time for Jeff to say
Good-bye to Breckenridge
Time to get warmed-up and leave the cold
of nature's fridge
And when he's back at work he'll be gettin' such a lickin'
The grateful owners will give him a lifetime supply of chicken
Bagels too
Sit a spell Check this beam out
Y'all come back now, hear?

I know this is probably not how you meant this, but I would like some clarification regarding one quote from your latest message. "I know you can't truly relate, dude; but think of really really *really* good sex." I'm guessing you're referring to the organic orgasm you seem to get from whooshing down a cold mountain at breakneck speed. One could, however, construe this message to imply that I have never had "really really *really* good sex." I have had outstanding sex, dear boy. If it wasn't outstanding, what were you hollering about? The mere fact that I was a consenting participant means it was really *really really* good sex. In fact, Joan Osborne dedicated that song "What If God Was One Of Us?" to me after she and I had sex. Yeah, that's the ticket. If, however, you are referring to godsporting like a fiend...hmmm....hmmmm....no sir, I don't like it! Therefore, I hope you had one helluva nice day of skiing, because you deserve it after all the chicken shit you've been through over the last month. And I? Well, I deserve some really really really good sex.

Good to hear you signed up for the tennis tourney. I played this weekend. Won, but did not look good doing it. You're going to kick my ass in July. Hope you had fun today and that you're rejuvenated enough to get you through until you can godsport again. And while I don't ski, I'm with you in spirit, because, like I say, Mexicans (for the most part) don't ski.

Bad tennis matches suck, really really *really* good sex rules. OUT!!

Buck Naked

Date: Mar 4
To: Duke
From: Jeff
Subject: Where Did All These People Come From?

PRESS RELEASE:

DENVER: Local bagel magnate Jeffrey C. Chacon, Esq. was arrested this afternoon after his second standoff with police officers in as many weeks. It seems Mr. Chacon went skiing at Breckenridge, and, when the ski area became quite crowded, he lost his mind and took a group of twenty Texans hostage. After a six-hour standoff with police, during which Mr. Chacon refused to come down off of the mountain "Unless they bring me a lifetime supply of bagels, give me the key to the city, and leave my mountain alone," he was subdued when the police distracted him by sending up a local architect. While Mr. Chacon was yelling, "Your stupid damned bagels. Why does the whole world need bagels?" and pointing his rifle at the architect, the officers were able to disarm Mr. Chacon.

It seems Mr. Chacon became quite distressed when the ski area became crowded right around 10 o'saka in the morning, at which point he began yelling and screaming something about "This is my God!! You are mocking my God!!! Why are you all here? Only I am to be here!!! Only I am to godsport!!! Vengeance is mine!!!! Bagels and Chicken forever!!!" At that point he saw a group of tourists from Austin, Texas, who were staring at his antics. He pulled out a rifle and took them hostage, refusing to come down off the mountain. Mr. Chacon is in city jail and cannot be reached for comment.

Yessir, it was crowded. On a Monday. I could NOT believe it. But it was worth it. I skied until one o'saka, then I came home and took a long hot bath. But before I talk about the bath, I'll tell you about my moment of cosmic togetherness. I was sitting in the warming hut at about 10 a.m. this morning at the top of Peak 8, drinking a cup of hot chocolate and eating a peanut butter and raspberry preserve sandwich, taking a short break from my battles with the mountain. I was looking at the map, trying to decide what to do next, and I noticed a run called "Duke's Run." At that exact moment, a woman walked into the hut who looked exactly like our old friend Lori would look if she skied. I kid you not. At that moment, I felt the cosmos align and the planetary system come together and I knew that I had to ski your run. So I did. I skied "Duke's Run" for you, dude. Because the cosmos told me to. Could you feel it?

Anyway, I came home and took a bath, because I had to wash off all that cosmic togetherness mushiness. In the bath, I watched Sally Jessy Raphael, who had on this couple; the woman was 31-years-old, our age, and her hubby was 73-frickin'-years-old. 73. And he was cheatin' on her with her sister. WHERE DO THEY GET THESE PEOPLE? Imagine Julie dating your grandfather. And the woman said, "This man is my life. I love him." And she took her normal 31-year-old lips and kissed his 73-year-old dried-prunes-that-pass-for-lips. I couldn't believe it. I thought I'd seen it all. Where was this girl's father to say, "Uh, punkin, your man is a might bit old, don't ya think?" It was pretty sick.

Of course, I was talking about really *really really* good sex that you've had, you numskull. I DO have eyes in the back of my head, after all. I wouldn't ask you to think about it unless I know that you have had it, would I?

Well, *amigo*, you have yourself a wonderful week. I go to work tomorrow refreshed, ready to take on the world of architects once again. Oh, and before I forget, I finished my "Spring Mix" music tape tonight. I'll be sending you a copy soon. Look for it in your mailbox, it's next to the envelope with Ed McMahon's picture on it.

Crowded Mondays Suck, Cosmic togetherness RULES!!!

-Alberto

Chapter 5
Slumlords and Toofless Little Punks

Date: Mar 5
To: Jeff
From: Anthony
Subject: Cosmo's Factory

Geez, you just can't win, can you? Sorry the mountain was so full of vacationing buttheads and the like. "Duke's Run" sounds like hell's own mountain. Actually, what it probably is a 15 degree slope with a tow rope and first aid stations placed 10 feet apart; complete with picnic benches for bitter people who've come to their senses and given up on godsporting, or for those who were knocked unconscious. Naturally, the bar isn't too far away. More than likely, while you were battling the horror of "Duke's Run," I was in a meeting of our company newspaper. But I think there was some sort of cosmic thang going on because, at one point, I felt a real icy chill and my head inexplicably crashed down on the table. I was out for a couple of seconds, but, when I started to come to, they said the first thing out of my mouth was, "Fuck, I hate bagels."

I've finally discovered what hell is. I work out at the local gym a couple of times a week and they provide a TV in the room for viewing pleasure. So, I went in there yesterday and, before I started working out on the stair-stepper, I flipped through the channels to see what's on. Nothing, so I turned it off and began my thirty minute session on the machine. Not two minutes later, this old woman came in, turned on the TV, and put on one of those talk shows you were telling me about in your e-mail. Today's topic, "My Mother Stole My Boyfriend." So, not only am I dying on a stair-stepper, but now I gotta listen to some cretin telling me why he dropped his fat ugly girlfriend of 16 for her even fatter, uglier mother of 50-plus. Not pretty, my friend, not pretty. I'm just about convinced, however, that a lot of this guano is staged. I pray it is!

Tonight, we have our first read-through for the play, which means it'll probably be a late night. I'm hoping that assembling the cast for the first time sparks some interest in me that, so far, seems lacking. Don't know what the problem is, but I just can't get cranked up for this. Oh well, like I say, maybe the interaction with others will prick my interest (or vice versa). Anyway, off to the world of science. Have a most blissful day and we'll be talking at you very soon.

Dumb ass talk shows suck, "Duke's Run" rules. OUT!!

Duke

Date: Mar 5
To: Duke
From: Jeff
Subject: Office Politics

Of course, "Duke's Run" was really a good mile of open terrain sloping downhill at a gentle 30 degrees, easily the best run of the day -- until I took those Texans hostage at the bottom and the police got involved, the SWAT team, the fire engines....

"Senator Chacon!!! Senator Chacon!!!" Kinda has a nice ring,, don't you think? I am now a political junkie. If you can't tell, I just returned home from my first WHNA (West Highlands Neighborhood Association, for the neighborhood where we live) meeting, where one Tony Chacon, a Denver City Planner, spoke about planning-type stuff. And you know what? I've decided to say "Fuck it!" I'm Hispanic. 'Cuz when this Tony guy asked me where *mi familia* is from and I said, "Well, I'm really adopted into the name," I felt like an idiot!!! So, from now on, I'm Hispanic. I'm Chacon. It's just easier that way. And, when I'm up for State Senator of Colorado: no, I did not inhale, or snort, and I do not know where the nanny Maria came from; and, yes I paid her Social Security. Ecstasy? What is that? Sure, I've been ecstatic, but I've never done any drugs......

And, now, our office politics' report. About a month ago, Boss #1 (I have two) approached me with this idea: They are turning an old sanitarium (where I lived until they let me out a few years ago) into lofts right close to here, and he wants to get into a couple of the units as an investment vehicle. With my background as a slumlord, he wanted Julie and me to go in on it with him. So we talked, and we agreed that he would be the cash cow. He would put up most of the money, and The Great One and I would be minor financial partners and the slumlords. So, we kind of hammered out a tentative deal, went to the jobsite, and put down a few bones on three of the units. We think we can sell them for a substantial profit a few years down the road. Anyway, Boss #1 and I have kept this pretty hush hush. But, last week, Boss #2 took me to lunch on the way back from one of our many Chicken and Bagel architect beating sessions, and, in the middle of a bite of gyro, he asked me, "So, how's the loft thing going?" As I choked on a piece of pita and scrambled for a reasonable answer, because I had no idea that anybody knew, I replied "okay" I then told him all about it, thinking that Boss #1 had already told him all about it, because somehow he knew. Anyway, today, Boss #1 pulled me aside and asked if I told Boss #2 about our deal. I said, "No, he asked me. I thought you told him." He said no, but he also said that Boss #2 pulled him aside and told him that this whole thing might not be a good idea, because "people in the office are a little jealous, and you are showing favoritism towards Jeff." EXCUSE ME?? JEALOUS?? I'm sorry that all you other putzes don't get to be the golden boy, but somebody's got to do it. And you all can KISS MY ASS if you don't like it. Set up your own deals, O.K.? I

37

cannot believe that this is a big deal. Who is jealous? Maybe they all realize that I have the inside track to success and my train is blowing right by everybody else's. Maybe they all see the future and it's a picture of my butt. Maybe I'm a little bit too clocky at this point. Or is that cocky? Anyway, I ate my lunch alone, because I was a little taken aback by the whole thing. Jealousy is ugly. Office politics have entered my life before, and I know I don't enjoy it. It's not easy being me. It's not easy being green. It definitely ain't easy being the chosen one. People envy you, spite you, try to keep you down. But it ain't gonna happen this time, nosiree. I'll own that company in ten years, then we'll see who's jealous.

Whooh. I got going there a little. "He's typically a humble guy, I don't know what got into him." Think tongue-in-cheek.

Hey, have a cool Wednesday. It's starting to snow as we speak, so our Wednesday certainly will be cool.

Jealousy sucks, golden boys rule. OUT

-Señor Teachers Pet

Date: Mar 6
To: Jeff
From: Anthony
Subject: Melrose Web

Boy did I get a wrong address on the 'Net this morning. Here I am looking for the morning e-mail and I accidentally turned to some idiot harping about office politics, jealousy, telling everyone to kiss his ass. Ooh, scary. For a minute, I wasn't sure what was going on. I figured the last thing on earth you'd ever do again is become a slumlord after the famous "Slobs R Us" (or whoever those loser tenants of yours were) affair. So, I'm guessing that I scrolled upon the *Melrose Place* page on worldwide web. Which is understandable since I was looking for the slutty chicks page. Looks like I also wound up on the civic-minded activist page. What up with you, dude? This e-mail of yours is filled with more politics than the editorial page. Politics? What is that? The next time we talk politics we'd better be talking about many-sided blood-sucking insects. And why do you continue to deny the fact that you are Mexican? You spent your whole life in South San Diego, you hork Mexican food, you drink like a *pescado*, you sleep all the time. Shit, you're more Mexican than I am. You didn't adopt the name, the name adopted you.

As for these small people who just can't accept the fact that your lips feel soft and moist on your boss's chafing behind, tell them to bleep off and go buy their own fuckin' sanitarium. Incidentally, I don't know that I'd live in a place that was once a sanitarium. I realize, of course, that you don't want to hear that, but I'd be afraid that the spirit of some Napoleonic wanna-be would still be stalking the halls. And, believe me, spooks is bad enough when they're derived from non-psychopaths. But, anyway, fact is when the trolley pulled into the station, you were there to get on board and your co-workers were resting on their fat laurels drinking coffee and eating bagels. I'm sorry you had to eat your lunch all by yourself, but let me tell you I got some news for you and you'll soon find out it's true...

As stated yesterday, we had our first rehearsal for the play last night. It never really dawned on me during the course of reading the script, but I have a very poignant scene with a small child who just endured an operation. Now, I'm sure you already know this, but, as an actor, you never work with kids or animals, especially when the kid is supposed to have just had an operation. So, I pulled Macaulay aside and shared a bottle of reality with him. "Listen, you dimply-faced toothless little punk, I'm the star here. If you upstage me, I'll have you living in the Gary Coleman Home of Obscurity so fast it'll make you puke." Nah, he's a great little guy and it'll be a while before I can get past laughing when he delivers his lines; not because he's funny, but because he's so good I have a tendency to laugh in amazement. I kinda had the same problem the first time Alden and I had sex. You can bet it was a while before we did it again.

Thus, I must take leave of e-mail as well as of my senses (too easy, I really shouldn't have done it). You have a very good day. I'll try even though I have to work and the weather is supposed to be around 80 today. Talk to you tomorrow.

80-degree days at work suck, leaving co-workers in your dust rules. OUT!!

Marlon

Date: Mar 6
To: Duke
From: Jeff
Subject: Will You Be My Running Mate?

I'd like to formally invite you to be my running mate. Yes, I'm asking you to be a candidate for Vice-President of *estos Estados Unidos*. We'll be the first Spanish candidates, you and I. Because you see, my friend, at the rate I'm going, we'll be running against Bill and Hillar...Al in 2000. Tonight, The Cranky One and I went to the Governor's Mansion to hang out with the Guv himself. Yes, this is not a typo. The Guv. Actually, it was an awards thing for The Arts. The local dance company that Julie is involved with was receiving an award from the Guv, so we went along to hob-nob with "the other half." Free champagne, all kinds of hors d'ovaries, chocolate-covered strawberries, and the Guv himself. It was cool. Next Tuesday, I'm going to hang out with our City Councilman at an early Saint Patrick's Day fiesta. Think about that -- three political moves in a week. That's more politics than I've experienced in 31 years! At this rate I figure I'll be ready to run for something soon. When I do reach that *El Presidente* level, I'll invite you to be my Admiral Stockdale, my Tipper Gore, my Dan Quayle. Hahaha.........Think of it. We'll make Railyard Ale the official beer of the White House. We'll pass resolutions that engineers and biologists switch salaries with doctors and lawyers. We'll make Shania Twain the official Every Morning National Anthem Singer (just for you). We'll make U2 illegal in this country. We'll outlaw rap, opera and Kenny G. And we'll make Michael Jordan come to the White House weekly for our own private basketball lessons. We'll open our state of the addresses with a five minute set of our own brand of comedy. We'll make *The Simpsons* required viewing for all residents of our great country. Lastly, we'll send all architects to go live on an island in the middle of Antarctica, where we'll visit them only when we really really need something from them, which will be pretty close to never. Oh, yeah, we'll also make all bosses give all employees of all companies a 50% raise -- which will come directly out of the bosses' salaries. Whaddya think?

You realize, of course, that your little co-star is a future talk show host, don't you? I mean, he'll go on to be this generation's Danny Partridge, and we all know where Danny Bonaduce is now, don't we? He's on "Danny!" So, tell your little co-star that you are a lesbian nun, and you'd like to be on his first show. It must be fun to work with a kid. I've done some readings with kids before, but none of them were very good. I did see a kid in the last live play I went to who was excellent. That would be weird. I mean, when I was a kid, all I wanted to do was build skyscrapers out of sand and run from bully girls who chased me all over the school yard. I didn't have time to be an actor.

Well, that's enough e-excitement for today. Let me get sappy for *uno momento* and tell you again that this e-mail thing on a daily basis is quickly becoming a fun habit. I really do enjoy these little blasts of e-thoughts. It's a great creative outlet. I find myself during the day thinking about what I'm going to write that night and, as soon as I get your message, I read it, laugh a bunch, and respond -- through rain, sleet, or snow. Have you thought of working for the post office? Anyway, bro, just wanted to let you know how I felt, even though you can probably tell by the way my e-mails get longer and longer all the time and my point-of-view gets more and more abstract. No, that's not me losing my mind, that's just me expanding my creativity in these things. Thanks for your support.

Kenny G sucks, Hispanic Presidential Candidates Rule!!!

-Guillermo Clinton.

Date: Mar 7
To: Jeff
From: Anthony
Subject: What the hell?

Sure, let's make a a run for the Casa de Blanca. I would build our campaign on a few other issues. We get to shoot all our opponents, Sting is banned from ever showing his face in the U.S.A. again, we get to have a First *and* Second Lady, Jim Rome gets to be Secretary of State, luxury boxes and free Railyard at all sporting and concert events, and implementation of a "Public Stoning Day" where people get to throw rocks at societal low-life. Talk-show hosts and lawyers come to mind.

Extremely tired today. Last night, we blocked Act I and it was a total zoo. The little kid I was telling you about went completely delirious with boredom. This kid has one scene in Act I and, in that scene, all he does is lie in a hospital bed and moan. For this, he had to wait in the theater from 7:00 until 9:30. All told, he was on stage for about ten minutes. Now, I don't profess to be Dr. Spock or any of the "Star Trek" characters, but don't you think that an eight year-old boy is going to get bored after a while? And what, pray tell, is an eight-year-old doing up at 10:00 p.m. on a school night? For that matter, what the hell am I doing up at 10:00 on a school night? The kid's blocking directions go like this: enter from behind curtain stage left, lie in bed, act, exit behind curtain stage left, done, finito, "Good night now." Plus, there's a cat (Elvis) in the play and he was there last night, so we could see how he'd handle things and he was pretty much freaking out. Overall, a bad scene and I'm praying it gets better.

Let me take a moment to echo your sappy sentiments regarding the daily e-mail. I, too, relish the opportunity to exchange in a little verbal foreplay with one of maybe three people who are tuned to the same frequency as I (my cousin Dave and Bugs Bunny come to mind). I've said it before (and I should've gotten a lawyer to deal with a certain beer enterprise), but I love you, man. Okay, enough of this sentimental squid shit, we're men dammit. I'm going to go have my lunch now. Then, I think I'll undo my belt buckle, clean my guns, and holler vulgarities at women. Have a great weekend.

Stupid rehearsals suck, cats named Elvis rule. OUT!!

Admiral Dukey

Date: Mar 7
To: Duke
From: Jeff
Subject: Just Call Me Bjorn

The pre-season polls came out today for the Men's 3.0 Spring Ladder at the Denver Tennis Center, and -- yes -- I am ranked #1. Can you believe it? I've never been #1 in anything! Although it is a random ranking, of course, I now have to spend the entire season defending my #1 spot in the polls. Since nobody has even called me yet to challenge my throne, it is officially one day down on my quest to finish the season undefeated and undethroned. Cha. I'll be lucky to make it out of March with anything in the Top Ten. Although you never know. This could very well be the putz ladder. It'll be fun. At the end, the top eight dudes get to have a playoff, with the winner receiving some kind of certificate or some shit. I'm looking forward to it. I'm even thinking of spending some time with a ball machine so I truly can be prepared for the many opponents who will be gunning for my spot.

Let's talk wedding. Let me just say that it would be an honor (and probably a good idea to get you out of your woman's hair) if I could take you to lunch at Ye Olde Chicken Pie Shop on that Friday before your wedding thing. This way, you could be out of sight as your woman and her mother are absolutely bonkers with last minute wedding things. You probably know about this already. Plus, it's a tradition. I would certainly enjoy it, and you might enjoy taking some of that focus off the wedding and putting it on Chicken Pot Pies, which is where it rightly belongs. Let me know about this, because we'll be making our arrangements for the trip soon, and as soon as people get a whiff that "Jeff's coming to town" everybody's gonna want some.

Well, I gotta go do some work -- I'm getting ready to issue a shopping center (liquor store, Starbucks, another bagel place) and I gotta backcheck some drawings. Yeah, yeah, yeah, it's late. But what the hell? You have a *bueno* weekend with your #1 woman, take her to see *Muppet Treasure Island*, and we'll be typing at you on Monday. If you e-mail me today (Friday), I won't see it 'til Sunday night ('cuz we're going to Chicago for the weekend), but don't let that stop you, O.K.?

Nothing sucks today, Chicken Pot Pies the day before you get married RULE!!!!

-Bjorn.

Date: Mar 11
To: Jeff
From: Anthony
Subject: Bjorn again

Sorry I'm not getting back to you until today. I flew up to see Alden Thursday night and took Friday off. Big doin's while I was gone, huh? The number one seed? I'm sure you'll occupy the position for a while. If you're in a bracket with a bunch of other dudes at your skill level I don't see why you can't advance. Just play your game. It can't be any harder than playing in a band, and you've already done that. Play smart, play hard, keep smiling, and good things will happen. If that doesn't work, cheat.

This past weekend is a good illustration of why I hate the land of Northern California. We looked around three different cities and not one was showing *Muppet Treasure Island*. But if you want to see *Beautiful Girls* any number of theaters are showing that one. Actually, it sounded rather enticing, but then Alden explained it to me and it sounded like nothing more than a chick-flick with an exciting title. As far as I'm concerned, this borders on entrapment. Then there's the NoCal driver. Know what they call a good driver in NoCal? A tourist.

"Dear, I think we're lost."

"Okay, I'll just drive slowly so we don't get even more lost."

"Dear, the traffic is backing up behind us."

"No problem, I'll just stop and let them pass me."

"Dear, maybe you shouldn't stop in the middle of a two-lane street."

And for real fun, on Friday morning in Santa Cruz, the overly politically-correct arrange for the recycling stations to whisk away their recyclables -- at 6:00 in the morning. If you've never heard the sound of 400 glass bottles being dropped into a metal truck from a height of about twelve feet, then you, my friend, are a lucky guy -- especially at 6:00 a.m. when you're snuggled up next to some sweet little scooter pie enjoying some luscious slumber because you don't have to work that day. We still managed to have a nice weekend. We went shopping for Alden's B-day and I dropped a big dog-choking wad of bills on clothes for her. You'd think that 200 bucks would get you an entire wardrobe, but it actually gets you three pairs of shorts, three tops, a light sweater, and a skirt -- at clearance sale prices. But what the hell, she's happy.

Did ya notice there was no loud "splash" this morning? That's because our engagement announcement showed up in the local newspaper yesterday, but it's such a shitty picture of me that all the women in the county never even considered suicide as a way to alleviate their grief. Oh well, perhaps it's better this way. The Coronado Bridge couldn't have held up under the strain, anyway. Could it?

I'm guessing I'll probably wind-up taking the Friday off before the wedding, so we are there at the Chicken Pie Shop. It is tradition and, even if it wasn't, it's damn tasty. I was worried that all this negative energy about chicken lately would somehow adversely affect your attitude towards all things chicken, but I'm glad to see that's not the case. Anyway, time to head to work. By the way, enjoy the tournament. Enjoy.

NoCal drivers suck, NCAA Tournament rules. OUT!!

Dicky V.

Date: Mar 11
To: Duke
From: Jeff
Subject: Bjorn Free

The Conversation That You Wish You Never Had To Have Department: Boss #1: "The reason I'm being so hard on you, Jeff, is that you are so close to being excellent." Jeff: "Uhh, yeah, mister boss man, thanks." And, you know, I'm starting to get a little tired of the "Jeff, we're checking this project very very closely, because (insert reason here)." Standard Jeff response: "Well, gee, Wally, I really appreciate the input. It's my life's dream to become all the engineer that I can be." Yeah, right. Can I go now? Sorry to bitch a little, but this topic came up today.

Julie's in Chicago for some conference still, so me and the girls...ur, computer, are just sitting around nake...uh, typing e-mails. Yeah, that's it. Ooh, I'm in trouble now. Once Julie reads this, she'll say "Jeff, did you really have naked women over? Did you?"

Uh, dude, there may not have been any "splash" when your picture appeared in your local newsrag; but there sure was a collective "splat" here in Colorado when the local womenfolk found about your impending doo...marriage. We don't have an ocean.

Winter? What's that? It's been 70 degrees the last two days, and it's supposed to continue that way the rest of the week. I really should get out and play some tennis. But why jeopardize my ranking? I've been number one for five straight days now, which oughta be some kind of record, don't ya think? I guess I'll play. But, first, one of the lowly not-number-one saps has to call me to challenge my dominance. Then -- and only if he begs on his hands and knees and brings me beer and lots of dinero, and only then -- will I play.

Hey, have an excellent Tuesday, won't you? And watch *NYPD Blue* tonight; that is, if you are not out acting like an insane Norwegian guy or something. It's a great show.

Kissing everybody's ass sucks, Naked e-mails RULE!!!

-Bjorn to be wild

Date: Mar 12
To: Jeff
From: Anthony
Subject: Bjorn in the USA

First of all, I owe you an apology. I turned on the computer this afternoon and was shocked to find no e-mail waiting. I figured maybe it was late, but after a while my mind began to think the most awful things. I was convinced you were having an e-mail affair behind my back. I was pissed, too. I was storming around calling you a cyberslut and all sorts of nasty shit. Needless to say, I was highly relieved when your message finally did show up. Relieved and embarrassed. I'm sorry, dude, I should know by now that I can trust you. You have to understand, however, that I am a bit on the defensive these days. The fallout from that engagement photo has been brutal. I've been getting comments like, "Great picture, man. HA HAA!" and "Why in the world would she want to marry *you*?" Harsh, isn't it? I'll send you a copy this evening, along with a couple of business cards and anything else I can scrounge up that might be of interest.

So why was your message late anyway? You taking the day off? Sounds like you may need to consider it. What's the problem, don't you want to be an excellent engineer? Don't you want your tombstone to read, "Here Lies Jeff Chacon...One Excellent Engineer"? Do you think they have need for excellent engineers in Heaven? Think of it: Structural Engineer Heaven, where the clients pay in cash and the architects are reasonable. No chicken, no bagels, no bosses questioning your shit. Just beer, pizza, and a new temp at the front desk every day.

So, how long is The Great One in Chicago? I trust you're being a good little sinner while she's gone? One thing: I guess I really didn't understand how the tennis tourney works. One of those low-ranked losers has to call and challenge you? Weird. Sounds like some kind of funky jousting tournament. "Sir Jeffrey, thou hast insulteth my honor and what's left of my fair maiden's. Preparest thy racquet, o' beam-checker of chicken shacks. Thou hast forced me to kicketh thy arse." My guess is that should any of these pussies find the stones to actually call you, you'll squash them flatter than a diet pancake.

I think I'm suffering jet-lag or something. No zest for writing today. Have a great day and I'll talk to you soon.

Writer's block sucks, and when you have writer's block nothing rules.

uh...umm...fuck it. Anthony

Date: Mar 12
To: Duke
From: Jeff
Subject: Where was ya Bjorn?

The number two seed finally called me today and challenged me to a match to be played today (Wednesday) at 11:00 a.m. I, of course, accepted, not being one to back down from challenges, mind you. Here's how the whole thing works: Every ladder participant has to play at least once every two weeks. When you challenge somebody above you, if you win, you take that putz's place and he moves down a slot. If you lose, *nada*. So you see, my good friend, all I have to do to retain my ranking is to NEVER LOSE. It's that simple. You record the results in some little book there at the tennis center, and every two weeks they come out with a new ranking based on what everybody did. Also, both participants bring a brand spankin' new can of tennis balls. You use one can and the loser takes that can home, while the winner takes home the new can. So, if I never lose, I never have to buy balls. Seems simple enough. Now, all I have to do is win, win, win. So, today at around 10:00 a.m. your time, think *bueno* thoughts for me as I sweat and toil at the net here in the Mile High City.

Old cans of balls suck, new cans of balls RULE!!!

-Jeffrey Agassi

Date: Mar 13
To: Jeff
From: Anthony
Subject: Bjorn on the Fourth of July

So have we officially exhausted this Bjorn thing?

Sometimes I just don't understand the levels of stupidity some people possess. A bunch of college students were arrested yesterday because they were protesting the possible abolishment of affirmative action. The arrests were a result of the fact that these people thought they could best present their case by locking arms and wading into the middle of La Jolla Village Drive during rush hour and stopping traffic. Now, call me stupid; but, if I want the rest of the world to come over to my way of thinking, I don't believe that insulting it, hurting it, or making its life an undo pain-in-the-ass is going to help me in the least, Especially if it's "The Man" you're trying to sway. And we all know that the fastest way to "The Man's" heart is to impede his progress as he tries to drive home at night. Duh!

Oh joy, tomorrow is the start of the NCAA Tournament. Got my office pool in front of me, my highlighter, my television is on, and I've got various odds and ends that I can throw in disgust as my teams drop like the proverbial flies. You gotta love it. Go Valparaiso!! Go Cal Poly SLO!! Okay, maybe not this year or the next, but someday we'll be able to tune into a major network and watch our mighty Mustangs take down the UCLA Ruins.

Pretty tired today. Last night was the first night I actually tossed and turned with regards to the wedding. I made the mistake of calling my mother to confer with her about the guest list; she wanted to talk about the food, the tuxes, etc. Politically speaking, weddings are a pain-in-the-ass. Guest lists are a pain-in-the-ass. Thank God we're having the reception at a place that makes beer, lots and lots o' beer. I figure Alden's got me for the rest of her life, so I'll probably spend the reception hunkered down at the bar with my dudes. Yeah, uh huh, bound to happen. "Anthony, come on, we have to cut the cake." "Can't you shee I'm shitting here with Jeff having thome beerth? Jeethuth, we're married two hourth and you're nagging me already." Yeah, it's a wonderful life.

Okay, I'm through bitching for the day. I guess I finally found some mental Ex-Lax to eliminate that foul blockage that was dulling my creativity. Had lunch with Alanis...uh, Carol today and we're looking forward to the gig in July. In the meantime, I'll be occupying myself learning my lines for the upcoming play. Hope all went well regarding your defense of your hard-earned number-one ranking, and welcome home to The Great One. Talk at you later.

Dumb-ass protesters suck, bitchin' on your soapbox rules. OUT!!

Rush

Chapter 6
What Are You Wearing?

Date: Mar 14
To: Duke
From: Jeff
Subject: Kevorkian Tennis

Kevorkian Tennis: When one player mercifully puts the other player, who is getting his blood spilled all over the court, out of his misery. I knew I was in trouble when the number-two seed called me a half-hour before our scheduled game today and asked "What are you wearing?" "Uh, dick, I don't quite know what you mean. What am I wearing? Well, right now I've got a newly pressed shirt and tie on, but when I come out to kick your ass, I'll be wearing shorts and a sweatshirt, which, when I get warmed up, will be removed to reveal my secret weapon -- a T-shirt. WHAT KIND OF A QUESTION IS THAT?" This bozo replied "Well, I couldn't decide if I should wear jeans or shorts." Yeah, yeah, you read that right. Jeans. I knew that this guy was in over his little head. He showed up in shorts and a Hawaiian print T-shirt; and he had his "Tennis for Dorks" book in hand. And he went over how to keep score with me, because it's been a while since he played. I tried to be nice. I really did. So, I kicked his ass, 6-0 6-0, all the while daydreaming about the weekend and what it might be like to play a real opponent. I tried to encourage this guy a little, because he probably could use it. I mean, I've never heard of a disgruntled tennis player coming back to the courts with a gun and killing his oppressor, but it could happen. So, I'm like "Yeah, nice shot, dude," trying to keep his spirits up. And, at the end, he said, "That was fun. Maybe we can do it again." NOT! I do not think so. This is not why I play this game, buster. I play to compete. I play for testosterone. And I play to bring my ability level up, not down. This was like Mike Tyson against Peter McNeeley. So now I'm thinking that maybe I've underestimated myself, or overestimated this ladder thing. Maybe I need to move up a level. I figure I'll play one more guy from this ladder, and if he is half as bad as this joker today was, I'm going to ask to be brought up to the majors. Because this was *boring*, and probably detrimental to my game.

I finally caught The Great One's cold. Getting sick sucks. So, I left early today, came home and took a nap before going to pick up The Great One at the *aeropuerto*. She's at the store now picking up some good drugs for me.

Well, I'm gonna go back to bed, eat some Chicken Gumbo soup, watch my *Stevie Ray Vaughan Live At the El Mocambo* video, and take some good drugs, of course. Have a nice Thursday, won't you?

Kevorkian tennis sucks, getting sick sucks, Making your wife go out for drugs RULES!

Date: Mar 14
To: Jeff
From: Anthony
Subject: Tennis Menace

Oh, brother. "What are you wearing?" Is this guy for real? "Well, currently, I'm sporting a Georgio Armani shirt, Docker's slacks, and a tie painted to look like a rainbow trout. However, for our match thith afternoon, I was going to wear thith darling little white thkirt with matching white polo." Apparently, what you should have told him was, "I'm going to wear the grubbiest clothes I can find. Do you think I want your blood all over my nice duds?" 6-0, 6-0? Geez, I took you to 5-5 with a broken racquet. Perhaps you should reconsider moving up in the world. Playing with underlings will do nothing to make you better. Also, remember, there *are* a few rules to keep in mind when choosing opponents:

1. Never play a guy with a wooden racquet or one that costs more than twice yours.

2. Never play a guy wearing jeans or a sleeveless sweater.

3. Never play a guy who brings orange balls or balls with funny designs to the match.

4. Never play a guy in a polyester sweatsuit.

5. Never play a guy who wants to drink from your water bottle.

6. Never play a guy who brings a cellular phone to the match.

7. Never play a guy who brings a gun to the match.

8. Never play seemingly shitty players who always want to bet.

9. Never, never, NEVER play a guy who suggests playing on courts with metal nets.

10. Always play cute girls in white skirts.

Bummer that you're sick, but you have the luxury of having a loving Great One there to nurture you. Me, I have to suffer alone, languishing in my own diseased body fluids. I've been very fortunate this year however; I haven't gotten sick. But this is par for the course. Usually what happens is I skate through cold and flu season and, just when the rest of the world starts to get better, I get sick. But because of my strict regiment of exercise, eating healthy, and Bible study, perhaps this year I'll ward off all potential viruses, bacteria, and funky fungi. Anyway, enjoy your Chicken Mocambo and SRV at the El Gumbo video. Hope you feel better soon. AND NO GOD-SPORTING FOR YOU, YOUNG MAN!!

Kevorkian tennis does suck, nurturing Great Ones rule. OUT!!

Anthony
President of "Dudes Against Metal Nets" (DAMN)

Date: Mar 18
To: Duke
From: Jeff
Subject: Who's the Joker?

Dear Batman,

Although you may think you have seen the last of The Joker, I have recently discovered that he is still around these parts. Not in Gotham, mind you, but in a little town called San Diego. I was thumbing through a recent *San Diego Union* and I noticed on the "Engagements" page a handsome young man. I realized this man has a smile that could be no other -- The Joker. Beware, Batman. He is alive. And he's masquerading as one "Anthony Reynoso," set to marry one "Alden Kidd," who, for all we know, could be the next Batgirl. I mean, she does look a bit like that Alicia Silverstone chick we hired for the part. Anyway, Batman, just thought you'd like to know.

-A Concerned Citizen of Gotham

Needless to say, I got your engagement photo in the mail. Dude, what up with that? You look incredibly like Jack Nicholson in the first Batman movie. Classic.!
Well, after a quick recovery from whatever bug I had, the weekend was meant yet again for skiing. We just got back. Legs tired. Soul at peace. But skiing in powder sucks, especially today, when there was about 12" of powder and it was snowing all day. I can't quite get the mph up in powder; it's just too heavy. Then we had a three hour drive home. But in the end, it's all worth it. Strap some 193 centimeter-long fiberglass boards to my feet and drop me off in Heaven, 'cuz skiing is where it's at. But now, alas, it's time for bed. *Yo estoy* very tired. And I have to go to work tomorrow and design middle schools so the children of the land will have somewhere to go come Fall. Ain't I just a total provider-type guy? Chicken, Bagels, Alcohol, Video, now *las esceulas*. What will they think of next?
Powder skiing sucks, The Joker RULES!!

-Commissioner Gordon

Date: Mar 18
To: Jeff
From: Anthony
Subject: Wait'll they get a load of me

Yes, I must admit, I do display some of that Nicholsonesque charm in that photo. Trust me, the next time any picture of me appears in any type of publication for any type of reason, I will have the final say as to which one it will be, for it is clear that my darling little old-bat-to-be doesn't have my best interests at heart.

Speaking of old-bats-to-be, I've discovered the surest cure to a lasting marriage: take your betrothed to a 30-plus singles party. I actually attended one of these little affairs last Saturday night; it had all the educating value of one of those "Perils of Drunk Driving" movies they show in traffic court. Scary, my man, scary. For one thing, I would estimate that a more correct term for the party would've been 40-plus. Realistically, everyone was there to get paired-up with the "ideal" person of their dreams, so they should've grouped people accordingly. Categories could've included "Real hair vs. fake," "Real boobs vs. fake," "Clothing's cotton content greater than 50 percent," "Shirt unbuttoned to navel," "More jewelry than Deion Sanders," "Can be out in the sun for no longer than 30 minutes before body parts start to melt," and , of course, "Supplements income through alimony." In case you're wondering what I was doing there, I went because all the boys wanted to go there instead of to the Las Vegas-type art museum I told you about. I just don't understand some people's choice o' culcha. This, naturally, was the follow-up to the Tyson-Bruno "fight" we paid for because we're all basically stoo-pid. Frank Bruno applies the same strategy to boxing as Tommy Lasorda does to managing: keep hugging and everything will be fine. Bruno apparently thought, "Well, maybe if I convince him I love him, he won't kill me." Hug, hug, hug. Tyson just said, "I love you, too, but I gotth to kill your thtupid ath." If it hadn't been for the two chicks who fought it out in the undercard, the evening would've been a total loss. Yeah, women boxing. Actually, there really wasn't any boxing; it was fighting. The bell rang and these two alley cats walked into the center of the ring and proceeded to beat the hell out of each other. By the time it was over they both had that "Calgon take me away" look about them. All in all, an education on how not to spend a Saturday night. Hope you're feeling better this week and glad to see you got some godsporting in. Talk at you soon.

Chick-boxing rules. OUT!!

Swinging single

Date: Mar 18
To: Duke
From: Jeff
Subject: You The Man

You The Man. Chick boxing? Paying to see yet another Mike Tyson "opponent" sacrifice himself in the name of Don King and Cash? And a swinging over-the-hill singles' party? Instead of a Las Vegas-type museum? Dude, what kind of guys are you hanging out with these days? I'm just gonna have to come out there and take names. 'Cuz this singles partying has got to stop. Now. Not because you're about to become un-singled, but because you blew off an opportunity to go to what I'm sure was a world famous museum for this. I'm really scared. For mankind. And for dudes in general. But, I gotta tell you, the social commentary that accompanied the "swinging single" party review was probably worth your pain, because that is some funny shit.

Well, time for bed. The Great One and I just got back from showing The Brother Of The Great One and his buddy around Denver (we skied with him yesterday, and he's actually been up skiing for a whole week). We ended up, naturally, at the Wynkoop, on a Monday night. What could be better? So I'm tired, and a little buzzed, so I'll head off to bed now. I'll try to write a longer and better, or kinder and gentler, e-mail tomorrow night. Have a Groovy Tuesday.

Clothes with cotton content less than 80% suck, Excellent E-mails RULE!!

-El Borracho

Date: Mar 19
To: Jeff
From: Anthony
Subject: No, no, you The Man

In all fairness to the boys who didn't want to attend the art museum, they actually had gone the night before. I don't know that this totally forgives their actions, for great art should be appreciated as often as possible. I'm guessing that if they would've gone again, perhaps they would've seen a particularly nice piece they really hadn't noticed the night before. With new companions along, you're also able to get new opinions and thoughts regarding the works on display, which could lead to stimulating discussions about which piece was the most provocative, daring, or satisfying to the senses. Indeed, you could even make a game out of it. Judge the pieces and award prizes for "Biggest Piece," "Best Presentation," "The Piece You'd Most Like to Own," and, of course, the "Booby Prize." Yes, one should never squelch culcha.

As I write this morning, I continue to listen to the bitter grumblings in my tummy. I do not feel well at all today. As bad as Saturday was, at least there was beer and even a few laughs. Yesterday, it was all dentist. I had to go to the dentist for a check-up, supposedly. Don't know if you're on a dental plan at work, but this HMO/DMO thing is for the birds. When I called for the appointment it was still mid-February and they weren't able to see me until yesterday, March 18th!. Okay, they're busy. But I went in there and naturally I had to fill out four hundred questionnaires with the nosiest questions in the world. "Any allergies?" "Had any operations?" "Liver condition?" "Skin condition?" "Ever had sex?" "Do you still call her?" Etc. Well, I always have to answer Y to the one about do you have a heart condition, and that sends dentists into a tizzy fit. Yes, I know what you're asking, "How do the two relate?" Well, it has been determined that 12 (yes, 12) Americans die each year because they have certain heart conditions and, when a dentist cleans your teeth, you always bleed somewhat and little bacterias get into the blood and race right down to your heart and build a little bacteria-ball that clogs your arteries and make you fall go boom. OUT!! So after waiting four weeks to get my choppers cleansed, I was turned away and forced to have my physician call to assure them that I wouldn't croak in the chair. The dentist did, however, examine my teeth and determine that my body has now started to reject my false tooth and I must now see a specialist to decide how best I should spend a couple-hundred bucks -- either on a bridge or some other procedure designed to make what's left of the tooth acceptable to Anthony-as-a-whole.

Now the fun starts; because I'm on the DMO, the insurance company wants to know why I need to see a specialist and, if they're convinced I do, they will decide who I get to see. This process should take about 4 to 6 weeks. Meanwhile, I already have an infection, so the dentist prescribed erythromycin; 5000 mg 4 times a day. So, I downed these huge, bright pink pills (these things would've gone over well in the sixties, "Let me take you down cuz we're going to...") without realizing that these things cause more stomach upset than a Bob Dole speech and a Michael Bolton concert combined. Thus, today, my stomach has become a contortion artist and is twisting itself into more shapes than Gumby trying to impress the chicks. Thus, I'm in pain, I'm pissed at The System, my teeth are still dirty, and I'm sitting here drinking warm ginger ale in an attempt to make myself belch. Charming, huh? I'm seriously contemplating lying down and watching *Cartoon Network*.

Anyway, sorry to dump all over you with that. I'm going to get to the business at hand now, so I can call the dentist later and tell him what he can do with his bright pink pills. You have a great day.

Bad reactions to medication sucks, art museums rule. OUT!!

Charlie Brown

Date: Mar 19
To: Duke
From: Julie
Subject: Your stomach

Hey, Anthony, I was just enjoying your e-mail. Sorry about the tooth, DMO, antibiotics situation. Bummer. However, just a reminder, make sure you are taking the meds with food, it should help the stomach thing. Erythromycin is pretty intense and will kill off anything resembling bacteria in your body (I'm sure you know this). Anyway, eat....it should help. Feel better, I'm sick too. The second time around with the same damn cold. I got it from work, gave it to Jeff, now it's back. Never say "No, honey, I can't get the same cold twice." Ya right. Out!

-The Great One

Date: Mar 19
To: Duke
From: Jeff
Subject: Your Teeth.

So The Great One sent you some health-care smack, eh? Don't believe the hype. Dentists really really really do suck. I had a root canal a couple of years ago, shortly after I arrived in our fair city. Actually, it started out as a small pain in my mouth, which turned into Painzilla; at which point, I was downing six Advils at a time and calling all over town for a dentist who would see me NOW. I found one, and they did as much "root canaling" as they possibly could, at which point they sent me to a specialist. I went to this "root canal specialist," a young twenty-something gal, and shortly before she began excavating my face, I asked her, "So, uh, what made you decide to become a 'root canal specialist,' because, in my book, there is no greater form of sadism. It's a bizarre career choice, at the very least." She responded, "Well, young victim...ur, patient, I don't like blood." I was thinking, "Yeah. You don't like blood. But you sure like pain, don't you?" At this point, I must have had this pained expression on my face, because she said (with a face that was probably supposed to be reassuring but was really more "Psychopathic Root Canal Specialist Kills 4"), "Oh, don't worry. This'll hurt me more than it will hurt you." She proceeded to excavate my face, and she actually found a hidden fifth root (run that on your calculator) which the previous batch of mad doctors didn't find. So, needless to say, I had an enjoyable visit.

Later, the first dentist -- who is a very mellow, calm, older woman who lets me listen to a Walkman and says nice things to me like "How are you? And how are your happy little fillings today?" as she sticks various metal picks, jackhammers, and crowbars down my throat -- had to give me a crown on the tooth that was canaled. I basically spent close to a gazillion hours at the various sadists...ur, dentists for this one frickin' tooth. Now, my dentist, the nice older lady, wants to crown about six of my teeth, because the old bowling ball-size molten steel fillings, which are all bigger than the teeth themselves, look like they might eventually fall out. Eventually. So every time I go in for a "checkup," they remind me that I need to "come back for those 20 crowns!!" "Uh, yeah, NOT!" I'll take my chances. Plus, they keep reminding me that I have all four of my wisdom teeth which are going to do some damage to my mouth, so I need to go to a "Specialist" and get those removed as well. Yeah, well, those teeth have been coming in for about 10 years now, thanks. Besides, all this destruction to my poor mouth costs dinero, which my lame insurance (which, ironically, is managed by The

Cranky One's organization) only covers about half of it. Because, as they say in the insurance biz, the crowns and the wisdom teeth yanking are "Cosmetic." Cosmetic, my ass. Give me a boob job, and I'll file it under "cosmetic." Then maybe I can go to swinging singles over-30 parties and fit in.

Well, *amigo*, try to have a pleasant last day of winter. With the tooth and drug thing going on, I know it won't be easy. But try. You know what they say. No Pain, No Gain.....and what is the gain? That is the question.

Dentists suck, Spring Anticipation RULES!!!!

-El Mariachi

Date: Mar 20
To: Jeff
From: Anthony
Subject: Concerned in Denver

Thank you both for your kind words regarding the perilous state of my choppers. I have an appointment with the endodontist today (they upgraded me to emergency status, which probably means more money now because they're "doing me a favor"), so I will hopefully get this all resolved soon. I'm going to go see this person, sit in the chair, and ask, "So, do you need a pick?" At which point, I will produce a Fender medium guitar pick and pray that my biting wit will save my biting teeth, not to mention my fiercely-clenched ass. Regarding the E-mycin, I just followed the directions on the bottle, which said to mix one shot with orange juice and top off...oops, wrong bottle. Actually, I took an hour before eating like it said, so it's not my fault I got sick. Anyway, I don't want to talk about no stinking dentist anymore. 'Tis spring! The fog is falling and it is time to undo one ceremonial button on the jacket (around mid-May, we'll lose the jacket completely). I want to focus my attention on the lighter side of life Unfortunately, I can't forget that I'm about to shell out big cash to someone who's going to strip-mine my face. I don't wanna die!! I'm too young to die!! Ironically enough, after the dentist gave me the bad news about the endodontist he poked around in my mouth and said, "My, you have beautiful teeth. No cavities. Never wore braces, huh? Well, well. It's a shame." Yeah, and you and your kind are sadistic, pain-peddling, cash-sucking, lawyers-in-labcoats. Gad, I hate this.

Had rehearsal last night which was kind of a drag, but it gave me an opportunity to rehearse with the girl who's playing the nurse and she's,...well, not to mince words, a babe. Interesting, because she looks like Madonna and I can't figure out why I find her attractive, whereas Madonna no longer interests me in the least (rumor has it that I once tried to crawl into the TV screen while watching Madonna perform "Like A Virgin"). I guess the biggest difference between this chick and Madonna is personality; this girl is really nice, whereas I think Madonna's kind of a piranha. Hey cool, that rhymes. Madonna the pir-an-ha, Madonna the pir-an-ha...

Allll rightee then. Time to get to work and look busy. Pray for my pathetic off-brown ass today as I am subjected to ungodly tortures at the hands of the endodontist. Doesn't our Constitution say something about "cruel and unusual punishment"? Thank The Great One for her note and tell her to chiiiill. Later.

    Facial strip-mining totally sucks, foggy "first day of Spring" rules.

Canyonface

Date: Mar 20
To: Duke
From: Jeff
Subject: Spring

    Ah, yes, spring. *Primavera es mi corazón*. The weather warms up, the birds and plants come out to play, and the overall mood just gets better.

    That is, until I decided to sit down and work through the taxes *de mi familia esta noche*. It's not April 14th, I know, when I usually do the taxes, but I had a sneaky suspicion that this year might be trouble. And it is. Two thousand bones of trouble. Can you believe that? *Dos mil dólares*? I'm a bitter, bitter man. Unless I can find some more creative deductions, The Cranky One and I will be forking over some serious cash. I think I'll ask José, who owns Sabor Latino down the street (where we stuff our faces two or three times a month) if he can make his restaurant a charity. And maybe the Wynkoop is a charity. Yeah, that's it. And maybe Guitars and CDs are business expenses. Yeah! And maybe all of our trips are for business, as well. Yeah!! If the IRS ever sees this e-mail, I don't know what you are talking about.

    But what can we do? Next year, it'll just be worse. And we both have the maximum taken out of our paychecks every time. Which leaves me with five of my ten earned dollars every two weeks. Ah, well. Death and Texas. The only things in life that are certain. At least we have beer. And, tonight, I bottled my second batch. So, the house smells like a brewery, which is the second best smell in the world. So, life's not all that bad. Spring has sprung. And I loves me some spring, dude. Especially now that I'm in a place that has a winter, because after you've been through a winter, spring is the thing you want to see. Yessir, spring. Almost time to go plant some fresh little daisies, marigolds, and start to think about tuning up the ol' lawn mower. Ah, yes, spring -- When you sit outside on warm nights, watching the stars and drinking homebrew. When you invite your neighbors over for a 'cue. When you ride your bicycle all around the barrio on the weekends. When you climb mountains. When it rains like a bat out of hell each and every day for about an hour. When you catch the Rocks on the TV or the radio, beating the heck out of all those California teams. Springtime is all of these things to me, and more.

How're the teeth doing? Root canals are loads and loads of fun, let me tell you. They put this little screen type thing around the tooth in question that basically blocks the rest of your mouth from the dentist's view and holds your mouth completely open at the same time. Once you get used to the pain in your jaw from having your mouth held open at an unnaturally large angle, it's really not much work at all. You just sort of lay there and do nothing, feeling the rhythms and the sounds of the mad scientists at work around you: "Drill? Drill. Scalpel? Scalpel. Clamp? Clamp. Super-duper root-sucking machine? Super-duper root-sucking machine." You can actually kind of feel it when they get your roots out -- it's kind of like they are removing a teeny-tiny sliver of your brain from deep within you. You can feel it being slowly and deliberately removed. Like trying to retrieve a prize from the bottom of a Cracker Jack box that's just been opened. It's kind of weird, actually. Enjoy, won't you?

Well, hombre, time for me to jump into the shower. Have a nice weekend and we'll be e-talking to you later.

Root Canals suck, Fridays rule!

-Mister Spring

Chapter 7
Adjust Your Straps!

Date: Mar 22
To: Jeff
From: Anthony
Subject: The Taxes Tornadoes

Hey, thanks for setting my mind at ease regarding my impending root canal. You're just a regular Florence Fuckin' Nightingale. Brutal tax story, dude. How come you and The Great Cranky One owe so much money? You're a homeowner now and I thought that meant you get some kind of break. I guess you really don't want to hear this, but I got both my federal and state returns this week and I'm now about 1000 bucks wealthier. I also lucked-out as much as I could at the endodontist's yesterday. Seems that if the problem is what the endodontist expects, he'll have to go in and patch up the root canal which can be done under local anesthetic, takes about 20 minutes, and will cost me zip, zilch, nada, because of my wonderful, caring, charitable, helpingest-to-old-ladies-crossing-streetest DMO. Naturally, this is all best case scenario. Worst-case scenario is that the endodontist is wrong, in which case I've been gutted for nothing, I'm looking at implants and bridges, and those bastards at the DMO will only pay 40%. No matter what, there will be pain and blood involved, which will make the doctors happy. Thus, next Tuesday, I will take that long walk to the chair and do my best to bleed all over the endodontist's Doc Martin's.

I didn't get to see *Must See T.V.* last night because I was at rehearsal and couldn't tape it because Alden's mom decided that, for the first time in six months, there was something on the tube she just had to see -- figure skating. Buckle up my friend, we're going for a little ride. Let's talk figure skating. What is the fascination women have with this "sport"? This "sport" is useful only in terms of ice hockey and, if you don't have a big curved stick in your hands (remember how much more exciting figure skating became when someone did pick up a stick and apply it to a knee?), it's basically ballet on ice. And I think we're all in agreement that ballet is not a sport (albeit you do have to demonstrate high levels of athleticism if not testosterone to do it). Thus, if all you change is the medium on which you perform, how does this automatically qualify figure skating as a sport? 'Nuff said. But this still doesn't reveal why women are so taken by this event. The only plausible explanation I can come up with is that (for the most part) men hate it. Thus, if men hate it, women will flock to it like fleas to a fat dog. Yes friends, it's "The Neanderthal Hour." Julie, this is one of those little blips in time Jeff was telling you about where you don't pay attention to anything we say, because we're basically talking to rile someone up. One undeniable fact remains, however: I fuckin' hate figure skating and every woman I know will leave a mall early to get home and be mesmerized by it. And God forbid, you don't give up the remote control because they'll basically pull a gun on your ass. And then they get really pissed off if you sit there and make fun of it. For the unenlightened viewer of figure skating, the intrigue and the passion climax only when the skaters fall down and you can do your best Nelson (of *The Simpsons*) impersonation and go "HA HA!!" This is sort of akin to the same psychological explanation as to why people pay money to watch cars go around and around; because they know that at high speed, crashes are pretty dramatic. The one thing skating does have going for it, however, is that the some of the chicks are total babes. But you can't even give it credit for this, because then the woman with the gun and the remote calls you a shallow pig. My guess is that, if you look at the domestic violence calls received by police stations last night, it was up dramatically because they scheduled this shit at the same time as the NCAA Tournament! Great idea. Sports bars must've loved it. Ah well, if you can't beat it, exploit it. When figure skating's on, I can get away with shit I wouldn't even consider any other time of day. I've thrown out Alden's old clothes, shoes, and make-up -- right under her nose. Of course, this could explain why during football season I can't ever find my guitar.

Anyway, big weekend in store. Alden's coming in this morning for Spring Break. She has to leave early though because she's going to deliver a lecture at a conference in Utah. So, she's all excited about that and because "some of the guys are going to take us skiing (godsporting)." I'm pretty happy about this fact, as you can well imagine. I would remind Alden that while I don't ski, snow doesn't last forever, and any snow weasel that tries to "adjust her straps" will have to deal with me on solid ground at some point. This weekend, however, she's having a bridal shower. This "cluckfest" will take place on Saturday; then Sunday we're going to go to the San Diego Wild Animal Park. All in all, it looks like a great weekend and hope you guys are looking forward to the same. Better put this novel to rest. You guys take care and we'll talk to you next week.

Figure skating sucks, Wild Animal Park rules. OUT!!

Marlin Perkins

Date: Mar 24
To: Duke
From: Jeff
Subject: The Taxes Rangers

Man, do you realize that we have been going at this e-mail thing almost every day for the last two months? Are we in love, or what? This kind of reminds me of the 10th grade, when I used to hog my parents' phone to talk to my "Annabelle" (yes, that was her real name) for hours and hours and hours on end.....

So, Mess Aldiente is going skiing? One word of advice to you, *hermano*: "Adjust your straps" is an expression that really has nothing to do with skiing, and if you say something like that around a group of real skiers, you'll probably get laughed at wholeheartedly and thrown out of the lodge into the cold wet snow. There are no straps on or around skis, you see. Maybe "Adjust your bindings" or "Adjust your boots" would be more apropos. Just trying to save you from a possible awkward social scenario, *amigo*, and keep you warm and comfy.

Concur on the figure skating thing. In a sport where the performers are nearly perfect all the time, the public yearns for a moment of mortalness, a sign that the performer is merely human, a screwup of some kind like us normal folk have each and every day. This approach seems to work for hockey as well. The crowds at the few games I have seen couldn't care less about the event until a couple of Ducks and Sharks take off their gloves and begin to lay into each other as though one had stolen another's wife. At this point, the crowd goes nuts and starts to yell and scream like they were cheering for something important. I don't get it.

One last thing, before I let you go on to do that voodoo that you do so well. Disturbing Signs of Growing Up and Domesticity: Tonight, The Great One and I made some pizza dough and some pizzas. When I was trying to decide what to put on my own pizza, did I choose something cool like Canadian Bacon and Pineapple? No!! I chose Pesto, Tomato and Mozzarella cheese. And I like it that way. It's tough getting old. Help me. Have a beautimous Monday, won't you?

Figure Skating Sucks, Money Trees Rule!

-Farmer Jeff

Date: Mar 25
To: Jeff
From: Anthony
Subject: And the winner is...

Point of clarification: I apologize to all you godsporters for my erroneous statements regarding the use of straps on skis. I must plead ignorance, for I am not a godsporter and I only ask that you don't make fun of me because it is very important to me that I be highly regarded in your social circle. Yes, even though I liken the sensation of your chosen sport to paying two-hundred bucks for the privilege of running headfirst into the wall of a walk-in freezer, I still hope I'm cool in your eyes. Because, hey, you're cool in mine. Still, however, should any of you rad dudes endeavor to warm your hands on MY little snowshoe hare I'll shove a godsport pole up your ass and call you a popsicle.

Had a wonderful weekend with the fiancé in town and even managed to take care of a few things. Hawaii is a "go" and I even managed to reserve the tuxedos for the Big Day. By the way, we'll need your tuxedo measurements by the first of July. The Wild Animal Park continues to rule even though it is always populated with the most obnoxious displays of bad parenting the world has ever seen. Aside from the normal disconcern for letting their little brats run amok, scream endlessly, and create general mayhem, some parents truly stand out in their stupidity. Case in point, the genius who casually sat on his fat ass while his two-year old daughter played with the latch of the monorail while it was stopped fifty feet above the lion pit. Fortunately, Little Genius inherited her father's brain power and couldn't figure out the sophisticated security system. Overall, a valid endorsement for condoms.

Tonight the world turns its attention to Oscar (which tends to piss-off the other residents of *Sesame Street*) and answers the looming question of whether a movie about a talking pig can really be deemed as the Best Picture of any year. No chance, but I still contend that it's a great movie. Hopefully, my boy Nicolas Cage will walk off with one of the golden midgets as will *Leaving Las Vegas*. If Tom Hanks wins again, I'm going to start wondering whether or not he's managed by Don King. Naturally, as an aspiring actor, I will be spending Oscar night learning my lines so that I, too, may one day stand up before Hollywood's elite and babble endlessly.

Tomorrow is my date with destiny (don't tell Alden, she's insanely jealous) as I journey to the endodontist for interrogation. From here on out, my policy regarding dentists is to always lie to them. I'm going to get tortured anyway, so I might as well make 'em work for it. That's about it for today. Oscar smack tomorrow. By the way, have you heard that our boy Val Kilmer is mole-munching with Cindy Crawford? More to cum...uh, follow.

Parents suck, Nicolas Cage rules. OUT!!

The Critic

Date: Mar 25
To: Duke
From: Jeff
Subject: I'd like to thank....

"Great Baked Potatoes, Jeff."
"Thank you honey. Thank you very much. I'll try to keep this short. I'd like to thank the microwave, General Electric for their quality workmanship in making the microwave, Public Service for the electricity that they provide to our house, Benjamin Franklin for discovering electricity, the fabulous state of Idaho for their great potatoes, the great earth in which the potatoes grow, the bag company who made the bags in which the potatoes came, the guy who made the cupboards in which the potatoes sit before they

are made, Blahblah Mortgage for lending us the money to buy this house and the microwave within, my mother for taking me to potato-baking classes over on La Jolla Boulevard when I was 12 years old..."

It is my belief that they should really rename the Academy Awards "The Boob Show." Because, from the pre-show where they show all the *fabuloso* actresses and what they wear to the end, it is one big ol' booby fest, served up on a platter. There are more boobs at the Oscars than in a good porno movie, and you can see every last one of them. Amazing. They could pass out awards like "Best boobs barely contained in a formal dress," "Best see through outfit," "Best headlights on Oscar night," and "Most pointed dress." It's almost like a contest to see who can show the most breast and remain formal without actually showing the nip. I was glad to see that *Mi Familia* actually got mentioned a couple of times. Once for some awards, like "Best Accent in an Ethnic Movie" or some shit and the other times as, "Here's Jimmy Smits, star of Mi Familia!!!" With the seemingly lack of good movies last year, why wasn't it nominated for more awards? And why wasn't *Toy Story* nominated for best picture? That was the best movie that I saw last year, hands down. It's a must buy.

Don't worry about the godsport social *faux pas* (now there's a big couple of words) that you committed. I was merely trying to make sure that you don't make that mistake in the wrong situation. Besides, non-godsporters are people, too. Barely. Have a Groovy Tuesday, won't you?

Toy Story RULES! (no matter who wins Best Pigture)

-Blackwell.

Date: Mar 26
To: Jeff
From: Anthony
Subject: Can you smell that Mel?

Thus, another Academy Awards show has come and gone and I'm left to grouse about the outcome. I knew I would always have trouble with this show the year *Star Wars* lost to *Annie Hall*. Don't get me wrong, *Braveheart* was a great movie, but doesn't it seem like the easiest way to get an Academy Award is to put a guy in a skirt? First *Tootsie* and now this. Far as I'm concerned, the pig still rules. There is nothing you can say that will convince me that any of those other movies will stand the test of time like *Babe* will. Besides, it may not have won the Oscar, but people are buying it up faster than yesterday's bacon. Something else I decided last night: I may have sex, I may go for a roll in the hay, I may bop like bunnies, but I'll never make Whoopi again. Fortunately, they gave Nicolas the Best Actor Award, which restored my faith in the people that vote for these things. Actually, I didn't see the show. Did any of those well-exposed double-scoops belong to Elisabeth

"Woo Hoo" Shue? And was Val there with Cindy? Ah Hollywood, and there but for the grace of God go I. By the way, got my lines down.

Had dinner with Alden and her Mom last night at a BBQ joint in Solana Beach. Yep, right off the I-5 in the heart of Solana Beach is a BBQ place where you are encouraged to throw peanut shells on the floor. Unfortunately, it's also one of those places that believes that in order for anything to be BBQ you have to put sauce on it, LOTS O' SAUCE. I hope that if I taught you anything about BBQing it's that you don't have to douse the meat in four gallons of overachieving ketchup for it to be good. My theory about BBQ sauce is, if you have to have it, emphasize flavor rather than heat. In other words, if you have bad sauce, don't try to cover up the flavor by adding more pepper, Tabasco, and gasoline, start over. Overall, however, the place was kinda cool. Good to see there's a redneck bar so close to home featuring live entertainment. Have to mosey on down there some Saturday night, rustle up some vittles, have a few cold ones, and listen to some good ol' boys pick away.

Today's the day. Today, at 1:45 the dentist will use various objects with sharp pointy ends to put the hurt on my ass. This means that my status for correspondence tomorrow is up in the air. Guess it depends on how much pain I'm in and whether or not I get any sleep tonight. I guess what I'm saying is think happy thoughts for me this afternoon and don't be too surprised if I'm not able to write tomorrow. I'll do my best, however. And with the help of my friends Tylenol and Codeine, who knows what I can accomplish?

Well anyway, man, time to get to it. Like I say, no promises for tomorrow, but we'll see. Have a good one. Excellent message this morning by the way. Very clever.

D-Day at the dentist sucks, *Babe* rules. OUT!!

Dead Man Walking

Date: Mar 28
To: Duke
From: Jeff
Subject: The E-mail Patch

I've got my e-mail patch on my right arm, just up at the shoulder area, to help me deal with the withdrawal symptoms I'm experiencing. Instead of cutting off the e-mail cold turkey, it merely reduces my daily intake a little at a time until I'm receiving no e-mail at all. This way, I won't experience the nausea, morning sickness, and vomiting that normally occur when one is suddenly cut off from e-mail, either voluntarily or involuntarily. Ah, yes, the miracles of modern science.

What happened to you yesterday? I suspected that you may be "under the weather" as it were. I know how it is when a dentist works you over for hours at a time. You just want to go home and cry and sleep a little and grab the nearest stuffed animal (in my case, Gorilla) and lay in bed all day eating 'Nilla Wafers and watching talk shows. I can relate. I've been there.

Concur on the BBQ thing. Some of the best 'cue that I've ever had (next to your 'cueing, of course) was in Memphis, where they believe in "Dry" ribs, which are ribs with the sauce cooked in, so that the final product is a clean dry piece of a former pig. YUMMY!!!! Plus, they are not quite as messy to eat that way.

Opened up a "preview" bottle of the second batch of homebrew last night. A preview bottle is when the beer hasn't quite been in the bottle long enough, but you just gotta taste it anyway. This preview bottle was pretty darn good, I must say. Dark color, decent taste. A vast improvement over the first batch. Goes to show what a little hops can do. By May, I should have this thing down.

Well, time to get in the shower and, yes, find something to iron. Have a nice Wednesday if you go to work. Have an even nicer Wednesday if you stay home. If you stay home, I expect a full update on all of the daytime talk shows. "My cousin is a transvestite lesbian alcoholic incestual architect, and I think she should stop being an architect" on the next "Danny!"

E-mail withdrawal sucks, 'Nilla wafers RULE!!!

-Jeffrey Coors

Date: Mar 28
To: Jeff
From: Anthony
Subject: Back from hell

Whassup my friend? I have returned today, battered, bruised, but never beaten. The last two days have been hell. In hell, there is a skinny recliner with a hydraulic jack. In hell, they strap you into this chair and provide you with a choice of wonderful reading materials (*Sunset* and *Good Housekeeping*). In hell, a guy in a crisp white jacket comes in, settles next to your chair, and produces a shiny silver table to display the shiny silver instruments of torture he will use to make you sorry you ever broke a commandment. In hell, there is anesthetic that hurts more than anything else. In hell, the guy in the crisp white jacket always has a shitburger and chili fries (with onions) for lunch. In hell, you hear the sounds of flesh being ripped away from teeth. In hell, smoke comes out of your mouth without the aid of a cigarette. In hell, there are stitches. Fortunately for me, a call came in from the afterlife governor saying there had been some mistake, I was not supposed to be in hell at all. Seems there's some guy in Colorado I have a tendency to be mistaken for. Anyway, off to Heaven. In Heaven, there are angels of mercy such as my Alden, who brings me milkshakes, fluffs my pillow, and wipes my sweaty brow. In Heaven, there is Vicodin. In Heaven, Pay-Per-View channels almost come in through ordinary cable hook-ups. In Heaven, there is no work, only sleep. In Heaven, the Lakers kick the snot out of the Magic. And, in Heaven, there is the Great Father who cares for His flock with an unmatched love. We call Him the DMO.

Thus, the ordeal is over and it played along the lines of best-case scenario. I don't have to go back, I don't have to worry, and, best of all, I don't have to pay. The only problem is that the root was worn down to a nub and any trauma in the area could mean problems down the road. Thus, I won't be able to engage in any more barroom brawls with you. I did stay home yesterday because I had the worst headache and I was having trouble sleeping through the pain from my tooth. It still hurts a bit today. Problem is, I can't take my Vicodin because I have to work and it makes me loopier than a loon.

Anyway, off to work to find out what I missed yesterday. Have a great day and glad to hear your new batch of Jeffbrew looks like it's going to turn out well. But don't get your hops up too high. HA HA. *Hola* to The Great One.

Pain sucks, pain-killers rule. OUT!!

Toothless

Date: Mar 28
To: Duke
From: Jeff
Subject: How Loopy Is A Loon?

Oh, shit. Now I'm in trouble. "If I come home and you're lying on the couch watching *Wheel Of Fortune* again and the house is a mess, I'm gonna take out all of your roots" myopia is pretty much what I got ahold of today. The Cranky One does not do her justice at this point. More like The Naggy One. I guess I had better start to clean the house once in a while, huh? Damn, as soon as she reads this I'll probably be forced to sleep out under the stars for a month or two. Ah, yes, women.

You know, it's amazing how many dentists eat those shitburgers for lunch, and for breakfast, I might add; and possibly as a light snack between patients. There must be some particular restaurant they all go to where all that is served is shitburgers and chili-cheese fries with extra onions. Maybe the dentists all sit around eating shitburgers and relishing the thought of excavating the next poor soul's face. Maybe they all dream of new ways to use the Super-Duper Root-Sucking Machine on their patients. Maybe they give each other points based upon how much pain each dentist has caused that day. The winner being the dentist who dishes out the most pain, of course. Because in order to even consider ever becoming a dentist, one has to be a sadist in a big way.

So, I need help with names for the Jeffbrew products. Some names already thought of: "Go Directly to Jail Ale," where the label would be decorated with various *Monopoly* characters, "Buzz Light Beer," "Alehouse

64

Rock," and some others that I can't quite think of right now. They are written down somewhere, of course. But you, my man, can help out, because you are the "Idea Master." And, I'm sure, you've got some gems in you somewhere. So feel free to suggest some names. One day, you too may appear on a beer bottle.

Tonight, we're going to see Chris Duarte at the Fox Theater in Boulder. I already have the guitar wood in my pants, and it's unlikely to go away until well after the show is over. I may have trouble walking all day, I know, but I'll do my best to just sit at my desk and never get up. That way no one will notice my funny limp. If they do, I'll plead "Hey, it's guitar wood, not female wood!" Because Chris is an amazing guitar player. I'll tell you again -- Go see him -- for inspiration, at the very least. He'll make you want to learn your blues scales faster than you say "Austin, Texas." I just kind of stand there in the Theater with my jaw on the floor and my wood sticking out of my shirt the whole night. If you can't already tell, I am looking forward to it tremendously. And, tomorrow, we Godsport. Although that's really in jeopardy now because of my Doghouse status. I hate it when crankiness ruins a good time. Or a good weekend. But I ain't kissing butt to come back inside the house this time. Spring is almost here, the weather is getting better, I may actually like being outside and in the doghouse. Yeah, that's it. That'll show her. I won't come back inside until October. Did you ever see *The Simpsons'* episode where Marge kicked Homer out? That was a riot. Here he was, dressed in rags, growth of hair on his chin, in Bart's tree house, and he said "Gosh, I've been out of the house for ten whole minutes already!" Classic.

Well, it's time for beddie-bye. I really ought to go outside and climb into that doghouse and go to sleep, because that's where I'm gonna end up anyway. You have a nice weekend now, you hear?

Women Suck, Chris Duarte RULES!!!

-Homer

Date: Mar 29
To: Jeff
From: Anthony
Subject: Lassie come home

Sorry to hear you've taken up residence at the Hound-a-day Inn. Troubles me to hear that you and The Great One brawl. That means that Alden and I are capable of brawling. That sucks. Look, why don't we both admit that marriage is a stupid idea and get back to what it used to be. We could be a real-life Joey and Chandler. Come home to me, roomie. No more of these filthy girls. Only I know what's best for you, Jeffrey. Only I can love you. On second thought, you don't put out enough. You tell The Great One to let you back in the house and YOU quit watching *Wheel of Fortune*. For

God's sake, watching *Wheel of Fortune* while the house is a mess. Surely there must be a ball game on somewhere.

While you sweep the floor with your jaw at Chris Duarte tonight, I'll be entangled in a softball game. We started our Friday night league last week and swept both games of a double-header. Looks like we're going to be a force to be reckoned with this year. Being the "man of many positions" (just ask Alden), I find myself this year at rover. That's right, buddy. This year I'm doing it doggy-style. Actually, thus far, I haven't exactly been excelling at the position (just ask Alden); but within the next few games, I'm sure I'll get a handle on things. I do have to be extremely careful about my tooth tonight. After all, the last thing I need to munch on is a softball.

I am stalling because I can't think of any potential names for your new line of custom-made beers. Uh, how about "Head Beer" (it would make it a lot of fun to order), or "I Can't Believe It's Beer," or anything along the lines of "Yogi Beer" or "Smokey the Beer." Yeah, "Smokey the Beer"; the story of how a young brewmeister and his babelicious wife go camping for the weekend. While they're out hiking, a young, orphaned bear cub wanders into camp and proceeds to drink all the new beers the young brewmeister was working on. When the couple returns to camp, they find the bear cub sitting in a chair, smoking cigarettes, and belching like a fiend. Then the cub tries to pick up on the young brewmeister's Great wife. When he sees that's not going to work, he wanders over to the next campsite where three female modeling majors are sponge-bathing and parties with them all night long. Thus, the legend is born.

Actually, there is a true story behind the name "Smokey the Beer." At my brother's bachelor party, we were barbecuing when a piece of meat caught on fire prompting some fool to run over and pour beer all over it and extinguish the fire. For the rest of the night he was "Smokey the Beer." True story, ask my cousin Dave, he was hysterical.

Well, time to get busy in an attempt to hasten the weekend's arrival. Have a monstrous weekend and good luck in your escape from the dog pound. Enjoy.

La casa de perro sucks, "Smokey the Beer" rules. OUT!!

Rover

Date: Mar 31
To: Duke
From: Jeff
Subject: Play Ball!!!!!!!!!!!!

I think the greatest compliment an opponent can give you, and I never heard this before my tennis match today, is when he's winning, and he's hitting the ball all over the court and you are running after it and returning just about everything, and he says, "Damn! You just won't go away, will you?"

That was a compliment of the highest order in my book. Because, no, I will not go away. I also knew, at that point, that I had this guy right where I wanted him. Ahead, but a little scared. But you know what he had that gave me problems? A great net game. I tried everything. Initially, when he was at the net, I returned his shots right back to him, but he was able to cross-court me like a fiend. Then, I tried to lob him. It worked a few times but, more often than not, I hit the ball out. Finally, I settled for doing my damnedest to keep him back away from the net, which worked the best. But I learned that a great net game is dangerous. And you know why I finally won? Aggressiveness, my dear boy. The lesson that you preach. I was aggressive as often as I could be. I hit the ball where he wasn't, back and forth and left and right; then, when he caught on to that, I hit the ball right back at him, right around his knees -- which gives most tennis players fits. When he caught on to that, I hit it again where he wasn't. And changed the speed of my returns. There's a concept. First, I hit it medium speed a couple of times to soften him up; then I hit a zinger way into the corner, which he had a hard time returning. Ah, yes, tennis. What else is there?

Well, there's guitars for one thing. I do not want to be LIKE Chris Duarte, I want to BE Chris Duarte. Last night, we watched him play his Stratocaster at the Fox Theater in Boulder from about 10:20 p.m. to 1:30 a.m. That's right. We got out to the car, turned it on, looked at the clock, and could not believe it was that late. He rocked. He rolled. He's a maniac.

Julie talking now: I will add -- He's hot, too. Long curly locks attempting to be tamed in a ponytail, bulging muscles, and he performed the whole show in Converse hi-tops and a kilt. Is Duarte Scottish? Anyway, the encore was sans shirt, so we were able to enjoy the washboard stomach complete with a series of tattoos -- I mean, enjoy the incredible finale of awesome guitar stunts. He's The Man.

Cool! A little Great One smack. Yeah, she's The Great One again. All I needed was a little "I'm sorry I was a butthole last night" to make me happy. And a little ass kissing. So, anyway, Chris is a maniac. If you get a chance, go see him. Grab yourself a cold one or three, kick back, and be prepared to have your mind blown.

Sunday now. We didn't godsport today, because He brought us excellent weather instead. So, we started our second annual "Let's work on the garden until it hurts" campaign. And, boy, do I hurt. I think it's a combo of the tennis war yesterday and the gardening today. But I loves me some gardening, dude. It may not be *manly*, it may not be *macho*, hell, it probably isn't even up there with *sissy*, but gardening is all right with me. Out there in the bright sun, just me against the ivy that I am trying to dig up, and its roots which are all 3" diameter by 400 feet long; and the rose bushes, which last year, when we were "just letting things grow to see what is really out there," really took over the yard. They are beautiful, but they grow like weeds. So I had to prune *las rosaledas*. It's kind of a calming thing, really. Getting my hands into mother earth, caressing her until she is beautiful, planting tiny seeds that will grow into forty-seven million tomato plants that will threaten to take over the world by September. Oh yeah, it's cool. We haven't really planted anything yet, because the last frost probably hasn't hit yet, but we're getting ready. We are starting some things indoors: squash, sunflowers, green peppers, money trees, beer bushes; you name it. When you and Aldiente get your first house, maybe you'll get this bug, too.

Well, *amigo*, it's time to go rest my tired body from this rigorous weekend. Heck, I need another day to recover from the weekend!! You have a nice Monday.

Chris Duarte is King, Tennis Rules. OUT!

-Garden Boy

Chapter 8
Minus Penis

Date: Apr 1
To: Jeff
From: Anthony
Subject: A Dark Day

Well, dude, the wedding's off. I'd like to be able to expound a lot more detail to you at this point, but, fact is, I'm numb. Considered not going into work today, but didn't really think it'd matter one way or the other. Seems that while Alden was in Utah, she had a ski lesson from some guy and...well, you get the picture. All right, the obligatory April Fool's joke is outta the way and, while I have no doubt that you saw through that little facade, now I can get on with life. Damn, you know how to spend a weekend. Mine, basically, looked like this: Friday night, rehearsed, played softball, went to bed; Saturday, got oil changed, bought running shoes, went for costume fitting, watched basketball, played guitar for two hours, bandaged fingers, went to bed; Sunday, ate, went to store, ran, showered, watched TV, went to bed. On the up side, the mighty many-times morphosized softball team is now 3-0. Interesting to see how the complexion of a team that's used to losing changes once it starts to win. No beer is consumed during the game, there's meaningful chatter, people actually show, and there's a lot less bitching at the umpire.

Well done, Grasshopper. Glad to see you can win "the close ones." As far as guys getting to the net, you were right to keep him from getting there in the first place. This, of course, means you must dictate the pace and the flow of the game. This is important because, once you play to an opponent's strengths, you're dead (see UCLA basketball). I haven't played tennis in ages. The guy I normally play hasn't been around, so I'm basically out of commission. I gotta find a new patsy, I mean partner. Now, correct me if I'm wrong, but the last time you and I played, didn't I yell, "Die, won't you?" which, in my eyes, is a much better compliment than the one *he* paid you. He just wanted you to go away. You pissed me off so much I wanted you to drop dead on the spot. I still plan to play you in July. Hopefully, I can get some practice in before but, if not, that won't be my excuse for losing. I'll think of something else.

Uh, Julie...why salivate over the masculine attributes of Chris Duarte when you have a carved hunk of male marble occupying your boudoir on a daily basis? Why is it so important that a guy have a washboard stomach? If you women were expected to actually use a washboard, you'd have a conniption. Therefore, I think more recognition should be given to those of us guys who can boast of having a stomach like a washing machine. Yeah, modernize. You women gotta get with the times. Would you rather have a

69

hard, immobile, labor intensive piece of machinery, or one with a rotating basket and spin cycle? And, besides, Jeff plays guitar and HE doesn't wear a dress. Well, there was that one time but we'd been drinking tequila.....So, love your man, even though it sounds like he'd do Chris Duarte faster than you would. And, uh, if anyone's interested, I played my guitar for a long time on Saturday and I've got the "ow-ies" to prove it.

Aah, little Jeffrey working in his garden, "Jeff the Gatherer," "Reaper of the Harvest," "He Who Would Wear the Shoes of the Humble Man." So when did this become such a hobby, Fertilizer Boy? I shoulda known, you always did like working with hoes. HA HA!! Get it? Hoes? Ah, go root around in the dirt some more. So whatcha growin' in your garden, Jeff? (Wink, wink) "Oh, we got some radishes, corn (we call it "maize"), brussel sprouts, mushrooms (wink), and grass (wink, wink)." What you ought to do is grow your own barley and hops. Just yankin' ya, buddy. I think that tending weeds is a sign of maturity. Besides, it provides me with countless opportunities to make fun of you, because now I can use such words as hose, trim, bush, buds, and tuber. Hey, Arnold with a cold: "Ees not a tuber."

Thus, I take leave of you for a Monday. Have a great day and we'll see ya tomorrow.

Washboard stomachs suck, Dodgers rule. OUT!!

Maytag

Date: Apr 2
To: Duke
From: Jeff
Subject: whlkdjlajdflkiiop

Gitr owis rul, dde. Let me try that again: Guitar "owies" rule, dude. Sorry, it's early in the morning and the first sip of coffee hasn't hit my bloodstream yet, so I'm a little out of whack. But I'm glad to hear about your guitar owies. This is your first step on the road to becoming Chris Duarte. Let those fingers bleed, so that one day you won't be able to feel a thing on the end of 'em. Now, the real trick is to play your guitar again tonight until those fingers are owie-ing all over again. That's the tough part. Playing guitar with previous owies is a bitch.

Bravo!! Bravo!! Once again, we are on the exact same wavelength, only 1200 miles apart. I don't understand this myopia about women: They think it's not okay for us men to admire the physical attributes of any women, including themselves; then they turn around and say to us, "Why don't you do a thousand sit-ups tonight, dear?" Uh, yeah, isn't a washboard stomach a physical attribute, much like a nice pair of perky succulent breasts or an ass that just won't quit? I rest my case. And I'm glad to see that you feel the same. And what if I don't want a washboard stomach, what if I want a nice fluffy pillow stomach, the better for you to snuggle up your pretty little head, my dear? Besides, you know what they say, don't you? Washboard stomach, tiny penis.

So your softball team is 3-0, huh? I am impressed. And I'm sure it's because of your doggysty...uh, rover playing. Back in the old days, I used to feel a quiet calm come over me whenever I would hear "Anthony Reynoso, Rover," because I knew you would shag all those fly balls that no one else could get, and I knew we would win, because you were our rock. And don't even get me started on those home runs.....I wish I had a team to play on, but I haven't played in all my years in the Mile High City, because I don't really know anybody in a company large enough to have a team. I'll stick to tennis. In tennis, there is no jealousy between the second baseman and the lesbian first baseman. In tennis, there are no ex-girlfriends showing up to rattle you. In tennis, you can play in the nice part of town, which is conveniently located next to the office. In tennis, the "leader of the team," or actually "just the biggest guy around" doesn't decide where you play and when you hit. It's just you, the ball, the court, and your opponent. Nobody to blame but yourself. I like it that way. And maybe, by the end of this week, I'll be 3-0 as well.

Tiempo para mi to get into the shower, hombre. I guess I gotta go to work.

Washboard Stomachs (Tiny Penises) Suck, Guitar Owies Rule!!! And the caffeine has finally hit my bloodstream.

-Mr. Coffee

Date: Apr 2
To: Jeff
From: Anthony
Subject: Tuesday

Some days just don't warrant a catchy title. I can't get a break. The problem that prompted me to see the dentist in the first place has reared its ugly little pus-filled head again. So, I called the endodontist to sound the alarm and the receptionist said, "Uh, he's not here, he's out at an emergency extraction." Translated: he's extracting his ball from a sand trap on 11. So, I explained to her the problem and now I have to go in at 11:30 this morning so he can look at it. Some possible scenarios she gave me: (1) antibiotics, or (2) "Root Canal-The Sequel." Do you know how bitter I'm going to be if I have to go under the drill bit again? Let me explain. Take a truck load of lemons and squeeze the juice out of them. Now add 1000 bottles of finely ground aspirin, and mix well. Now go brush your teeth, then come back and immediately drink the lemon-aspirin mixture. Can't you just taste it? That's how bitter I'm going to be.

Yeah, yeah, same wavelength. Damn women! Yeah, perky ass, breasts that won't quit. Hah! Uh, Jeff, did I really say all THAT? Wait, I'm reading the e-mail I sent you yesterday...uh huh...washboard stomach... modernize...spin cycle...Jeff in a dress...yeah, I guess I did. Sorry, buddy. Damn women! You, you purveyors of double-standards! Washboard stomach. Know what you get with that? Teensy weensy weenie, that's what. Yeah, so small it's almost a negative value. "Minus-penis" is what it's called. Come on over to Positive Country. Cum to where the action is. Damn women!

Well, my friend, I'd love to get you started on those home runs, but, unfortunately, there were none. I'm not a power hitter. You must have me confused with YOU. Yeah, I can imagine that when one hits as many home runs as you, one has a tendency to sort of project them onto others after a while. It's your subconscious mind saying, "Damn, I wish the rest of these weaklings could go yard once in a while. Must I constantly carry these leeches?" Then your conscious mind snaps into action and you say things like, "Nice bunt Anthony, way to keep the rally going." But in your mind you're thinking, "Boy, you sure pounded the crap outta that one. The third baseman would've thrown you out if he wasn't laughing so hard." Until you get so lost in thought that you aren't even aware that you're up again and you've hit another homer. So, when you DO come back to reality, you don't know how we got so far ahead and you just credit someone else with the homer. That's you, buddy -- Mr. Generous. Now, I smugly take leave for the day. Have a nice day, won't you?

Root canals suck harder than ever, "love bundles" rule. OUT!!

Señor Bitter-boy

Date: Apr 3
To: Jeff
From: Anthony
Subject: Weirdnesday

You know what? I have a co-worker who thinks he's my secretary. "Uh, Anth, don't you have a meeting this morning?" "Uh, Anth, don't forget to fill out your time card." Needless to say, this is driving me right out of my fucking mind for lots of reasons, such as: (1) Me a big boy now, take care of self. (2) He seems to take great pride in doing this. (3) He honestly believes he's doing me a favor. (4) I always envisioned my secretary as being a woman in an obscenely short skirt. And (5) I hate being called "Anth" by anyone who's not earned the right to call me whatever the hell they want. WEIRD! (And possibly detrimental to someone's health.)

Well, let's see, Dustin Hoffman has *Ishtar*, Jack Nicholson has *Wolf*, Nicolas Cage has *Trapped in Paradise,* so I guess it's only right that I have a project I can look back on with horror. Mine is *I Remember Mama*. Realistically, it's still too early to judge the final product but all indications point to a bomb of Hiroshima proportions. For one thing, last night's rehearsal was scheduled to start at 6:30, but at 7:00 only about a third of the cast was there prompting the director to go "ballistic" and say, "Do you think we could all be on time next time?" Uh, excuse me, I think it's time to get in some faces and lay down the law -- not quietly plead with us to adhere to our schedules. Also, she was ready to cancel tonight's rehearsal, because tonight is Passover which is legit in my eyes. But only one cast member is Jewish! So, we're rehearsing after all and, Lord, do we need it. I dunno, buddy, the work ethic of this cast is really bad but the director doesn't push it either. WEIRD!

Finally, I'm constantly being reminded of my mortality these days. This naturally occurs every time somebody in a white coat starts poking around my mouth. Latest news is that the root may or may not stabilize enough to function correctly. We'll have to wait and see. Then, this morning, I'm driving to work and some dumb mofo turns left about thirty feet in front of me without noticing that I'm traveling about 50 MPH. Best part is that once he's entirely blocked my lane, his morning coffee kicks in and suddenly he's aware he's about to get a green Toyota in his passenger seat, so he does what any inept asshole would do and he slams on the brakes. Do you realize that the biggest tiff you and I have had in our friendship was caused by someone named Mary Jo? I ask this only because, as my life flashed before my eyes, this fact sort of peaked my curiosity. The rest is a blur and a tribute to the power of fear and its influence on reflexes. Somehow, I realized that if I hit my brakes I was going to be part of a sandwich, so I notice that the lane he just turned from is vacant, and I steer left then quickly jack-knife right and fish my rear end around the side of him. Don't ask me how I maintained control, clean living I guess. The postscript to this story is a tirade of four-letter words that probably make no sense when used in conjunction. So, in the great scheme of life, a problem tooth ain't no biggie -- all that matters is enjoying life to the fullest. But I am feeling pretty "Smokey and the Bandit" about now.

Hey, I gotta split. Have a hap, hap, happy day because that's all that matters. Talk to you soon. And thanks for helping me enjoy life.

Idiots behind the wheel suck, life rules. OUT!!

Bjorn again

Date: Apr 3
To: Duke
From: Jeff
Subject: Ice Cream in Bed...

"Ju seem like a decent fellow. I hate to keel you." "You seem like a decent fellow. I hate to die." So it goes in the world of tennis. I come to you fresh from a 6-3, 6-4 victory over a very nice guy. In fact, he was the #2 ranked player in our little league. Actually, that won't change. Anyway, I have found the killer instinct and the aggression that you, the master, so eloquently preach. I wouldn't have won today if I hadn't been aggressive. The aggressiveness was paying off in big ways, let me tell you. I won a butttload of points on dropshots (he wasn't as fast as you or my other favorite opponent) and wicked zingers down the baseline. And I played the net particularly well. I actually returned a bunch of his lobs for winners. It was a good time.

Sorry to hear that Mary Jo was brought up in your mind again. That is one episode that I had hoped we would all quietly forget. Talk about a weird time of life. I am actually looking towards writing an autobiography about growing up in the 1970s, 1980s, and 1990s, and 1986-1987 would be a couple of chapters. Because it was a weird time. I was being brought into the career thing kicking and screaming and was looking for anything to keep me out of it. I was also hornier than Bill Clinton on the set of a porno movie, but that's another story. Anyway, every once in a while it's good to face your own mortality; it reminds you to never stop pushing the envelope, to never stop trying new things and to never stop living life to the fullest, because you never know when it might be over. I recently attended my first funeral and had these revelations. So, you see, there was probably a good reason for some idiot driver to cause you to poop in your pants.

Well, Anth, I gotta go. Defending my number one slot in the tourney all the time makes me tired and, besides, The Great One and I are going to go lay in bed and eat ice cream now. Adios!!!

Shortening your name when you didn't ask for it sucks, Aggressiveness on the court RULES!!

-Ben *y* Jerry

Date: Apr 4
To: Jeff
From: Anthony
Subject: Enter The Court

This impending tennis match of ours is shaping up like a bad kung-fu movie (as opposed to a good one). The story of a Master who takes a young man under his wing and teaches him the finer points of an ancient art. The lad learns well and, one day, snatches the sacred tennis ball from the hands of the Master. "It is time for you to go now, my son. Time for you to seek out greener grass courts to call your own. I arm you only with a sports bottle and a can of balls I found in the closet. Remember, honor forever what I have taught you." The lad does well in competition, but soon falls prey to the temptations that success in a capitalistic society can sometimes hold. No longer does he respect pathetic opponents, and the drop shot has become an integral part of his game. Word has it he's even flooding the streets with homemade beer. But, one night, as he sits in his plush Denver estate staring at a trophy case and imbibing gallons of homebrew, his wife Elvira comes stumbling in and asks him what's wrong.

"Ees thees all d'ere ees? Ju know, tennees, eating, drinking, fucking, sucking..."

Elvira replies, "Look at you. You're a mess. I'm telling you to get your shit together or we'll lose everything."

"Don't ju give me no fuckin' orders. Cuz baby, the only theeng that geeves orders is balls. Tennees balls."

As Elvira is packing, she cries, "You used to speak of honor, powerful serves, and a good net game. What would the Master think?" Which sends our hero into a rage.

"Hey, who put thees theeng together? ME! I don't want to hear about that old man again. I'm the Master now and I'm going to prove it to all of you!"

A story of revenge, a story of courage, the story of a legend and the man who couldn't live with it. Starring Jeff Chacon as Grasshopper and Anthony Reynoso as The Master. "ENTER THE COURT," coming this Summer.

Speaking of theatrical productions, we spent a lot of time last night working on the scene I have with the Madonna look-alike. It is actually a confrontational scene between my character and a nurse so she and I have to get in each other's faces, quite literally now. We play out the scene and the director says, "Let's try it again but, Anthony, when you're arguing with her, get as close to her face as you can." And I, of course, being the suave, de-boner fuck that I am, start freaking out. About the only time I ever get close to anyone's face is when I'm about to kiss them and now I have to get into this gorgeous face and holler at it. So, now, we're doing the scene and, on cue, I get right up in her face and the director says, "Cut. Try it again, Anthony, but get closer." So, now, I'm practically sweating bullets but, as we say in show biz, "What the fuck?" So, this time, we're nose-to-nose. Now, the other problem is that, because my character has a thick accent and I'm supposed to be older, I have to alter my voice quite a bit which produces a lot of, not to mince words, spit. So we're french-kissing noses and she's yelling at me and I'm trying to holler at her without hawking all over her and I sound like Charlie Brown's teacher. I swear dude, a simple pucker is all that stands between me and bachelorhood again. Hopefully, I'll get over this problem because I was blushing like a jerk. Afterwards though, she did ask me how many other plays I'd been in and, when I told her this was my third, she was surprised because she thought I was a professional. SCHWING! This is her first play; so, while she may not be speaking from experience, she is a real sweetheart.

Anyway, gotta split. Enjoy the rest of the day and we'll tawk tomorrow.

Spitting on beautiful actresses sucks, French-kissing noses rules. OUT!!

Gerard Depardieu

Date: Apr 4
To: Duke
From: Jeff
Subject: French Kisses

Yes, master, the sacred tennis ball may be snatched from your hand this summer. Or, if I have my way, it may be forcibly removed in such a way that you won't even know what hit you. But it'll be all your fault, of course. You encouraged me. You taught me about aggressiveness and playing the net. Ju were dee one. I was merely another "lay back and let the opponent make the mistakes" player until you preached to me the wisdom of winning instead of not losing. Now I don't wait. I go for the jugular. And it's starting to work nicely. You have created a monster. So, don't blame me for your demise in July.....I'm merely a mirror image of yourself, only with a little more practice.

Do you realize that we are a mere six weeks from Vegas? Six weeks? Time will fly, and soon we will be in the land of Oz. Needless to say, I am looking forward to it. It's really the one weekend of the year where I can really let my hair down, drink like a *pescado*, wander around in a stupor, eat steak and eggs at 3:00 in the morning, smoke stogies, and be a general nuisance to the world. Kind of makes me feel like an architect. Vegas is really the next time I'll be getting on a plane, so I'm starting to look forward to it now. Besides, I get to hang with you for an entire weekend, and soon you will be ball and chained.....uh, married, and everything will change. Nonetheless, we need to make this trip an annual event, with or without marriage as an excuse. Just a bunch of guys in Vegas. Once a year. To remind us where we came from and where we're going to. To remind us what it's supposed to be like to be guys. Whaddya say? On that note, this October will be the ten-year anniversary of that infamous trip to Magic Mountain and the humble beginnings of our subsequent friendship. We've talked about marking it with a trip to *El Montaña* -- have you given that much thought?

Well, bro, time to go hit the proverbial hay. Have an excellent weekend; hope the play thing works itself out. But you are right. Everybody who's anybody has had a bad part. Look at Nicolas Cage in *Honeymoon in Vegas*. Or Kevin Kline in *French Kiss*. Bad, bad, bad movies.

Laying back sucks, Vegas Anticipation RULES!!!

-The Munchkins

Date: Apr 5
To: Jeff
From: Anthony
Subject: Blank

Yes, my son, you may indeed beat me in tennis; but, in a way, I will be kind of proud of ju, ju know? It'll be like the day I finally beat my Dad in a one-on-one basketball game. Of course, there is the slimmest of slim possibilities that you may indeed lose, realizing that this is a far cry from reality but not outside the realm of possibility. Just remember that a true master never divulges all of his secrets and will resort to dirty play, fake injuries, and even broken racquets if need be.

Yes, a mere six weeks is all that separates us from "The Land of the Desert Sin." Ah Vegas, t'will be a most epic sort of vacation. That's the one thing I notice about getting older: those weekends where you really let your hair down are fewer and further between. Also, being older, the hair doesn't fall quite as far as it used to and there's alarmingly little of it. But, still, I don't feel as though I wasted too much of my youth. I was kind of a stick in the mud before college but, then, I sort of made up for it. A lot of it was due to a certain weekend when we packed up a Volvo with beer, pillows, and girls, and sojourned off to the happiest place on earth -- the Motel 6 in Ventura. Then, the next day, we were at Magic Mountain playing "Jostle the Hangover." Ah yes, perhaps it would be a good idea to mark the anniversary of that fateful trip with a return pilgrimage. Why the hell not? Question is, do we bring our women? May not be a real good idea if we start having flashbacks. I can just see me yelling "passout" in my sleep and you taking roll call when you get in bed. Ya know, come to think of it, that time of life was far too cool to try and do it justice in a day or two. We should try and take some time to see if we could live through a typical weekend such as those we had in college. We could start in San Luis Obispo at McCarthy's on Friday afternoon and just sort of make our way down the coast for a bonfire at the beach, then sneak into the hot tubs, find a corner where we could stand and drink wine, go to Weinerschnitzel for breakfast, play guitar all day, then go see *Rocky Horror Picture Show* at midnight. Nah, I'd be dead after one beer at McCarthy's.

Hey, if it's snowing, that must mean another two weeks of godsporting, right? By the way, Alden said she didn't really enjoy godsporting; but she also said that the guy she took a lesson from was a real prick. So she's thinking she'd like to try again sometime, so maybe we'll fly out next year and you guys can give us lessons. I know I said I'd never ski again but what the hell? I said I'd never get married again either. Anyway, y'all be cool and we'll rap wit' ya next week.

Aging sucks, vacations rule. OUT!!

Toast

Date: Apr 7
To: Duke
From: Jeff
Subject: I play the drooms....

Let me see if I got this straight -- You want to fly out here next winter so Julie and I can take *su y su novia* skiing? Skiing? Godsporting? After all these years of, "They don't have any mountains in Mexico; therefore, Mexicans don't ski?" After all those opportunities for you when I woke up at 4:00 a.m. in the morning with my little brother, ground some coffee beans, thus waking up your ass which was on my couch, and went skiing? You could have come, you know. Yeah, right. I ain't buying this for a second. It must be an April Fool's hangover that you're experiencing. Or maybe you're going to do it because Aldiente wants to. Don't sell out, dude. It's kind of like my golf thing. Don't sell out, not even for your wife. Not that I would mind, of course. I welcome everyone to the world of godsporting, especially those who share the same type of existence I do. If you were a godsporter we would be even closer to being on the same intellectual plane. At this point, that's very hard to imagine, because we already are -- on the same intellectual plane, I mean. So forget about it. Because you must be joking.

Happy Easter, *amigo*. We got up before sunrise and went to Red Rocks for a "Sunrise Service," which was kind of cool. I really wanted to see the sunrise, which is why I went. I am not a follower of organized religion; therefore, I didn't pay too much attention to all the "God will send you to hell" stuff that was going on there. But the whole Red Rocks at Sunrise thing is pretty cool, and a good way to start the Spring. After it was over, we came home and took a nap, one of my favorite things to do on weekends, of course.

ITEM: The artist formally known as "Prince" recently got married, and the happy couple is expecting, sometime before the end of the year. *MY VIEW:* What the hell are they going to name the kid? "^," or possibly "#?" Maybe he could have a middle name, at which point his name could be "@)," or "?!." Of course, if the kid is a girl, look out. Prince has a penchant for naming women the stupidest things he can think of. Remember "Vanity" and "Appolonia?" He could name his daughter "Flatulence," "Smellybutt," or "Guanogirl." Personally, I can't wait.

ITEM: The three surviving Beatles turned down $500 million bucks to do a twenty minute set at Shea Stadium. *MY VIEW*: Yeah, Paul may have turned it down, but do you honestly think George and Ringo would turn down that kind of money to go play somebody else's (Paul and John's) songs for twenty minutes? Songs they already know? I doubt it. I bet Ringo is calling Paul right now: "Ya bloody wanka. What the hell were ya thinkin, ya bloody blouse wearin' poodle walka? Sure, you and John wrote the tunes, but I was Ringo and I played the drooms. Why didn't ya ask me how I felt about it, ya bloody wanka? How am I supposed to go on leevin when all I gots is me two million from the television thing?" Because, you know, Ringo and George don't have nearly the bank that McCartney does at this point. And if George and Ringo had it their way, they'd do the set, take their portion of the cash, and be happy for at least a couple of years. I wonder if Ringo and George decided to do it without Paul, would anybody care? "Uh, yeah, Mister Club Owner? This is Ringo, and I play the drooms. Listen, about that five hundred million. George and I will do the gig for three hundred thirty-three million. Whaddya think?"

Today (Sunday) is easily *mi favorita dia del año. Porque?* Because Daylight Savings Time begins, which makes me a very happy boy. Coming home from work in the dark sucks, but coming home from work with a couple of hours of light left rules. I can work in my garden, sit on my front porch playing the blues, go for a bicycle ride, light a cue, and swill some homebrew; whatever. It makes life seem that much better. And work seem that much less awful. Yeah, right. I still wouldn't show up the day after I won the lottery. But, now, I can come home from work and it seems like there is actually some time left in the day. That is the difference. Have an excellent Monday.

Daylight Savings Time and Waking your ass up at 4:00 am with a coffee grinder Rule!!

-The Fifth Beatle

Date: Apr 8
To: Jeff
From: Anthony
Subject: How soon they forget

Well, looky here, another e-mail from Jeff who's distressed that I'm about to sell out to my woman. This coming from the same guy who used to stash cigarettes in kitchen cabinets because he didn't want a prospective girlfriend to know he smoked. Jeez, I thought you'd be happy about this. As to why I didn't get up with you and your brother at 4:00 in the morning, well I guess some questions just seem to answer themselves. You gotta understand, dude, aside from walking, Alden and I share absolutely no recreational interests. Well, there is that one thing. You know, THAT thing. So when I find out that there is some sport out there she may actually enjoy, I'm all over it. Also, while it is true that the guy who gave her a lesson was an asshole, she also happened to mention that he was "kinda cute."

Yeah, Easter services at Red Rocks must've been a sight to behold. Happy Easter to you, also. I celebrated the day by getting in my car and driving home from Santa Maria. Amazingly enough, I didn't hit one traffic jam in Los Angeles and made it back in four hours. Had a good weekend, but I'm always exhausted when I return. There just isn't enough time to get to Santa Maria and relax. Plus, this time-change has really thrown me outta whack. I agree. it's nice to have some daylight in the evening. but I was driving to work in the dark this morning and the only darkness I was interested in was the inside of my eyelids. We did manage to find time this weekend to buy my wedding ring though. One of the key advantages to being a woman is her wedding ring. Not because they're generally fancier than ours, but because she's out only about one-sixth the cash I paid. She also got it installed with the new interlocking mechanism which, when activated, will insert tiny hooks down into the bone of my finger which will prevent me from removing the ring in bars and art museums.

Good calls on the "artist-formerly-known-as-Talented" and the three remaining Beatles. Some other possible names for the baby could be "Seehesnotgay," "Purple Jane," "Insertnamehere" or "The-child-formerly-known-as-embryo." Can you believe some fool would pay $500 million to see John-less Beatles? Yeah, I have a hard time believing Ringo and George would turn down that kind of cash. And can you imagine if Ringo and George did it alone? "Right now, we'd like to do 'Twist and Shout' but, uh, John sang that one so we can't. So, how about 'Yesterday'? Uh, no, that was Paul's. So, here's another rousing rendition of 'Yellow Submarine'!"

Artists with punctuation marks for names suck, no traffic jams in Los Angeles rules. OUT!!

The Fifth Cockroach

Chapter 9
Guanogirl and Diamond Nancy

Date: Apr 9
To: Duke
From: Jeff
Subject: Guanogirl

I'll believe the skiing thing when I see it, O.K?

One way around the million dollar wedding ring for the intended-to-be: Don't buy her one. Just use her engagement ring as the wedding ring. That's what we did. Although I suppose that I'll be indebted to my bride forever until I buy her some fancy piece of jewelry to make up for it.....

I had yet another tough day at work yesterday, but let me share with you exactly what this e-mail stuff is doing for my outlook: Whenever I think of the word "Guanogirl," (which, as you recall, was a possible name for Prince's daughter), a terrific smile passes across my face and I start giggling. "Uh, Jeff, you're fir....what the hell are you smiling about?" "Sorry, Boss, it's Guanogirl." So, I got to thinking......What if Guanogirl were a superhero for the nineties? Sort of a shitty antithesis to "Batgirl." Born Shania Hemingway to a dirt-poor family who lived in an abandoned warehouse on the east side of town, Guanogirl fell into a big pit of guano one day while playing in the warehouse. When she was pulled out of the pit forty-seven hours later by local law enforcement officers, she somehow had absorbed superpowers from the guano -- plus a smell that just won't go away, And a couple of bat-type ears that appear only when she's really really pissed off or she's at that time of the month. So, now she can fly, she can...she can...hmm, what else can bats do? They are supposedly "blind as a bat." But Guanogirl can be the superhero for all the down and out-ers of the world. She can have a sense of humor that is not quite as stupid as most superhero's senses of humor. She can care about the bats, because she is one of them. Maybe one day she will meet a boy who will make her happy, maybe "Cacaboy" or "Cowpieman." And Smellycat could be her trusty companion at all times, although I don't think the producers of "Amigos" would like that too much. What do you think?

Million Dollar Wedding Rings Suck, Guanogirl RULES!!!

-El Cacaloco

Date: Apr 9
To: Jeff
From: Anthony
Subject: Cynic's Corner

That's not a bad idea about the engagement ring doubling as the wedding ring -- if you can get away with it. Problem is, my little bride-to-be knows my mother; a.k.a. Diamond Nancy. Trust me, any woman who catches "diamond fever" will go out of her way to infect others, so, for the sake of your anorexic wallet, keep Julie away from Alden's fingers after the wedding.

Hey, that's interesting that you should bring up the point about bats. I've often wondered why Batman never employed one particular power of the bat: ultrasonic hearing. Bats home in on things by emitting high-pitched shrieks that bounce off the object which the bat then detects and interprets as something to eat or, "Watch out for that tree." Therefore, Guanogirl can use her ultrasonic "nag-waves" to stun male criminals into submission. She can also use her built-in radar to help her when she gets lost on the way to a crime scene. One of the general misconceptions about bats is that they are rodents. This comes as a shock to many people because they believe anything that small, furry, and ugly must be some kind of rat or lawyer. One of the true misconceptions about Guanogirl, therefore, is that she is a woman. But, after being pulled from the guano pit, little Shania Hemingway began a startling transformation. She began watching sports on TV regularly, drinking beer, and frequenting Vegas-type art museums until, one day, while watching pro-wrestling, she decided the best way to anonymously fight crime was to incorporate the natural powers of the bat and the supernatural powers of the typical American female. Thus, Guanogirl. Run with it if you want, but I think I've pissed-off half the population enough for one day. OUT!!

Expensive rings suck, androgynous superheroes rule. OUT!!

Duke

Date: Apr 15
To: Duke
From: Jeff
Subject: 67 hours

67 hours. That is what my timecard will say today about last week. 67 hours. No human being should be allowed to prostrate him/herself to the client for that many hours in one month, let alone one week. And why do we do it?? Because of our "reputation." We "always meet the deadlines, so they keep coming back to us." Yeah, well, that's like saying, "The dog always shits on that one particular spot, so he keeps going back to it." I am starting to dread the smell of this dog's shit. The next time they tell me, "Señor Chacon, we have this little project, it has a tight schedule and a difficult architect, and we're going to give it to you, because you are so damn close to being excellent," I'm going to have to say, "yeah, well, mister boss man, I think I've proved my excellence in getting shat upon over the last few months; why don't you try send those dogs to some other spot this time??"

I write this to you at 7:30 a.m. from the Mile High City, because after working 67 hours last week, I am going to work today whenever the hell I damn well feel like going to work today. You see, we sent *la escuela* out yesterday. Then we had a little meeting during which Boss #2 basically told us we will be swamped for the next six weeks. We are "busier than we've been in ten years." So I said, "That's okay, but it my personal philosophy that everybody should take at least one day off per week, whether it be Saturday or Sunday. If this situation that we just went through comes up again, I will come to you (pointing at Boss #2) and say 'Dude, it ain't gonna happen,' because I will not do this again. I believe I'll take Wednesday off this week, so I may spend some time with The Great One who, at this point, doesn't even remember what I look like." They weren't too keen on my taking a day off in the middle of the week, but I told 'em I'd work the time out, and we'd somehow get all this crap done. And I better see some serious bank on all of these projects or else Village Inn (a family restaurant local to the area) is gonna have themselves one damn fine new waiter. So, this morning I slept in and am now writing my e-mail. I will go in late, because once in a while you just gotta send a message to people. This message is: "If I work 67 hours in a week, I need some good recovery time." Otherwise, the dogs just keep shitting and shitting and I keep getting closer and closer to excellent and.....

Typical Rockies slugfest last night: The Padres went up 5-0 in the top of the first, because, yes, the Rox have no starting pitching. We sat in center field for the longest time that inning, wondering if we were ever going to get out of it. Then the Rox come back behind some good hitting and finally won it in the bottom of the eighth on a Bichette homer, 11-9. They oughta play the Broncos some time; the Rox score more than the Broncos do on most nights. But, hey, this is what makes baseball in Colorado fun. I'd rather watch an 11-9 game than watch Hideo Nomo fan a shitload of people, to be honest.

And the baseball fans in Colorado? Don't get me started. On one side of us were the yuppie fans; you know, talking about business, the stock market, answering the cell phone in the middle of an inning, etc. On the other side of us, your typical 'neck Colorado fan. This 'neck is skinny-as-a-rail, with the shoulder-length sandy-brown hair and the 'stache and even the 'burns down the side of his face. He's wearing a black "Harley Davidson Rules" cap and a black leather jacket, with black jeans and black tennis shoes completing the outfit. He's got a tattoo (I, of course, am merely speculating at this point. But the previous stuff was real) on one shoulder that reads "I am the NRA and I vote," and a tattoo on the other shoulder that reads "Mop" because he misspelled "Mom" one night when he and his tattoo buddy were real real real drunk, pick any weekday or weekend night. So this dude is yelling at the top of his lungs for every batter to "hit it out here ya bastard" and every time somebody does get a hit he jumps up from his seat, raises his fist in the air, and starts a hootin' and a hollerin' no end. He's high fivin' everybody around him, even the even weirder dude next to him. He's turnin' to the kids behind him and sayin', "Remember when Vinny hit that grand slam last year against the Pirates to win the game? Wouldn't it be cool if he could do that again right now?" (even though there's only one man on base) This, of course, makes the mother of the children very uncomfortable, so she replies back nervously, "Uh, yes, that would be, uh, very nice." Then she gives her kids a hug and a look that says "Don't talk to the 'neck, darlings. He is a very scary man. He will take you to his cabin in Montana and make you serve as his love slave for the rest of your life and Mommy will never see you again." This guy is a baseball fan that can be found only in the lovely state of Colorado. He's probably got a big ol' wife at home who beats the shit out of him on a regular basis, so he comes down out of the mountains to escape her and to catch a Rox game once in a while. Only in Colorado.

Well, it's 8 o'clock in the a.m, I suppose I should face reality and go to the office. Lord knows, if I don't show up soon everybody's going to start poopin' in their pants. Did you know they actually called here lookin' for me Sunday morning after I already left for the office? At least today is payday, which means I take my five dollars and spend it on lunch. Finally, I truly know what "Overworked, Underpaid" stands for.

Company Loyalty sucks, Punk Yuppies RULE!!

-Jeff Vicious

Date: Apr 16
To: Jeff
From: Anthony
Subject: Help me...

"Ladies and gentlemen, we are pleased to present a production of *I Remember Mama*. The poignant, gut-wrenching tale of a Norwegian family's struggles to get by on hype and publicity. Starring Anthony Reynoso as Uncle Chris, the crusty patriarch of the family who sits in the back and wonders how he'll ever resurrect his fading stage career. Please pay particular attention to the wonderful photos adorning the lobby as you enter the theater. They are the results of an entire evening's work which could've been better spent rehearsing but, nah. Also, make sure you keep those ticket stubs because there will be door prizes for some lucky masochist who actually makes it to the end of this production which could surpass *Chariots of Fire* in both length and boredom. And keep those cameras rolling. At some point during the production, somebody's bound to make some kind of goof-up worthy of *America's Funniest Home Videos*. Yes, if you want to gain a new appreciation for post-football-season Sunday afternoon television, you gotta see *I Remember Mama*."

Quick, think of some way to get me outta this thing! I am not bullshitting you about anything in the above paragraph. Last night, we spent the first 90 minutes taking publicity photos. Naturally, we couldn't start taking them until everyone got there which means we STARTED rehearsing at 8:30.

Two hours later, we stumbled to the end of Act One. The biggest problem was that, with less than two weeks before we open, we still have some of the main characters crying for line cues. Plus, it seems everyone is more concerned with publicity photos and award nominations. Speaking of publicity photos, in a room full of actors dressed in 1940s attire, the award for Worst Wig went to the photographer whose toupee looked like he had a weasel asleep on his head. However, I continue to battle against all odds and am now starting to feel more comfortable in the role, despite the fact that I look like Teddy Roosevelt and occasionally sound like Boris Yeltsin. Ju gotta help me, mein! Oh well, at least 90% of my role is based around screaming in heavy Norwegian accent at everybody else, which is amazingly easy. Sort of like Sam Kinison visits Solvang.

Why does the winning team have to score in double figures at Coors Field? This is not baseball my friend; this is batting practice. Too bad about your "neck" friend in the stands. Reminds me of this one Padre game I went to. A few innings into the game this obnoxious drunk came hollering up into the stands, sat down a couple of seats away, spilled hot chocolate on people, high-fived some kids behind him, provoking that look from the mother which you described oh so well. But I got even with his stupid ass: I had to drive him home, so I threw him in the back of my truck and played pinball with him all the way. Yeah, some people.

I am becoming worried about your disenchantment with your chosen field of work. When you start talking like this, resumes addressed to Tennessee and Arkansas start showing up. That however, doesn't bother me as much as this desire to get back into food service. Lest you forget, this field isn't all glamour and glitz either. I remind you that the general public can be a royal pain-in-the-ass when it's hungry and even worse when it's hungry and drunk. Worse yet, when it's hungry and can't make up its mind what the hell it wants to eat. It's also very hard to please at times and people are...well...for lack of a better term, fuckin' pigs. I think ju just need a couple of days to get your head on straight. Take a couple of days and don't do squat. You'll be a new man for it. As far as them calling you at home on Sunday, that may be the biggest scoop of slimy, smelly bullshit I've ever heard. What is that!?

All right bro, I am outta here. Enjoy your day and don't stress too much or you will have a heart attack; or worse, go bald. See ya.

Living off publicity sucks, days off rule. OUT!!

Pinball Wizard

Date: Apr 16
To: Duke
From: Jeff
Subject: The dark and scary Past

Yeah, you had to bring it up, didn't you? The infamous "Jeff does his first ever dozen beer shooters" night at the Padres game. Now, The Great One is asking me, "Who's he talking about, Honey?" So, per the agreement I mentally signed when I married her, I had to tell the truth. And, now, she knows the truth about me -- that I am the same as that Rockies 'neck, only my neck is brown and I don't have a bigass hairbrush jammed into my back pocket like he did. Thanks, bro. Thanks a lot.

"Ladies and gentlemen, we are pleased to present a production of 'I Dismember Mama'. The poignant, gut-wrenching tale of a young extremely talented actor who has to deal with his co-stars' lack of sense of responsibility towards the theater, until one night he goes berserk and turns into Freddy Kruger and wreaks havoc on the entire set. Starring Anthony Reynoso as himself."

Sorry to hear about the play, dude. Why don't you just throw Momma from the train? Hahahaha. I recall fondly the misadventures of a musical reading that I did back in 1994. We called it *Low Budget, the musical that never stops sucking*. We had it all, including an actress who actually had a fight with the author: "What? Are you saying I can't sing? I *can* sing!! That's it, I quit!!!" I think he had merely asked her to practice her shit. Then on the night of the thing, the author, who had insisted on playing all of the music on his little Casio-type keyboard live, got tremendously nervous and screwed the pooch on virtually EVERY SONG. Actors were on stage, trying to sing in key, but the key they thought the song was in was not necessarily the key the Casio-author-guy was playing in. So they'd be singing, all the while staring over into the wings, grimacing and glaring at the dude who was screwing the pooch. It was a mess. In fact, the first applause from the audience came just after yours truly (playing a janitor) sang his first song, which was kind of cool. I mean, I was standing back in the wings waiting to come on, thinking "Oh God. Oh God. Nobody is clapping. The songs are all off key, and I gotta rip a tremendous fart and take a Godzilla-size dump." Because that's what stage fright does to me; kinda loosens up my innards a bit, you know? The climactic scene was where one of the character's sons got shot by a bad guy. At which point, this "actress," who was playing the kid's mother, got to do her thing. She sucked. Try this: Breath in all the air you possibly can. Get ready to shriek as though you were a cat stuck in a blender at its highest speed. Now, shriek at the top of your lungs:
"MY CHILD!!!!!!!
MY CHIIIIIIIILLLLLLLLLDDDDDDDD!!!!!!
MY CHIIIIIIIIIIIIIIIIIIIIIIIIIILLLLLLLLLLDDDDDDDDDDDDDDD!!!"
Like a million nails on a thousand chalkboards, I kid you not. Julie and I still make the occasional jokes about it, running around the house going, "MY CHILD, MY CHIIIIIIILLLLLLLLLLLLLLDD!!" Every time I see one my fellow actors from this thing, it's always like "Yeah, hey Jeff!! How ya doin'? Done any musicals lately? Heh heh heh...." So, yeah, I can see how theater can suck at times. And I do feel for you. Because being up on stage when

everything is falling apart around you is a very uneasy feeling. I imagine the feeling of being up in a hot air balloon when a plane rips the balloon in half is a probable, comparable feeling. Don't worry too much, because the audience will know. They'll know that you are the true star of the show and that everybody else sucks. That's just how it works, trust me.

Well, it's *tiempo para sueño*. I am dragging. I always notice that after a 67-hour week or a long weekend of skiing or drinking or Vegas-ing that I get tired on Tuesday, not Monday. It's like there's a one day drag on the body. The body on Monday thinks it's still going, but on Tuesday it says, "We're done? We're actually done? Yeahhhhh, nap time!!!" So, I am dead tired. The Great One and I are working half days tomorrow and we're taking the afternoon off. Kind of a little romantic midweek thing, you know? Plus, we could both use the break. You have a nice one, O.K?

Bad co-stars suck, Half Days RULE!

-Janitor Jeff

Date: Apr 17
To: Jeff
From: Anthony
Subject: The darker, scarier present

Yeah, I guess that was you, wasn't it? Funny, that facial imprint on the side wall of my truck-bed didn't LOOK like you. Ah well, what the hell, right? Just one slight blemish on the profile of life.

Don't you hate it when 90% of the blueberry muffin sticks to the paper?

So, our primary actress had a Three Mile Island last night. This is one of those plays where the narrator sets up the action, then sort of falls into character. Thus, this girl has a very big part with many lines to memorize and much blocking to coordinate; she has worked very hard to learn her shit, unlike most of the people she spends time with on stage. Thus, she naturally went exorcist on one of the guys whose acting style doesn't mesh with hers; he actually employs a new artistic movement in theater called "improvisationalism." That's when the actor is convinced the writer doesn't know what he's talking about, and the actor throws in his/her own lines and blocking to illicit more "real" responses from classically trained actors who have this annoying, archaic habit of memorizing lines. Now, the best part of all this is that the actor never settles on one mode of action; he/she changes it every night. These improvisationalists are really amazing, too. Sometimes, they change things around so much, I think I'm watching a play other than the one I'm in. Unfortunately, the 25% of us who are classically trained are making life miserable for those fun-loving souls who, in this age of "blooper" shows, work so hard to give the audience what they really want.

Thus, I bring this correspondence to a close. Have a major weekend, won't you? *Adios*, my man.

Improvisationalists suck, blueberry muffins rule. OUT!!

Talent scout

Date: April 17
To: Duke
From: Jeff
Subject: Kids and Zoos

Today, I found an excellent method of birth control: Go to the zoo on a weekday. There are children crawling all over that place. Not that I didn't enjoy hanging out with the kiddies, mind you, but they are truly a bundle of energy. On the go -- all the time. There were kids running all over the zoo, yelling, "Mommy, where's Simba? Is that Simba? Mommy, we're going into the snake pit!! Mommy, little Dukey just climbed into that elephant's mouth!!" There were few adults trying to keep track of all these children. I realized that, being the laid back creature that I am, children and I probably wouldn't quite mesh at this point in my life. Because they are all gogogogogogogo, and I am more inclined to rrreeeeellllllllaaaaaaaaxxxxx. It would be 24-hour-a-day questioning and hormones from a younger version of me, which is quite an ugly thought. Plus, they would cut into the hour-long, daily guitar practice I have set up for myself, and the beer making which, by the way, is getting rave reviews from my guinea pigs. I gave some of the latest Jeffbrew product to my project team as a gesture of thanks for the hell that they went through last week. Kids would even cut into my e-mail time. Not that I've ruled children out completely, of course -- because the Great One and I still wanna have a couple of little Jeffreys -- but it might be a while. Have you and the Mess decided on a plan about this?

So, *mañana* it's back to the grindstone for us. We took this afternoon and went to the zoo and to the Botanical Gardens; because, as you know, we have some of the blackest thumbs around and are always looking for help in making them greener. Then we went to a little restaurant and had some hummus and Railyard, which made us come home and take a little nap. Then we ordered a pizza pie and ate it and, now, it's about time for bed. Overall, a nice break for us. It was good for the soul. I think everybody should spend one day a year being a tourist in their own city. Now I'm ready (yeah, right) to go back into battle, retake my position on the front lines, and kick me some architect ASS!!! Have an excellent Thursday.

El Turistas de Nuestro Ciudad RULE!

-Jeff Embry

Date: Apr 18
To: Jeff
From: Anthony
Subject: Rested and relaxed

Jeez, one day at the zoo and the guy's ready for a vasectomy. You gotta procreate dude. If for no other reason than to listen to little Jeffrey tell one of his classmates, "Look, butthead, if you add another red Lego the whole thing's coming down." Also, I can't wait to hear your answers to such questions as, "Daddy, is brewing beer the same as making moonshine?" "Daddy, can I be a architect when I grow up?" "Daddy, I got a Good Citizen bumper sticker from school. Will you put it on the bumper of your new Mustang?" Even better, I can't wait to hear Julie's answers to such questions as, "Mommy, why does Daddy hate bagels?" and "Mommy, can I go with Daddy to see the Vegas art museums?"

So, I heard that Johnny Elway thinks he's going to survive another five years as Bronco QB. Can't see it. Considering the pounding he's taken over the years, it's amazing he can still count to seven let alone wear it. Don't get me wrong. When he retires, I'm going to lose a lot of interest in football, because he's always been my favorite player, but I would rather see him go out with all his marbles instead of a Super Bowl trophy. Of course, he is the biggest thing Denver sports can boast of, so I can see why they want to keep him around a while. I mean, look what happened to basketball as a whole when Michael and Magic retired. If, and when, they ever retire permanently that sport is up a creek. Nah, I can see both of those guys doing slam dunks from hydraulic wheelchairs when they're 80. And Michael will still be getting away with traveling. I've told Alden I'd try and take her to see the Chargers-Broncos this year, since I'm hopeful she'll somehow become interested in football. Hopefully, I'll get on TV again. Remember me? I was the guy in the orange jersey with a 7 on it, mouthing, "Fuck" as Jason Elam hooked a 35-yard field goal left.

Glad to hear you guys had a nice restful day. Alden will be home sometime this evening and we'll have a nice little weekend together, also. Do you realize the wedding is exactly three months from Saturday? Even better, do you realize that Vegas is a mere *four* weeks away? I can't wait!! For the wedding, that is. You guys have a good one, and I'll talk to you tomorrow.

Catatonic ex-quarterbacks suck, sleep rules. OUT!!

Uncle Duke

Date: Apr 21
To: Duke
From: Jeff
Subject: *Para Bailar La Bamba...*

First things first: Walk out...no, run out and buy *Papa's Dream,* a little known album by Los Lobos. It's really a children's album, and it's hard to find, but it is great. Los Lobos play a bunch of songs and some older guy tells a story between the songs. The songs are the best part for us adults; they do a couple of versions of the old standby, "La Bamba," and they do "Woolly Bully," and a bunch of very cool Hispanic tunes. I'm digging on it right now, as a matter of fact. And I think it will be really great for the triplets, when we have them. Because the three Jeffreys are going to know how to sing and play "La Bamba" and "De Colores" by the time they are two. Guaranteed. I may even have to find them some big ol' *guitarrons*, which is what the Lobos play on stage when they do the Hispanic tunes. Although, at that young age, the *guitarrons* will probably be bigger than the Jeffreys. That's okay, because I'll have to build them some *Guitarron* Playing Stools to sit on as they play "La Bamba." Anyway, the Jeffreys will also enjoy the story, because it sounds like they get into some Hispanic words and meanings and that kind of thing. And the Jeffreys will be required to know an extensive amount of Hispanic words and meanings and that kind of thing if they expect to ever graduate from preschool.

As we type, I am currently making the "Bachelor Brew" for the Vegas trip. I'm taking the last recipe, which turned out truly *delicioso*, and adding some more goodies to try and bring the alcohol content up. Let's face it: Good tasting beer is not actually "good" unless the effects of alcohol can be felt, and there just aren't that many effects of alcohol from the last batch. So, I add more malt extract to try and increase that. Right now the house smells like a brewery, which is a good thing, because the Wynkoop also smells like a brewery. Which means that my two favorite places to be in Denver smell like a brewery right about now. And I can handle that.

Hopiness is mine. It's time to go add the hops to the wort. Isn't that a cool word? "Wort." Makes me think of wort hogs screwing for some reason. Where did I see that? Back in a second. Back now. Hops added. Now, we boil the wort for another twenty minutes. Then, we add the remainder of the hops, for aroma, and boil for a minute and a half. Then we let the whole thing cool for a couple of hours, until the temp is in the 60s, then we add the yeast, stir vigorously, and put the lid and the airstop on the pail and let it sit, probably until Thursday or Friday, at which time we'll transfer the yummy beverage into the "carboy," (like Mom used to say, "get into the carboy, we're going to the store!") which is really just a big ol' Sparklett's Water bottle. This will enable us to remove some of the gunk from the bottom of the pail. Then, a couple of days after that, we add some sugar to stimulate the yeast (too bad women aren't that easy to stimulate, huh?). Then we bottle, and, in a few weeks, we drink. Thus, this beer should be ready in time for the "La Fiesta de Matrimonia en Las Vegas." I still haven't figure out exactly how I'm gonna get the brew to the hotel, but I will.

Well, *hermano*, I should probably go upstairs and begin my work. Yes, I am still working weekends. In fact, it is a strong possibility that I may not have a day off between now and Vegas. Which means that I, like you after the disaster called "I Remember Mama, But I Forgot My Lines" will be in rare form for that weekend. I've seen it before, you probably have, too. We work too hard and too long and with too many stupid actors and architects; then one day, five weeks later, we're let out of our cages to play, in Vegas even. It will be epic. I am looking forward to it with an excitement unmatched in a long time, except when my wife is already at home naked when I get home from a long day at work. Or when my wife is naked anytime, for that matter. But that is a different topic for a different time. This is now, and Vegas is only four short weeks away!

Working like a dog sucks, Guitarrons Rule!!!!

-Woolly Bully

Date: Apr 22
To: Jeff
From: Anthony
Subject: Betrayed, bewildered...

So much on my mind this morning. Coming off a big weekend with the wife-in-training where we got quite a bit accomplished and didn't kill each other. One question: What sadistic pig ever came up with the concept of a wedding? I mean consider the wedding. It starts off as a labor of love. It is fussed-over, fed, overplanned, overhyped, overbudget, until it becomes this carnivorous monster with big pointy teeth that noshes on your sanity, serenity, mentality, and emotions, until it becomes so big and all-encompassing that you eventually start thinking of ways to kill it. Its only ally is the parents of the poor people it is seeking to destroy. These days, as things continue in preparation for the Big Day, the most minor of accomplishments are met with sighs of relief rather than shrieks of anticipation. But we did manage to get the invitations taken care of with only minor injuries, so now we can invite people to sacrifice to the monster. Damn, Alden and I have not brawled in three previous years the way we've hooked in the last six months. Thank God it's almost over. But, in preparation for life after the dragon is vanquished, we managed to secure an apartment over the weekend and we put a deposit down on a TV set. Priorities is priorities. I mean, normally, you'd think the TV comes first but you do need a place to put it and plug it in. Next, we'll attempt to find something to sit on while watching it.

Ya know, I've heard of that Los Lobos album, but I've never actually seen it anywhere so it looks like I've got another project. Thanks a lot, buddy, as if I didn't have enough to do. Speaking of which, four more days until the opening of "I'd Like to Forget Mama." This may be a first for community theater as an art form. I know that Broadway plays can close because of bad reviews and I think we make a strong case for applying this principle to community theater. I bought a can of hair color and spent some time trying to make my hair look gray this weekend, and I've come to the undeniable conclusion that baldness IS an option. After I sprayed that crud in my hair I knew immediately how Richard Gere got grayed-up for "Pretty Woman" (contrary to popular belief that he was actually forced to watch some of his own movies). I'm going to cake the make-up on in an attempt to become as unrecognizable as possible. That way, as I make my way through the angry crowds clamoring for refunds, I can say I was just a stage hand. As I've stated, I'm happy that I'll be in Vegas the following weekend because I'll need a few days of culcha to forget this whole miserable affair.

Hey listen, I think I've come up with the perfect hook: Guanogirl's identity will never be discovered, because her alias is another superhero. The idea came to me Sunday morning. Alden and I got a room Saturday night so we could spend some quality time together. Seems the hotel was bordered by a large grove of trees and the birds therein started chirping at 5:00 am. Now this doesn't bother me, but Alden can't sleep unless it's totally quiet, so she throws a pillow over her head to try and muffle the noise. So when I wake up, I look to my right and see this huge sandwich where Alden was, thus she was dubbed "Sandwich Head" for the rest of the day. So when Guanogirl isn't Guanogirl, she can be "Sandwich Head" and naturally her side order...uh, sidekick could be called "Chips." Food for thought. Okay, I'll shut up now. This is where I take my leave for the day. You have a good one and we'll wrap it down to you tomorrow.

Weddings suck, quality time rules. OUT!!

Hoagie Head

Chapter 10
Lefty's Wet Dreams

Date: Apr 22
To: Duke
From: Jeff
Subject: I'm Gonna Wash That Gray Right Outta My Hair....

Dear Mister Grecian Formula: Have you tried primer? I mean, good quality long lasting gray autobody primer? It really does work.

Weddings are really kind of stupid after you get into the whole thing. I mean, all it really is supposed to be is a chance for your friends to spend some time with you as you make the mista....commitment of a lifetime. So, I say live it up. When I got home tonight, The Great One was watching the video from our own day of infamy and, as she watched the rehearsal party/fiesta, I thought "you know, that was really fun." Because we made some name tags, we had *Señor* Chacon make some *Carne Asada Mas Excellante* and we basically had a good time, which is the way it should be. But, boy, did we have some battles getting there. Especially about the invitations. She wanted single cards with art and words printed on them, while I wanted a fold-over type card with our own handiwork on the outside and our own lettering on the inside. So, as you know, we compromised. And, yes, I did get something out of it. The handiwork. As this kind of thing (planning a wedding) went on, I was inclined to try to end the fights by using the old "Honey, look, I don't care" routine. "Whatever you want is fine." But she would never allow that. It was always, "No, this is OUR wedding, and you should really be involved in the decision-making." Yeah, right. Let's face it. The wedding belongs, for the most part, to the bride and the bride's mother; they are the two people who are most excited about it by the time it arrives. You, as the groom in the bunch, are probably feeling something like "Fuck it. Let's get this over with so that we can go back to our lives." That's kind of how I felt by the time it arrived. But the actual event really affected me, in ways I couldn't previously imagine. It was truly magical, and I hope that yours is, too. It will be. And there will be beer. Good beer.

Today was officially BLOW day. First of all, I went to get my haircut by my usual guy, Jimmy, who may be a bit of a flame. But there's nothing wrong with that. I start to tell him that I play the guitar, the electric guitar. How we got on that subject, I'll never know. And he says "Have you ever blown an amp?" And I reply "No, but I've blown a mic." And he replies "Really? Oh, I've blown a Mike too!!" Then I'm getting ready to go to my harmonica class (which you probably haven't heard about up to now). It's a six week beginning class, and it's a lot of fun), so I'm walking around work telling everybody that I have to go "blow my instrument." Tomorrow, the new

93

Hootie and the Blowfish CD comes out, which you know I'm looking forward to with much celebration and anticipation. I mean, another summer with nothing but all Hootie, all the damn time. What could be better? Well, I suppose a root canal. Two root canals. A 36-hour meeting with a hundred architects. A whole month of eating nothing but chicken and bagels. Hell, a dozen root canals. Why do you think they call them the BLOWfish anyway?

Speaking of harmonica class, I have a hilarious story to tell you. You probably need to be sitting down, before you read. I'll wait......................O.K. Are you sitting down? In the first week of class, the instructor tells us that we can practice our harmonicas whenever we want, and that many people practice in the car while they are driving around town or to work or to the Chicken and Bagel Shack. So this one dude has been driving around practicing his harmonica in his car, and he rear ended somebody while doing this. No kidding. He came into class the next week saying, "This class has cost me $1500 so far....." Hilarious. I feel sorry for the dude, but you gotta admire his 'nads for actually coming back to class and telling us all the story. Lord knows *I* wouldn't have told anybody.

I am getting so into this little e-mail thing that my typical day -- which was today -- goes like this: Arrive at work around 7:00 am. Get first of three cups of coffee. Get first e-mail idea. Pull first piece of pink "While you were out" paper from the pad, write idea on back, fold in half, put in pocket. Spill coffee on new shirt as boss walks into my office. Think to myself, "You know, if I were laying on a beach somewhere this morning and that spillage was actually a *piña colada*, I wouldn't be quite so pissed off at the world right now." Then think to myself, "That's a good e-mail topic," so I pull out the little "While you were out" paper from my pocket and write it down. Put paper back in pocket. Get new coffee, being careful not to spill it again. Work for a couple of hours making schools stand up so that the little children will have somewhere to learn. Think of Hootie and the Suckfish as another e-mail topic.....

So you see, by the end of today, I had been carrying around this pink piece of "While you were out" paper folded up in my shirt pocket all day long and it was full of e-mail ideas. That's how far into this I am. I actually have a backlog of topics right now, which doesn't faze me a bit. Because, occasionally, I can't think of anything witty to say (there are those who would argue that "occasionally" should be changed to "always"), then I can just refer to my notes for a fresh topic. It's pretty cool. And it puts a little spring into my step each and every day; because, as I'm slaving away over a hot set of drawings, I'm watching the world around me, taking notes, thinking, "You're gonna make my e-mail tonight. And, uh, let's see, you're NOT."

Well, *El Hermano Loco*, it's time for me to hit the proverbial hay. And where did that saying come from exactly? "Hit the hay." I suppose that in the olden days the people would go out to the barn, take a few swings at the hay, then come back in and go to bed. Musta been some kind of boxing thing.

Nonetheless, *sayonara* (Oh goodness, a third language, my brain hurts) and have a groovy Tuesday. Remember, "Nobody Will Remember Mama."
Blowing sucks, "While you were out" pads RULE!!

-Rob Blow

Date: Apr 23
To: Jeff
From: Anthony
Subject: Pleasant thoughts

If it is, indeed, true that what doesn't kill you will only make you stronger, by the end of this play, I'll be ready to tattoo a big red "S" on my chest. If I live through it. Just think, in a mere four weeks I can begin to reclaim this life I once dared to call my own. I think the toughest thing these days is trying to accomplish everything I need to do while being limited in the fact that I have only one body and one mind and both are slowly going to hell. For instance, today the printer faxed me a copy of the wedding invitation to proofread, and I accidentally stuck it on the back of a report I was doing at work. Fortunately, I got it before it made its way to anyone of importance.

Speaking of Hooters and the Blowjobs, I have an interesting tale to spin. Now, you know that while Alden is my little pimento in the martini olive of life, she has a rather limited knowledge and appreciation of rock music. Therefore, when we are riding around in the car, I like to quiz her about songs we hear on the radio. So, we were toolin' around San Diego recently when Pearl Jam's song about "not calling me daughter" came on, so I asked her, "Hey baby, who does this song?" Now, Alden likes Pearl Jam and I know she has this song on tape, so I figure she's got it. Anyway, Eddie launches into some melodic angst and she beams, "Oh, it's Hootie and the Blowfish." Now this is rather horrifying BUT, if you listen to the two of them, I think at times it's an honest mistake. Granted, when Pearl Jam is blasting away at full-force, it's pretty easy to make a distinction; but during a quiet tune, Eddie and "Hootie's" voice are kinda similar, don't you think? I mean Axl Rose DOES sound like Ethel Merman, so why is it beyond the realm of possibility that Eddie sounds like "Hootie?" Just one of those facts of life that nobody wants to accept. This should stir up a nice potent little brawl.

Speaking of Alden, I have replaced her understudy. Now, as we all know, to this point, Alden's understudy has been Shania Twain; but, as the director, I am at liberty to make a change when I feel it would benefit the production at large or I get a wild hair up my *culo*. Thus, in the event that anything should happen to my lovely little "s'more," she will have to be replaced by Helen Hunt. For the record, I would like to make it known that Shania has done NOTHING to warrant this decision and there will be some lovely consolation prizes waiting for her backstage. But Helen RULES!! There's a picture of her in May's Vanity Fair where she's standing next to a boat wearing a bikini that really "raised my sail." Besides, Helen is very much like Alden from what I could tell in the article; she stars in my favorite TV show, and she's going out with Hank Azaria, who is a very cool dude in his own right. Congratulations, Helen Hunt!!

So, now, I must go and, through the magic of stage make-up, transform myself into a bitter, crabby old fart. You have a nice evening and I'll talk to you tomorrow, my friend. For the record, didn't people used to sleep on mattresses made of hay?

Working for "The Man" sucks, Helen Hunt rules. OUT!!

Anthony Buchman

Date: Apr 23
To: Duke
From: Jeff
Subject: Swiss Family Architects

Hootie, Eddie. Eddie, Hootie. Nossir, I don't like it.

As far as Helen Hunt goes, the entire fantasy wet-dream thing with her ended (for me, anyway) when I saw an old episode of *Swiss Family Robinson*. She was the daughter of the stranded *familia*, and she was all of 12-years-old or something. And I'm not THAT much of a pervert. But the episode was cool, kinda like a primeval McGyver. The father of the *familia* performed heart surgery on some dying dude, probably an uncle or something, using only jungle vines and bat dung. Intense. And let me get this straight, *Mad About You* is your favorite T.V. program? Sorry, dude, do NOT concur. Julie will concur, though. Paul Reiser's character is truly truly truly annoying to me. Maybe it's that whole New York stereotypical Woody Allen-type neurosis thing; it just doesn't do anything for me. In fact, it annoys. Sorry. Maybe it was an annoying neurotic guy in my childhood. Then, again, it was probably some architect early in my career who ruined the whole thing for me, I've met some neurotic annoying architects in my time.

Since you are making your big debut as mean Uncle Chris this weekend, I thought I would join you, at least in spirit. So, I signed up for an "Open Mike Night" Sunday night at Swallow Hill, which is the same place where I take my 'monica (harmonica) classes. And Phoebe classes. And Rachel Classes. It's a three song gig, where each person gets up and plays, yes, three songs. So, I'll be making my musical debut on a stage in Denver on the same weekend you are Uncle Chrissing it out in San Diego. Cool, huh? I figure I'll play "Something," "Granola Head," and one other. I still have never played a stage in Denver, if you don't count my backyard stage, and I'd like to get some stage time in before the big reunion gig in July; if only to cut down on the nervousness, which, as you probably know, is virtually impossible. I'm always nervous before going on stage for any reason.

One more thing. One of my co-workers comes into my little "cubicle from hell" this morning and starts to ask me about the summer schedule for concerts at Red Rocks and Fiddler's Green, both here in Denver.

"Did you hear that the Scorpions and Alice Cooper are coming?" he asks. "And Boston? And Cheap Trick?"

"Uh, Bob, hang on a second, would ya?" I check my calendar -- it DOES say it's the 1990s.

"And Jeff, did you hear that Chicago is coming? And Styx? And, just the other night, my wife and I went to see Night Ranger!!! Man, I am gonna spend a lot of money on concerts this summer."

I check my calendar again. I close my eyes for a few minutes, thinking that I'll wake up, it'll be 1981 all over again, and I'll be talking to Annabelle on the phone in my old bedroom with the Cars posters on the wall at my parents house. I open my eyes. Nope, it's still the 1990s......What up with this "old dudes touring" crap? It's "Eagles myopia," dude, wherein every "star" band from the 1970s and 1980s has realized that, since their bank accounts have long been drained of any substantial cash by all the drugs and paternity suits, they can go on tour and swindle gazillions amounts of cash out of fans like Bob who never moved past that phase of music, who think that Cheap Trick really does want them to want them. Because, heck, look at the Eagles and their bank accounts! Can't you just see the fallout from this? There'll be new Cheap Trick videos, *Unplugged* albums, and *Grammies* for everybody. Fuck.

Enough of my ranting and raving for today. Enjoy this long-winded e-mail, my friend, and we'll be eeeeeeing at you *mañana*.

Eagles myopia sucks, Bitter Crabby Old Farts RULE!

-The evil opposite of Paul Reiser, the anti-Paul Reiser

Date: Apr 24
To: Jeff
From: Anthony
Subject: Something old

Uh, I am with much confusion. You do not lust after Helen Hunt, because you saw her in a *Swiss Family Robinson* episode when she was 12? Are we to infer that you cannot lust after anyone who was once under the age of legal consent? Sort of limits your choices, don't you think? Did you think she was ugly as a youngster? Please to explain. Yeah, I didn't figure *Mad About You* would rate highly in your mind. But I like it because Jamie reminds so much of Alden and I like neurotic, New York humor. Also, the dog cracks me up. Last weekend was actually paradise for me. For some strange reason, NBC moved *Mad About You* to 9:00 which meant I got to watch *The Simpsons*. This is still the most consistently funny show on TV. Yes, if NBC would decide on a schedule for all this *Must See TV* shit and stick to it, maybe we would all get to watch our favorite shows when we want (and expect) to see them. And smack Paul Reiser all you want, but he's getting PAID to kiss Helen Hunt on a weekly basis.

Yeah, I was noticing that the newspapers are filled with outbreaks of "Eagles myopia." Although, if you think about it, I'd much rather have all these "once-was-es" on tour than on welfare. Cheap Trick? God, I remember what they looked like in '87. Can you imagine the horror now? Of course, you and I are not without fault in this whole affair. For we are also getting the band back together in July. The difference being that we don't need to do it for the cash, we just like being the center of attention.

And speaking of getting the band back together, I have taken the liberty of writing the flier for the gig. Let me bounce this off ya......

"In 1964, in a small village outside Chihuahua, Mexico, a young secretary at a nuclear waste dump gave birth to twin sons who were joined at the testicles. Because she was too poor (and proud) to raise these two on her own, she left them in the care of a traveling band of mariachis who, after years of opening for Julio Iglesias, managed to save enough pesos to have the twins extricated from each other. But they were forced to share two testicles between them. As time grew on, the mariachis found that they could no longer care for the infants and sold them to gringo parents. The infant with the left testicle grew up practical with his gringo parents in Santa Maria, while the right-testicled infant dabbled in music and photography with his gringo parents in and around San Diego. Years later, the infants were reunited by accident when the mariachi band reformed (because they had no money and no more infants to sell) and played at Cal Poly-San Luis Obispo where the twins were obtaining degrees in maintenance engineering and law (truly respected fields of work). The twins were reunited and vowed never to be apart again. That is until the right-testicled one was told he could make more money in Colorado. But their testicular bond transcended the miles and took the form of e-mail. Now, they are reuniting for one night and one night only and you have the unique opportunity to come and listen to their songs and stories..... There's Jeff (right testicle), the multi-talented, whimsical storyteller who sees the world through rose-colored glasses. And there's Anthony ("lefty"), the wise-cracking bundle o' love who knows the best way to remain standing is to keep both feet on the ground. Hear their songs, feel their pain....."

Anyway, we'll throw it out in the water and see if it floats. I really think I need to go away for a while. Anywho, that's all for today. You have a nice evening with your lovely Great One and I'll talk to you tomorrow. Peace.

Eagles myopia does suck, Murray rules. OUT!!

Expensive Treat (the evil opposite of Cheap Trick)

Date: Apr 25
To: Lefty
From: Jeff
Subject: Helen, Alden. Alden, Helen.

Epic flier, very funny. In fact, you will from now on be "Lefty" and I will be "Righty" so that we may honor that long lost *mariachi* band. And where did I put my rose-colored glasses?

You see, my man, the reason Helen Hunt doesn't do anything for my wood is that she still looks exactly like the little girl she was in the *Swiss Family Robinson* show. EXACTLY. Except, of course, for some well placed curves. But she has the same face and the same hair. So you see, I cannot look at Helen and think "woman." Instead, I think "cute little girl." And "cute little girl" doesn't quite get Mister Happy singing. Know what I mean?

Speaking of Mr. Happy, let me talk about tennis for a minute. Yes, watch how this tennis bit turns into yet another bit about sex. Seems like most things do turn into yet another bit about sex. Not a problem with me, though. So, here we go. Bought a new racquet yesterday. Yessir, a Prince Extender-Maxi-Super-Duper-2000 or something. It was actually a demo they were selling for fifty bones, so I bought it, because fifty bones for a good racquet is about fifty bones less than I thought I had to spend. Then I promptly went out and lost with it. O.K. Ready for the sex part? I attribute my loss to not quite knowing my racquet. The first time. It's kind of like the first time you are trying to make love to your new *ingenerio de amor*, who is the cutest thing you've ever been with. You know, you've never been with her, you don't quite know how she operates, and when it gets down to crunch-time, and you need Mr. Happy to stand up at attention like a big old oak tree, he is laying on your belly eating Twinkies and watching reruns of *Star Search*. So you plead and plead with him, threatening him with, "If you don't stand up at attention and sing for me, Mr. Happy, I'm gonna wear boxers for a week!!!" But it's no use. By now, Mr. Happy has slipped into a Twinkie-induced coma and is lying there snoring like the little shriveled up log that he is and dreaming about fried peanut butter sandwiches. So, you apologize to your new woman, try to make it up to her, and give up for the evening. That's about what I did with my new racquet yesterday. I lost, because I couldn't quite get the thing to get up for me. But today, I shall avenge that loss with a wood that is twice as big as usual, which just means I'll have to let it dangle out of my shirt sleeve as I play.

Ain't nothing like a little penis talk to get your Thursday up and running now, is there? Have an excellent day.

Twinkie induced comas suck, new racquets rule!

-Righty

Date: Apr 25
To: Jeff
From: Anthony
Subject: Prima Donna

Well, it took almost 32 years and three plays, but last night I had a "I can't work under these conditions" episode. Oddly enough, it worked, too. We'd had grand aspirations of using sound effects during the production, but there were two distinct problems. The first was that each effect was preceded by about 30 seconds of dead time and the sound guy couldn't figure out how to get around it. The second was that once the effect actually came on it was so poorly recorded you couldn't hear it. Now, I was supposed to make my entrance after one of these sound effects, but the timing threw me so far outta whack that I just simply said, "This isn't going to work, I can't hear the stupid thing" and all of a sudden I'm Paul Newman. "Yessir, sir. Hey, sound effects. OUT!! Anything else, sir?" This will save a lot of headaches, because we didn't even start trying the stupid effects until this week and that's not enough time to learn the cues. So, actually, we're all happy. But to give you some idea of what I'm up against, last night one of the main characters -- who STILL doesn't know his lines -- didn't show up to rehearsal. Yeah, pray for me.

I'm in a pretty foul mood today. I didn't sleep but maybe four hours last night. Let me ask you: What kind of low-life, yellow, demented, butt-sniffing, crotch-licking, yeast-infected pussy do you have to be to continuously call people on the phone and hang up? I mean, what purpose does this serve the caller other than giving themselves something to do with their fingers other than jack-off or pick their nose? Some annoying little piss-ant kept calling over and over last night and hanging up. Finally, I just took the phone off the hook, which I don't like to do, but I had to at least TRY and get some sleep. Then about 3:00 a.m. Rocky Raccoon decided to defend his heavyweight title against some local varmint and they brawled outside my window for about half an hour. Ever hear two raccoons battle it out? Sort of sounds like Black Sabbath played at 78 rpm.

So you're going to play open mike night at Swallow Hill, huh? You know my best wishes will be extended to you that evening. So you've decided to switch to "the racquet formerly known as Prince"? Good call, my friend. But do give yourself some time to get used to the feel of the shaft. Feel your way up the neck and caress the curves bordering the oversized head. Feel the powerful sinews of the strings as you roll your fingers back and forth, faster and faster. Touch him, love him!! Then go on out and play some tennis. And, by the way, there ain't nothing like BIG penis talk to get your Thursday up (hee hee) and running now, is there? Thus, in a cold sweat, I leave you. Have a most productive day.

People who call and hang up suck hyena dick, Rocky Raccoon rules!!

Sleepy in San Diego

Date: Apr 25
To: Lefty
From: Jeff
Subject: There's no place like Vegas, there's no place like Vegas.....

Mijo, don't you worry. Tonight is the first night of the rest of your life. If your co-stars start forgetting their lines, improvise with them. Like this example, straight from the annals (now THAT is a cool word; methinks I will use it more often), like I said, the annals of Acting 101: "I coulda been a contender. I coulda been somebody." "Uh, yeah, like, right on, dude. Maybe you coulda, but I wouldn't know, because I can't remember what you were gonna be!!! Righteous!!!! Line!!!" Nossir, I don't like it. But it sounds like you are going to be the star and the show stealer of the whole thing. Go get 'em, dude. I would say something like "break a leg," but whenever anybody tells me that, I get the heebeegeebees about the fact that "If I really do break my leg tonight SOMEONE's going to pay." Just go out there, have a good time, and make me and your #2 to #4,098,123 fans proud. I'll be thinking of you as I partake of some Railyard (only because I am out of Jeffbrew for the time being) on this Friday night. Tomorrow, you can look back on this and laugh. Or you can call the director and tell him to take his Uncle Chris role and shove it up his nose, you quit! And remember, it takes a man to get on stage at all, but it takes a stud muffin to get on stage with a bunch of people who may or may not be up to the task at hand. And you are my stud muffin. But don't tell Alden that, because she'll want you to be her stud muffin. Then we'll have a problem, won't we?

Misunderstood lyrics department: I always think that the UB40 version of "The Way You Do The Things You Do" has a line that sounds remarkably like "If good looks were mayonnaise, you know you coulda been a sandwich."

As far as the yeast-infected pussy-thing that calls you all night long, that's the price of fame, buddy. Hell, you got a starring role (by default; you WILL be the star, I have no doubt) in a big almost-Broadway production, you write a pretty mean e-mail, and you are generally just an overall good guy and a stud muffin to boot. What did ya expect? It's probably Brenda. She's always got a crush on some teen idol, and she has been known to call a few at home, listen to the soft timbre of their voice, and hang up, too nervous with 12-year-old shyness and angst to actually say anything.

Well, that's about it for now. As your co-stars are slobbering and stumbling all over themselves and the stage in a frenzy of trying to remember their lines tonight, just repeat these four magic words over and over: "There's no place like...." Whoops, sorry, wrong fantasy sequence. Try this: "Three weeks 'til Vegas. Three weeks 'til Vegas. Three weeks..." That, at least, will help you get through the massacre with a smile on your face. I'll be working all weekend yet again, when I'm not on the phone all night crank-calling the future stars of America, and those four magic words will help me also get through my own massacre with a smile on my face. Enjoy yourself tonight, and know that I am with you. In spirit, anyway. And have a good weekend otherwise.

Volleyball games instead of theater is stupid, Brenda crank-calling you RULES!!!!!!!!! And Uncle Chris RULES!!!!!!!!!!!!!!!!!! And Friday RULES!!!!!!!!!!!!!!!! And Rose-Colored Glasses RULE!!!!!!!!!!!!!!!

-#1 Fan

Date: Apr 26
To: Jeff
From: Anthony
Subject: Opening night

Question: Why is it that some guys don't flush the toilet in a public bathroom? Is this the manifestation of the mammalian urge to mark one's territory? This country boasts loudly about having the greatest sanitation system in the world, yet some people choose not to take advantage of it. This I do not understand.

We are, apparently, the Houston Rockets of the theatrical world. The Rockets basically cruise through the regular season. At times, they look brilliant but they just sort of go about their merry little way and by the time the playoffs come along, they're in fourth place or so and are not considered too serious. Yet, when the game's on the line, they somehow rise to the occasion. And so it is with our little production that somehow came to life last night, despite all our best efforts over the past four weeks to scuttle it. Last night was test audience night. You know, where you invite all your cheap friends who don't want to pay to see you perform and you ask them to be guinea pigs so the stage crew and actors can adjust to audience laughter, lighting, etc. True, there were some serious technical problems but, for the most part, the actors came through. So I'm now cautiously optimistic about tonight, but I'm still shaking like a chihuahua in a snowstorm. Last night, Mister Sound Effects Guy came up to me and said, "OH PLEEASE! I got the shit figured out. Can we have the sound effects, huh? OH PLEASE, PLEASE, PLEEEASE!?" And I looked around wondering when the director abdicated and left me the job.

So after my only scene in Act 2, I went back to the dressing room to wait for curtain call and Macaulay was in there taking off his make-up. This kid's amazing, he wears more make-up than a cheap hooker. Anyway, he was in there chiseling the shit off his face when he says, "I'm tired. I think I'll just leave after curtain call tomorrow night." So I, being the theater Pollyanna that I am, said, "But we're having a cast party." And he said, "No, I mean I don't think I'll hang around for autographs. As much as I like signing autographs, I'm just not in the mood." Oh, the pressures of stardom. Autographs? Has anyone ever asked you for an autograph? Apparently, they've asked this kid before, because he's convinced it's going to happen. Not only that, but apparently it's happened enough for it to become a pain-in-the-ass for him. I learned something else about actors. There's nothing funnier than an actor who doesn't know how to do his/her make-up. By the time this one guy was done with his make-up last night, he looked like Alice Cooper. And another guy looked like he was one of those painted professional wrestlers.

By the way, I never got a chance to tell you but, when we were picking out an apartment, I made sure that it had long walls so it wouldn't fall on us in the event of an earthquake. It's so useful to have a structural engineer for a friend. I hope my biology degree has served you at some point. Although the only thing I can think of is the time I was able to correctly identify the large rodent in our kitchen as a rat.

I see that Paul Westerberg is going to try another solo effort in the near future. Ya know, that's one guy I'd love to meet. Realistically, why don't the Replacements just get back together? Far as I know, Tommy ain't doin' shit and Paul just doesn't do the solo thing nearly as well. I mean, as long as Paul and Tommy were in the band it would still be the Replacements, right? Which brings up a point. How many guys do you have to lose before you're no longer the same band? Are the Beatles still the Beatles without John? The Stones are still the Stones without Bill Wyman, but would they be the Stones without Mick or Keith? I mean, The Snipehunters got a new name every time we got a new drummer. And, I forgot to tell you, there was a slight typo on my biography for the play. According to the program, I was "the former singer/songwriter/rhythm guitarist for local bands with many names." I distinctly told them "a" local band with many names.

Well, this is it. Time to put or shut up. You two have an awesome weekend and knock 'em dead Sunday night. Kick some ass, dude, and have a cold one on me.

Marking your territory sucks, schmoozing the fans rules!! OUT!!

Frank Booth

Chapter 11
Feeding Arturo and Bertha

Date: Apr 29
To: Jeff
From: Anthony
Subject: House of Blues

So tell me, how did it go at open mike night? Since I have yet to receive any messages from you today, I'm going to assume it went well and that you're sleeping in late fighting off the damaging effects of too much cheap whiskey and one high-class dame. So when your grizzled old ass regains consciousness and you've had your morning beer, go sit out on the porch, pat the coon dog on the head, listen to the river flow by, get out your laptop, and tell me what happened.

I must formally apologize this morning to one of my fellow actors. I bagged on the kid last week for complaining about autographs and, yesterday, I actually signed one. Yep, after yesterday's matinee, a lady (elderly, with husband, so let's not go there) came up and told me how much she enjoyed the show, then she handed me a program and pen and asked me to sign. Once I made sure it wasn't a subpoena, parking ticket, or paternity suit, I was left trying to figure out what the hell to say. This was truly a unique experience and I fear I didn't handle it like a seasoned pro, for the simple fact that I'm not. Imagine. Me. The little ol' left-testicled, practical *vato* from Santa Maria signing autographs in La Jolla. In the end, I finally went with, "Thank you for coming--Anthony Reynoso (Uncle Chris)."

As for the opening weekend, it went much better than expected, but far from perfectly. Most of the problems were with lights. There were a few times when actors were saying lines in the dark and a few times the lights came up too soon and the stage crew was up on stage adjusting props. But, hell, this is community theater after all. Most of the problems I have in the play stem from my death scene. In this scene, I wear a long, flowing night shirt and I have to get into a lawn chair made up to look like a bed. Sounds easy, but sometimes I move and the shirt doesn't follow. When this happens, I have a night shirt riding up the length of my leg. For this reason, the entire cast and about 30 lucky theater patrons now know that I wear 100% cotton boxer shorts. One piece of advice about theater: Never go see a play on its second night, especially if there's a cast party after opening night. I can sum up our second night's performance in one word: deflated. Two words, actually: deflated and hung-over (this is, of course, assuming that "hung-over" is considered to be one word).

Our reward for surviving the first weekend is that we don't have to rehearse every night. We only have to run through on Tuesday night to stay focused. Thus, tonight, I will attempt to scale that ever-increasing mountain of laundry I have growing in the corner of my room. How bad is it? I'm now wearing clothes that I relegated to "car-washing" status. While the laundry's going, I think I'll even attempt to play some geetar. WOO HOO!! Oh, how my heart cringes when I look at the soft, supple, pink tips of my left fingers. By the end of the night, they will be throbbing shreds of bleeding red flesh. By June they will be callused, white pads you couldn't shove a staple through. So don't worry, I will be in shape for the gig. Also, I may have found a new tennis partner. Be afraid, be very afraid.

By the way, when did you guys get an arena football team? I'm looking at the paper here and it says Montreal 21, Colorado 9........Holy shit, that's a baseball score! 21 runs?! What happened, did they just shut off the gravity entirely there yesterday?

Well, hopefully, at some point, I'll hear from you today. If not, then I'll just have to assume that Colonel Tom was in the audience last night and whisked you off to Nashville (or is it Memphis?) and you're now in the process of recording your first song for Sun Records. Just remember me when you start compiling your entourage. Have a good one and I'll talk to you soon.

Gravity-less baseball sucks, autograph hounds rule!! OUT!!

Big celeb

Date: Apr 28
To: Lefty
From: Jeff
Subject: Arturo and the Fright

Stage Fright is an amazing animal. It awakens about 30 hours before you are due to actually go on stage. At this early point, it resembles nothing more than a small cuddly kitten that has quietly got you thinking about the task at hand and how you are going to accomplish it. You are even a bit excited about the whole thing. Then it slowly grows and grows into various shapes and forms a dog, barking, "You're gonna screw it up, you're gonna screw it up!!!" A lion, roaring, "They're gonna laugh at you, they're gonna laugh at you!!!!" Finally, it resembles that big purple monster on Sesame Street (you know the one....Big Bird's best friend.....uh,. Snufflesomethingoranother) who is always there, mostly in the form of those butterflyzillas in your stomach, giving you a bad case of the constant willies about the whole thing for the hour before you actually drive the location of your demise. Your stomach is a mess, you start to feel hot flashes in your cheeks, your voice is sounding startlingly similar to Alfalfa's (of *Little Rascals* fame), and your legs tremble as though you haven't eaten in three days.

Then you pull up in your car to front of the location of your demise. You sit there for five, ten, fifteen minutes, trying to psyche yourself into actually going in and making a fool of yourself, wishing you still smoked so that you could have a cigarette or nine right about now. The Stage Fright creature at this point is a piranha the size of a ten-story building, eating away at your self-confidence at an alarming rate. Then, suddenly, you say to yourself, "Self, you know what? Anthony wouldn't be nearly this chickenshit at this point." All of a sudden, you've sent the piranha scurrying in search of easier, less self-confident prey, and you've gotten out of your car, grabbed your guitar, and are heading into the location of your next glorious life-conquering experience.

You walk in, tell them "I'm number four on the list tonight." "Oh, are you Jeff Charon?" "Uh, yeah, but that's Chacon. There's a 'c' in there somewhere." "Oh, well, Jeff, there's some rooms down the hall where you are welcome to tune-up and warm-up if you like." "Yeah, thanks, bro, I think I'll do that." You go into one of these rooms and you play a little, knowing full well that your guitar is in tune, because you did that at home. You play bits of your songs, thinking that it all sounds pretty good, which pretty much sends the piranha and his buddies into a different body of water to search for prey. You feel good, although the butterflyzillas are still lingering somewhere deep in your stomach. You go and grab a seat in the little performance hall, which really is about the same size as the hall at *Twigs* in San Diego, where you've played before.

You sit down, and they get started. Number one on the list, "Jammin' Jimmy," is a no-show, undoubtedly a victim of the Stage Fright piranha that almost got to you outside. So number two comes on. Now this place is mostly a folk-type place, and you realize this; but, as number two, a woman, starts to finger-pick her songs and sing them, sounding like an exact candidate for "Granola Head" status, the piranha slowly and quietly enters the room and your head, and you start to think that maybe you are in the wrong place. Because you don't finger-pick shit. Unless it's "Blackbird" by the Beatles, but you know that song ain't ripe for human consumption yet, so you ain't gonna play it. And *ain't* ain't a word and you ain't gonna say it. So, the whole Stage Fright Piranha thing is back, only this time it's an entire school of piranha. You start to think about making a break for it. You check the door, but the people who checked you in and know that you are number four are standing right there. Being that you have to come back for 'monica class tomorrow night, you don't wanna make too much of an ass of yourself, because it would be VERY embarrassing for someone to say to you tomorrow, "Hey, weren't you number four? And didn't you chicken out? We've got classes on how to deal with stage fright, you know."

So you remain in your seat; and, because the school of piranha is pretty much having an entire Thanksgiving Feast off of fright at this point, you start to go over the words to the songs in your head. "Something: Sittin' in front.......Got it." "Superman's Song: Tarzan, wasn't a ladies man......Check." "Granola Head: It ain't enough.......Hey, wait a minute -- WHAT THE HELL IS THE SECOND VERSE TO GRANOLA HEAD?" Then you are in a panic. You played the song earlier today; hell, you've played it four times this weekend, but, now, you cannot remember the second verse!!!!! At this point, the performer before you -- number three, a guy with a real nice voice and some real weird songs who, of course, is finger-picking -- is playing his tunes. You are in a bit of a panic, what with the checking of the door to find a way out and the complete brainfart about the second verse of "Granola Head." So, you go get a cup of water, because you know you are going to need it. At the water cooler, an idea strikes -- You decide to sing the third verse of "Granola Head" at the second spot, and sing the first verse again at the third spot. Yeah, that'll work.

Then, it's almost your turn. The piranha has been joined by a herd of lions, hyenas, and wolves at this point, all mercilessly eating at you and your self-confidence. Then, all of a sudden, it's your turn to hit the stage. You pull out your guitar, walk to the stage, and sit down. You get your microphones set up, and say something silly, like "Hi, I'm, uh, I'm, uh, I'm Jeff, and I am an guitaraholic....no, wait, I mean, I'm Jeff, this is my first appearance on a Denver stage, unless you count my front porch." Ah, yes, a little humor to set everything at ease. You get set to go, but you are shaking like you just jumped out naked from a hot tub in the winter time. You realize, "Hey, man, this is it. Time to put up or shut up." So you play a few E minor chords, a few G chords, try to hum the first tone of "Something," basically stalling. Because your body all of a sudden feels like it has digested an entire can of Beano and you are practically pooping in your pants.

Finally, you find somewhere deep within you the courage to go ahead. You close your eyes and start playing the first E minor chords of "Something." At this point, a strange transition takes place. The Stage Fright Zoo animals disappear, and a bizarre calm takes over -- because you have played this song a billion times. You are still a bit nervous, but that only manifests itself in the form of drymouth, which is a killer. Otherwise, you could very well be playing this song in your basement or your bedroom. So it's okay. People applaud, which makes you feel pretty good. At least they are not throwing things at you. You play "Something," "Granola Head" (with the whole weird verse thing), and "Superman's Song," not really screwing up anywhere. It sounds pretty good. You are not always sure of your timing, because you are not used to the whole crowd and microphone thing; but, hey, you've had a damn good time. And you basically got invited back to the next one, in three weeks.

I didn't even hang around for autographs. I really need to do this more often, just to relieve some of the stress involved with it. You know, I NEED to get on stage once in a while. I am now feeling this complete and utter calm about my life It's like I am again complete, at least for today. Does that make sense? I NEED to get on stage every now and again. It's my ego, which normally is suppressed as I am pandering to some architect's every whim, saying, "O.K, amigo, now it's my turn." If I don't listen to my ego, which we'll nickname "Arturo," if I don't listen to Arturo, he smacks me upside my head with feelings of complacency, boredom, and all around worthlessness. Arturo must be fed in order for me to live. You understand, better than anybody, I'm sure. Arturo doesn't rule my body, but he sure can make my life a living hell. Have a nice Monday.

Stage Fright Sucks, Arturo RULES!!!!

-Jeffrey Guthrie

Date: Apr 29
To: Jeff
From: Anthony
Subject: Well, looky here...

Well, cut off my opposable thumbs and call me a monkey! There you is! Missed you this morning, buddy, but I figured that once your message got here it would be epic and I was right. "It ain't enough to say you love, who knows what you're thinking of?" That's how the second verse starts. And Self, don't kid yourSelf, Anthony suffers from some of the worst stage fright in the world. Fortunately, my stage fright isn't borne out of the fact that I'm frightened of an audience; my stage fright is derived from the fear of fucking up. My guess is you suffer from the same problem. It's just a matter of knowing what to do and when and convincing yourself of that. For me, all stage fright disappears as soon as I hear that first reaction from the audience, so I try to make them laugh immediately. It just sort of reaffirms the fact that they're people and I'm a person, so we at least have that in common. It's also good to know that people don't normally go see performances with the hopes that the performer doesn't succeed. In other words, they're usually pulling for you. In the rare event that you do fuck up, I know you well enough to know that you can find a way out of it. For instance, I dropped the cap from my flask the other night, but, since I was in character and was supposed to be drunk, it was easy to reach down like a drunk and pick it up. Maybe the audience realized I made a mistake, but it didn't hurt anything. So, as far as your performance goes, I'm sure you were great. Any chance you taped it? And honored, yes honored, am I that you choose to perform one of our collaborations.

Concur on your Arturo theory! My ego (I'll call her Bertha) sits on the couch eating bon-bons most of the time, but she does require sustenance on a regular basis and she can be a voracious feeder. With that in mind, here's a little present for Arturo: As a former bandmate, I always knew you'd play the right note and the right chord. And here's a little present for Jeff: I wouldn't want to be in another band without you, because then it would just be a big headache without one-millionth the fun. And, yes, play again in three weeks.

Stage fright sucks, but fear of the stage would REALLY suck.

Calvin and the Hip Monks

Date: Apr 29
To: Lefty
From: Jeff
Subject: Warm Tinglies All Over

You know, even from 1300 miles away, you still give me the warm tinglies all over my body just like the old days. Thanks for the words of advice and encouragement for me and Arturo. And I am glad (for me, anyway) to hear that you too suffer from the Stage Fright Zoo, 'cuz it's nasty. But it really does make a person feel like he/she resides on a different plane than people who never get up on stage. Or so Arturo thinks.

Can I have your autograph, Uncle Chris? And am I to understand this correctly -- You have a drunk scene *and* a death scene? Man, I am proud of you. Hell, honored to even know you. Those are two of the coolest scenes an actor could wish for. You could complete the top five if you had a beach love scene with Pamela Anderson, a naked hot tub love scene with Shania Twain, and a band scene with Paul Westerberg. Then you'd be HUGE.

Well, I finally lost in my tennis league, and Arturo was not at all happy about it. It was Friday, windy as hell. I had played every day last week, and I was tired. Those are my excuses. Here's the real story: This dude, whom I'll call "Netboy," rushed to the net after every one of his serves or every one of his returns of my serves. EVERY TIME. I was dumbfounded initially, because I had never seen anybody do this before. So, I quickly lost the first couple of games, because he was good at the net. I tried to play my game, but he found a way to hit or smash every one of my shots back to me. So, I finally got a few lobs in, and, eventually, found my stroke (which always feels good) and started hitting zingers to the corners, which he had no way of getting to. So, I was finally in the set, down only 4-3. But I lost my momentum somehow and lost the set 6-4. *And* I lost my number one ranking. ~sigh~ But, hey, even though Arturo was so distressed that he locked himself in the back room of my brain and played Solitaire on his computer for three days afterwards, my logical brain, whom I'll call "Poindexter," tells me that this is good, because, after all, the whole reason we joined the ladder was to lose and get better by losing. So, Poindexter was happy, but Arturo was pissed off, refusing to come out of his room until last night's gig was complete.

Tonight, I'm sitting at work at 9:00 and my temper, whom I'll call "Oscar," flares up. Oscar starts to scream at me, "DO YOU REALIZE WE'RE THE ONLY ONES HERE? DO YOU REALIZE THAT WE HAVEN'T HAD A DAY OFF IN THREE WEEKS? DO YOU HAVE ANY IDEA HOW MUCH WORK THERE IS HERE? WHY DON'T YOU GET YOURSELF SOME *CAJONES* AND GO HOME AND GET SOME SLEEP AND TELL EVERYBODY TO FUCK OFF TOMORROW, YOU SPINELESS TWITCHING LITTLE PIECE OF GUANO?" So I did. I went home. Because I have totally run out of steam. And Oscar mentions this to me on an hourly basis these days. This working shit sucks, dude, and they tell us "It's going to be this busy all summer long." GREAT. What they really mean to say is, "There's a whole pack of wild dogs out there and we're gonna go and get as many as we can and bring them back so they can shit in all our spaces all the time. Won't that be fun?" As much as I love my job and career, I realized a long time ago that if Jeffrey and Arturo and Oscar and Poindexter don't have time to play the guitar, draw or paint a pretty picture, write some cool stories, go for a walk in the park, ride their bicycle, buy some Rollerblades, and go to smoky blues clubs once in a while, then their life just ain't worth much to them. See what I mean? I, quite seriously, would rather wait tables for thirty hours a week at minimum wage than work like a dog (like now) for 50 or 67 hours a week for the piddly wage they call "salary." You might think I am selling myself short, but I value my personal life over all other aspects of my life, and there ain't nothing wrong with that. It prevents me from becoming an old burned out yuppie living on the streets begging for money because he fried too many brain cells one night while working late on a project that some architect couldn't make up his mind about.

Well, I'm rambling. I should have learned long ago to not write after a long hard day at the office which ended up with Oscar yelling at me and me leaving because of it. So, I leave you for another day. Have a nice Tuesday, won't you? And if you get a collect call from "Jeffrey, Bartender at The Wynkoop," take it. Because that'll be me calling from my new job!

Oscar sucks, naming your emotions rules!!

-El gringo mariachi

Date: Apr 29
To: Lefty
From: Jeff
Subject: P.S.

Oh, I forgot a couple of things in my furious tirade:

"It ain't enough to say you love...." Yeah, yeah, yeah. I know that, but it's completely amazing what you can brainfart under pressure. I thought about that for about 15 minutes last night and couldn't remember it for the life of me. It's like saying, "My name is Jeffrey Ch....Ch....Chwhat?"

And, as an added bonus to our love-in this day, let me just say that if I -- *El Mariachi Gringo* -- were to ever find some real talent and take my guitar playing butt on the road for paying gigs, then you would be my rhythm guitar player. No ifs, ands, or buttocks. Because that would be cool. And playing paying shows for people all across this great country of ours wouldn't be one trillionth the fun it could be if you weren't there with me. So there. There it is. Now, can we end this love-in and go back to being men? Have a nice Tuesday, won't you?

-Jefferson Chacon Airplane

Date: Apr 30
To: Jeff
From: Anthony
Subject: End of the month

Thus, we bring April to a close and usher in the month in which we make our annual journey to worship the great god of the pyramid (a.k.a. the Luxor Hotel). We bring our humble offerings of gold (money) and heart (liver, actually) and place them onto the waiting hands of the high priests of the temple (pit boss). Late in the evening, we gather to celebrate the Festival with the Dance as several of the most nubile virgins in the land (well, nubile anyway) undulate rhythmically in an attempt to appease these visitors who worship within their holy land. And then we all go back to the hotel, throw up, and prepare for the next evening's services. Ah, a most blessed event.

But before we get to this most sacred time of year, we must endure life here on Planet Mundane. Dude, I can't believe you lost. Does this guy have a killer serve or what? Because it sounds like you're playing too far back at the baseline and allowing him too much time to get set up at the net. You're going to have to cut down your return time if you're going to beat him. But, as you say, live and learn. But don't find comfort in making Poindexter happy. *Au contraire, mon frere.* If Poindexter is happy, then you need to give The Great One your racquet, pull your pants down, and let her pound a few ground strokes on you. Uh, wait, you might actually enjoy that. DO NOT GET COMPLACENT! This infidel has violated the ultimate rule: I'M the only one who kicks your ass in tennis. Now, you call him soon and you get out there, take two small steps forward on your return, and show this guy that the only way to survive at the net against you is to get your e-mail address.

Poindexter, Arturo, Oscar? Are you going schizo, or what? I can imagine life for you these days:

Jeff: "I think I've worked long enough today. Guess I'll go home."

Oscar: "It's about fuckin' time, you puss. Just what the fuck are you trying to prove?"

Arturo: "I tell jou, one of dees days I'm goeeng to be dee next Stevie Ray Juan and I won't haf to put up wit' dis chit."

Poindexter: "Well, I think we should stay a while longer. It builds character."

Arturo: "Dis guy ain't big enuff for any more characters, cabron."

Oscar: "Let's fuckin' kill Poindexter."

Jeff: "Guess I better go home before they kill me, too."

My friend, at the very least, you need a vacation. At the very most, you need a lobotomy. But I think a vacation would do you wonders. And I don't necessarily mean to pack up and take a trip. Call in sick a couple of days and go find a cabin somewhere near a mountain stream. Take your woman, your guitar, a journal, and an obscene amount of alcohol, and don't do anything you don't want to do. Play, walk in the sunshine, frolic in the meadows, match a songbird note for note. God, I'm depressing myself.

Anthony: "God, I'm depressing myself."

Oscar: "Yeah, you sure TALK a good game, you mealy-mouthed puss."

Bertha: "I can act, I can write, and someday I'll prove it."

Poindexter: "Ya know, everything was all right until we started writing Jeff."

Oscar: "Let's kill Jeff."

Oh, uh huh huh, must've dozed off. Where was I? Yeah, get some rest. After all, if you don't have your health, you don't have anything. And don't underestimate the life of a bartender. It ain't the worst thing you can be. You could be a lawyer, a talk show host, or a biologist.

Anyway, if you're nearly as unhappy as you sound, then I would start checking the job market once again, because it goes against your nature to be miserable and work all the time. It just ain't conducive to an environment that will support Jeff Chacons. So stand back, take a look at the mountain on your desk, and either shove your face in it or push it on the floor, then jump up on the desk and do the naked chicken dance. Enjoy!

Poindexter sucks, naked chicken dancing rules!! OUT!!

Foghorn Leghorn

Date: May 1
To: Lefty
From: Jeff
Subject: I'm schizophrenic, and so am I

> Roses are red, violets are blue,
> I'm Schizophrenic and so am I.

"......ladies and gentlemen, JEFF CHACON!!!!!!!!!!!!!!!" Forty thousand screaming 12-year-old girls crowd the Sports Arena, screaming "JEFF!! JEFF!! JEFF!!" over and over again as I play the first notes of my latest hit, "It's Been A Hard *Dias Noche*" on the red Stratocaster. It's exactly like the scene out of "Hard Days Night" when John, Paul, George and Ringo couldn't hear a damn thing they were doing because of the din caused by all of the screaming pre-pubescent girls............And, slowly out of the fog, comes the sound of Jimmy Buffet singing "Margaritaville." SHIT!! I slowly realize that I am laying in bed in Denver and the preceding bit (brought to you by Leroy, my imagination) was merely a dream. DAMN! At least it's Saturday. HEY, WAIT A MINUTE!! THE ALARM NEVER GOES OFF ON SATURDAY!! Ah, hell, it's only Wednesday? I gotta go to work today? Shit.

I'm not nearly as unhappy as I sounded in yesterday's e-mail. Don't worry. I just bitch a lot. Everybody in my office is going about nuts right

112

now, at least those of us who are working 27 hours a day. Even Boss #2, who is normally as unemotional and straightforward as you can get, was losing his temper yesterday when I told him, "Uh, Boss #2, I've got about 32 hours of drafting here, and you say the draftsmen can't start on it until tomorrow, and how the hell are we going to get all of this work done by tomorrow night?" He kind of growled and scowled at me, grinding his teeth, and said something like, "It's been a long few weeks." As if I didn't know that. As you say, I merely need a vacation. And that vacation is in 16 days. VEGAS!! VEGAS!! VEGAS!! VEGAS!! VEGAS!! I'm merely slightly excited. Can you tell? And if the high priests of the temple are not satisfied with our offerings, maybe we can offer some sacrifices in their name? Also, after the Festival of the Late Night, we will partake of the holy meal (steak and eggs, of course). That is, if we can be revived from our stupor invariably brought on by the rhythmically undulating virgins and the alcohol imbibed while watching the undulations.

Well, I'm headed for the showers, much like the Rockies pitching staff in innings 5,6,7,8, and 9. Hell, throw in 1,2,3,4. By the way, that dude who pitched in the 21-9 loss to Montreal was sent down to the minors right after the game. Anyway, I'm off to another day of blissful fun and happiness at the hellho...um, workplace. Have a great Wednesday!

Waking up to Jimmy Buffet sucks, rhythmic undulations RULE!!

-Las Cucarachas

Date: May 1
To: Jeff
From: Anthony
Subject: No fun allowed

Hey, I'm wondering, does the contemporary use of the word "sucks" make it a verb or an adjective? Thinking back to those little cartoons on Saturday mornings, an adjective is something that describes a noun. Thus, when we say that "So-and-so sucks," aren't we using the verb "sucks" to describe "So-and-so" and, therefore, isn't "sucks" an adjective? This may or may not be the case, but one thing is truly undeniable: So-and-so truly sucks. But I think we need to come up with a new classification for words such as sucks, blows, bites, etc. Maybe they should be verbectives. Or maybe adjerbs. Or maybe we should name them after the guy who discovered them and call them Anthonys. Much to think about.

So, last night, we showed up for rehearsal. We've already done three performances, but we need to stay focused so we got together last night for a quick run-through. Now, you know this was not going to be taken extremely seriously. We bumped along saying our lines, laughing, and just generally goofing around. All of a sudden, this whiny, perturbed voice shrieked from the darkness, "If you guys aren't going to be serious about this, then I quit. I

113

need this time to learn my cues." From whence did yonder sniveling come? From Mister......Mister Light Guy. Then he grabbed his cigarettes and went out for a calming smoke, leaving us to wonder whether or not this play will actually ever become any fun at all. What Thomas Jefferson doesn't seem to understand is that this a run-through; he's not supposed to be learning shit. He is supposed to take the knowledge he's gained so far and apply it at predetermined times during the production. So, after that, we had to buckle down and stop laughing, so Butthead Lite could learn his cues. No more, dude. It ain't worth these headaches.

I may actually be playing tennis this evening -- I'm looking forward to that. Guess I'll take leave now. This was one of those days where I was busy as hell but didn't accomplish shit. Ever had one of those days? They suck (and it *is* an adjective). So you have a good evening and I'll talk to you tomorrow.

Whiny light guys suck, verbectives rule. OUT!!

Dark Prince

Date: May 1
To: Lefty
From: Jeff
Subject: Constipated Nouns

If grammar were outlawed, only outlaws would have grammar.

No, my grammar-ly-challenged friend, "suck" is NOT an adjective. Think about it. An adjective is something that describes something else. Such as "tremendous enormous gorgeous breasts." There. I used three adjectives to describe Julie's breasts. Would you ever say "suck breasts?" Well, not in public, anyway.

So, what exactly is suck? Well, "you suck" seems to be similar to "you smell like guano" or "you are ugly, U-G-L-Y, you ain't got no alibi, you ugly, uhh uhh you ugly...." So, that is an a....a....adver...adje...dang....verb.... parti.....What? I don't know. Let's call it a constipated dangling participle. Julie would know, but she's out at some "work party." Maybe she'll get home before I finish this e-mail, then we can know the truth. But you can't handle the truth. I prefer that we keep the given name of "Anthonys" to describe these fun-loving words.

And when you say "no more," are ju telling me that ju are giving up the acting career? Can this be true? NOOOOOOOOOOOOOOOOOO!!!!!!!!!! Oh, well, can't say that I blame ya. I have also given up on it, although many could argue, and many do, that my career never really got out of the gate. We have so many other talents to fall back on: writing, rock n' roll, sucking breasts, and retreating to Vegas to partake in "Male Awareness Weekend." I am truly sorry to hear that your play has not been nearly as fun as you would like it be. This Light Butthead Guy sounds like he's related to a certain

114

drummer named Eddie who lives in the East County there in San Diego. Remember him? That guy always tried to ruin our fun; because, frankly, he took the whole thing much too seriously. You and I were just out for some laughs and a little Arturo boost, and Eddie wanted to take it all seriously. "Uh, yeah, guys, could you at least try to sing on key? And I think we need to replace everybody in the band except me." That guy was a real party killer.

You know, the power of the wedding ring never gets much press. Yeah, well, I'm here to change that right now. Let's say you are in a very long and very boring meeting, and some cute little young architect is making googoo eyes at you all the time and is just about to get up the nerve to ask you out. You raise your left hand as if to stifle a yawn, place it a few inches from her face, and hold it there long enough for her to notice THE RING. It's as if you are saying, "Uh, no no no no!!! Don't touch the merchandise!!! You're cute and all, but where the hell were you B.J. (Before Julie)? I'm a taken and kept man now, sweetie. Don't worry, there are others like me out there." She says, "Uh, Mr. Jeff, Mr. Structural God of My Universe, uh, is that by chance a WEDDING RING?" "Yes, Brenda, that is. I'm married." Then she goes on to make it sound like she really cares. "Well, Jeff, how long have you been married blahblahblahblahblahblah....."

Ah yes, the power of the wedding ring. Now, just in case you might be making the wrong assumptions, let me just say: I'm not saying any of this actually happens. I'm not saying it doesn't. In fact, I'm just not saying. But the wedding ring is many things. A security blanket for you and your lovely bride, because you both know it means a commitment. A deterrent for keeping all of the cute young female architects away from the merchandise. And, of course, a symbol of your undying love for your wife..

Well, tonight, I am transferring the official "*Bailar Y Ondular* Party Brew" over into the carboy. It smells pretty darn good, let me tell you. Somebody told me that I could cover each of twelve bottles with a big ol' sock and put them all in a wine case box and check them at the airport. This kind of sounds like a keen idea to me. I think we need to have some *cerveza buena de mi casa a Las Vegas, si*? Of course, eventually we'll run out of the *cerveza buena;* but it won't matter. We'll drink anything at that point. I know. I've seen it.

Suck sucks, Julie's breasts RULE!!!

-Lord of the Structural Universe.

115

Chapter 12
Dog Days

Date: May 2
To: Jeff
From: Anthony
Subject: One of those days

I found myself in a rather Otto-esque situation this morning; I had to wish an obnoxious co-worker a happy birthday. "Happy birthday...happy birthd...FUCK YOOOOUUU!!" Not an easy thing to do. I would rather have swallowed a moldy apricot. I would rather have had sandpaper rubbed all over me, then been dropped in a tank of lemon juice. I would rather have slipped Marge Schott the tongue; uh, wait, it wasn't quite that bad. But you get the picture. And like any other large smelly stool, this too shall pass.

This has been a truly crummy day. This morning I get to work earlier than usual and, shortly thereafter, one of the truly fine secretaries from the other side of the building walks into our lab. And I'm thinking, "Hmm, interesting. I wasn't aware she came in this early. Maybe she's been waiting for me. Maybe she's taking the opportunity to throw caution to the wind in the hopes of one desperate fling with a REAL man." She leans against the door and breathes a warm, "Good morning." So, now, I'm throwing shit off the desk in anticipation of the big moment, when she says, "There's a leak in our lab over here. Could you come look at it?" Ah ha, the old "plumber adjusting the pipes" routine. So I start putting stuff back on my desk and I say "Sure." (I don't care who has the home-court advantage) Boy, imagine my surprise when I found out there really was a leak. Imagine my further surprise when I found out that she has a tendency to grossly underestimate the seriousness of a situation. Essentially, what happened was a water purification system blew up and there was water an inch deep throughout her lab. At this point, the only thing to do would be to turn off the water so I swim down under the sink to find about 27 assorted knobs. Knob #15 served my purpose. I'm thinking, "Hey, there's lots of water, we could still make the best of this situation," but she had gone back to her desk. Typical woman. Using sex to get some poor schmuck to do her dirty work.

Got in some tennis last night for the first time since the controversial "broken racquet" affair. Victory was mine at 6-2, 6-1 and, overall, I was pretty happy with my performance. Of course, toward the end of the match he cheated; he had his wife come out dressed in her workout gear, and this woman is beautiful. But that didn't stop me. I called upon the ancient powers of concentwation. Also, a little glimpse of her wedding ring made it easier to ignore the situation. You are right about the power of the ring. It's like a stop sign. Most people tend to follow the directions, but there's always a few

116

lawbreakers out there. A far as young architects making googoo eyes at you, remember, you hate architects. As much as you hate architects in general, imagine what a female architect must be like. Ooooh scary!! Overall, a lot of mammarian references in your message today. Can you say "fixation"?

Ah, my throat is achin' for some of that sweet brew you are currently stirring up in your cauldron of sin. Regarding my comments yesterday about the theater, I can't say I'm going to quit acting entirely, but I do plan to be a little bit more selective in my choices of projects. Hopefully, we'll all be able to have a little fun this weekend. After Friday night's performance, we're supposed to go kara..o..k...the Japanese word for singing over pre-recorded music. I have been besieged by requests to perform "Kiss" (by "The Artist"), but they'll have to buy me beer to make it happen. Talk to you soon.

Moldy Apricots suck, mammarian references RULE!!!

-Only a Mammary

Date: May 3
To: Lefty
From: Jeff
Subject: Spicy serve

Don't you hate it when you get a zit inside of your nasal cavity, right in the area where you feel the need to pick the most?

I was going to write something warm and fuzzy about what it's like to be married for a year, but since I'm seemingly in the doghouse again, that would be darn near impossible.

On May 2, Jeff Chacon finally learned how to serve. I was walking out to the court to meet my opponent and I started watching the classes which were going on all around me. I realized that a lot of the students had their racquets cocked up behind their heads before they served! So, being the ultra-curious dude that I am, I tried it. Much like a correct golf swing (which I never get right), I brought the racquet up, cocked it behind my head, which, when released, gave me an incredible increase in racquet speed. Heck, I even aced my opponent a half a dozen times with this new serve. This may pump some new life into my game yet. You don't have to worry, though. I fully expect to get stomped by you in July; because, after all, you *are* the master.

Well, I gotta go. I'm late, I'm late, for a very important date -- with a bunch of architects. We call it *architorture*. I'll be sitting in a conference room down in Colorado Springs trying to pick my nose but being unsuccessful because of aforementioned zit, while these architects try to decide "Where shall we put the blackboard in this room? What color are those drapes?" Oh, joy. Rapture. Ecstasy.

Doghouses suck, spicy serves rule!

-zitboy

Date: May 3
To: Jeff
From: Anthony
Subject: Dog days

Fortunately, I've spent the last few years building up an immunity to venomous e-mail. Here's a chance to use your harmonica:

"Relegated to the doghouse (da daa da DA)
no TV or a phone (da daa da DA)
got no whiskey in my dog dish (da daa da DA) and no place to bury my bone.
These are Dog Days, ba-bee, spendin' Dog Days all alone (nasty guitar solo)
I got no whiskey in my dog dish (da da da da) and no place to bury my bone
(twenty minute guitar solo)
Got a big zit in my nostril (da daa da DA)
sleepin' on cold cold grass (da daa da DA)
these Dog Days is nothin' (da daa da DA) but a big pain-in-the-ass.
These are Dog Days ba-bee, spendin' Dog Days all alone (nastier guitar solo)
Got no whiskey in my dog dish (da da da da da DUM)
...and no place to bur-y-y-yeeeee....my-y....Bo-o-o-o-one."

Thank ya. Y'all too kind. Hey, keep drinkin', and we'll be right back.

Your anniversary weekend and you find yourself in *La Casa de Perro*. Geez. Well, at least you can take some consolation in the fact that you feel you've developed a serve. Although I don't what the hell was wrong with the one you were using. But it never hurts to change up your game a little. Yes, zits in the nose are a definite nuisance, but ya know what is really painful? A badly skinned knee. Whereas, the act of skinning your knee hurts somewhat, it doesn't begin to compare to the constant pain you feel the next day when you slightly move your knee. And you never realize how much you move your knee during the course of a day until you skin it. I managed this feat last night during our company softball game as I dove for a ball in right field, to no avail. I really have to curtail this nasty habit I have of diving during softball games. I'm not a kid anymore and, one of these days, I may actually hurt myself. You know how these old bones can SNAP! so easily.

Weekend two of the play starts tonight and it'll be interesting to see if we can pick up where we left off. Meanwhile, you just set quietly on the porch with your head hung low in shame, and cast those big puppy-dog eyes up at The Great One until she caves and lets you back inside. I mean, really, this *is* your anniversary weekend. Play nice. Anyway, have a great weekend and I'll see ya Monday.

Skinned knees suck, burying bones rules. OUT!!

Scabman

Date: May 5
To: Lefty
From: Jeff
Subject: The Greatest One

  That's why we call her "The Great One." Friday, when I was feeling the dreaded "Doghouse Syndrome" that every man feels sooner or later, Julie called me at work and said, "What are you doing?" "I'm, duh, working, what do you mean?" "Well, you should come home now." Seems she called Boss #1 and Boss #2 the day before and interrupted their top-secret meeting to ask them, "Can I please please take Jeff away for the weekend AND take him early Friday?" They, because they knew who they were up against, said, "Yes, because Jeff is so unbelievably close to being excellent." So The Greatest One Of All and I went to Glenwood Springs for the weekend. And you know how this works, don't you? Five minutes after I walked into the house on Friday afternoon at two o'saka I'm a whimpering dog: "I'm sorry for being an idiot last night, and I'll never do it again. Promise." See how that works? The wife screws something up or acts like a total moron, and it's always me who ends up apologizing. Jeez. Needless to say, we had a good time. The Great One also eventually apologized, although somehow it still feels like I've been had, one way or another. But the weekend was fun. We got a room at the *Hotel Denver* which has a "Historical Art Deco Interior" (according to the flier), which is nothing more than spray on marshmallow texturing. At what point does one begin to consider suing for false advertising? The "Continental Breakfast" consisted of a coupon for $2.00 worth of grub at the bakery down the street. What can two bones buy these days? Half a bagel? Anyway, it was fun. We relaxed -- a lot -- ate -- a lot -- and generally did a whole lot of nothing. We drove down to this little town called Redstone on Saturday. My feeling is that Red Rocks was probably already taken. "This is Redstone. This is the Edge." (See? No matter how much they continue to let me down anymore, U2 will always be in my system) This little town has a population of 92 and a castle that is pretty cool. It's akin to Hearst Castle up there in the heartland of California, with one exception; this castle rents rooms. Very cool. I felt like riding up on my steed and rescuing the fair maiden, it was that cool.

  Bro, if I EVER start to really lose my hair, I'm gonna shave my entire head. I was sitting in my meeting Friday, trying to pick my nose but being denied that pleasure because of a certain well placed zit, when this dude walked in. He had on a seersucker suit, coke bottle glasses, a late 70s disco ball tie, which was about 14 inches wide at the bottom, and a little straw hat. He took off his hat and I started to guffaw uncontrollably. "Mr. Engineer," the lead architect asked, "are you okay?" "Yes, butth.....señor architect, sometimes I just think funny things." This dude, with white hair, was obviously balding. But he had tried to hide that fact by (1) Growing a beard and a 'stache, (2) combing his hair over the bald spot from left to right, and (3) cutting the hair on one side of his head so that it was exactly the same length as the other. In other words, and I'm doing my best to describe this to you, he had hair on both sides of his head cut straight from front to back at about the lobe level. Straight. Hiding his ears and everything. If you caught this dude during a windstorm, he'd have hair three feet long on one side of his head and six inches long on the other. I did my best to keep my eyes off him during the meeting, to no avail. If he was gay, or even straight, he probably thought I was VERY interested in him. You know how it is when you're sitting in a room full of very plain ordinary looking people and Krusty the Clown walks in. You just wanna stare!!!!! Then, I realized that the "Estimator" guy is also balding, only he isn't trying to hide it. He's got this thing where his hair starts halfway up his skull and continues back from there down to his neckline. So, when you're looking at him from the side, as in profile, he looks like he has half a helmet on his head. From the front, he looks bald. From the back, full head of hair. What is that? If I ever start to lose my hair, I'm shaving the whole damn thing. And I'll probably be seeing both of these dudes at the jobsite and meetings for the rest of the summer, which will only further my opinion that if one hair goes, they all go.

Well, we've been married a year now. And it's amazing to me the amount of people who actually remembered and called today. You sent a card (thanks, by the way), our 'rents called, some of our berry best friends called, it was enough to make a grown man feel loved. And I do. And I will write about being married for a year and loving it tomorrow, because now it's time to go and eat Chips Ahoy and milk in bed and get ready for the week. Have an excellent Monday.

False Advertising Sucks, Shaved Heads Rule!!!

-Kojak

Date: May 6
To: Jeff
From: Anthony
Subject: Whimpering dog

You sniveling little Shih Tzu. I can't believe you came crawling into the house whining, "I'm sorry, I was an idiot." What is that? Oh, well, glad to see you checked out of the doghouse in time to enjoy your anniversary. Allow me, as the former best man, to congratulate you and The Great One, wholeheartedly, for surviving the first year of what promises to be many decades of marital bliss. That is as long as you continue to tuck tail and belly crawl every time the two of you have a cross word. You puss! Much credit to Julie for fixing you guys up with a weekend in Glenwood Springs. Very classy move by a very classy lady. I was kinda worried about you guys today, because it just seems like love took a beating this weekend, so I was wondering whether or not the two of you would be fighting like *gatos y perros*

120

(Since you normally reside en *la casa*, you are the *perro*). Yeah, Paul and Jamie got into a big brawl last night on *Mad About You* and he walked out. Now, say what you will about Paul Reiser, but at least HE had the stones to walk out on Helen Hunt without groveling like a pud. I doubt you saw the show, but let me describe just how typical this situation is. On last week's episode, he met this chick at an awards show, they talked and he was very tempted, but he put her in a cab and sent her on her way. So, on last night's show, Paul was racked with guilt. Meanwhile, Jamie came to the reality that they were having problems and, when she couldn't find someone to talk to, she started smooching on her weasly co-worker. So, that night, Paul and Jamie both bared their souls; he got pissed, and walked out. THIS is typical. Similarly typical was Alden's take on the whole thing: "Well, he's just as guilty as she is." Really? I've often fantasized about robbing a bank, so am I as guilty as the guy who actually does it? This is your basic female logic at its best, and we men fall for it all the time, because we naturally assume that if it has to do with relationships *she* must be right -- for the simple fact that she's a woman and we don't know squat about relationships. Either that, or we know they can go without sex longer than we can. Anyway, don't be so quick to apologize. You may need to, but at least be sure you know why you're doing it.

Thus, we have rapped the second weekend of the play. It's amazing how an audience can change so dramatically from night to night. Friday's audience was pumped. They were laughing, they were clapping, you could tell they wanted to be entertained. Saturday's audience was desperately in need of CPR. I learned some things this night. First of all, if an audience isn't reacting, that doesn't necessarily mean they're not enjoying themselves; an audience will enjoy a show on its own terms. Secondly, you as an actor cannot change this so don't kill yourself trying. I figured the audience needed a little push, so I went totally bananas in an attempt to light a fire under them. All I wound up doing was sweating like a pig. So, from here on out, I play my part as I see fit to play it and let the audience decide for themselves. Two more shows and it's over.

Yes, I realize it's enjoyable to make fun of the bald, but you never really know how you're going to react in a crisis until you actually live through it. I like to think that when I start to seriously lose hair, I'll just let nature take its course, because I'll be so secure in my appearance and with myself as a person I'll be able to handle it. Then again, I can see myself shaving my armpits and gluing the hair on my head.

So it goes for a Monday. Once again, have a wonderful anniversary, and congratulations again. Remember, she is your love outlet, so plug in. You guys are something special. We'll be talkin' at ya tomorrow.

Female logic sucks, anniversary weekends rule. OUT!!

Best man

Date: May 7
To: Lefty
From: Jeff
Subject: Anniversary Time

Ah, yes, the morning after. How quickly life imitates art: After scarfing down some enchiladas and a bottle of Chilean Wine at Sabor Latino, our buddy José brought us a piece of *flan* with a candle in it to celebrate *nuestro aniversidad.* Veja Du?

You know what they call her in Paris? L'Great One.

Well, I gotta go to work, where it looks like an all-day session of A.C.T. (Ass Chewing Time) awaits me. I get to spend the day with Boss #2 going over what I did and didn't do on the schools. Joy. Rapture. Ecstasy. I can't wait. I think I'll give Arturo the day off; because, if he's around, it makes these humiliating sessions that much harder to handle. You know, Arturo makes me get all defensive, even about things I shouldn't be defensive about, like "'Bagel' *is* spelled 'B-A-G-L-E!!!!!!!!' Look it up!!" So I'll give Arturo the day off. Have a groovy Tuesday and, remember: 10 days 'til VEGAS!!!!!!

A.C.T. sucks, Anniversary Time RULES!

-L'Flan Man.

Date: May 7
To: Jeff
From: Anthony
Subject: Lack o' cash

Hey, Julie, best wishes and congrats to you on your one-year anniversary. But you're still in second place in terms of roommate longevity.

Hola, mijo. Why is it that the world seems so bent on acquiring what meager little stores of cash I have? It never ceases to amaze me how things can go along smoothly, then, all of a sudden, everybody wants money for something. Don't get me wrong, I have the money to make the wolves go away. I just don't want to give it to them. I'm sure you can relate to what I'm saying, especially because you were married a year ago and I know you couldn't have forgotten the outpouring of funds that accompanied the wedding. There's the deposit on the apartment, the first month's rent, the TV set, the car needs brakes, the registration's due, I had to buy a ticket to fly up and see Alden graduate, turn on the electricity, phone, and cable, clean the Persian rug her aunt gave us, rent a trailer to bring my stuff down from Santa Maria, and so on. Don't these people know that I'm going to Vegas in a mere ten days? And Hawaii in about two months? Not only that, but Alden's coming home this weekend and that usually winds up costing money, because we eat out all the time. By the way, since we're talking about wedding stuff, you need to go down and get measured at some point. I figure I wouldn't be too far off if I told them 36-22-36, but I figure it's better to be safe than sorry.

Sounds like you guys had a great evening of fine dining last night. You know what they say, "A plate of enchiladas, some Chilean wine, and thou." Unfortunately, the harsh realities of everyday life must head their ugly rears and subject you to some ass-chewing. My only suggestion to you would be to smear iocane powder all over your butt. By the way, let me ask you a question, since you are an old married man now and I am about to embark on said venture: Do you guys lump all your music in one big pile, or do you keep yours separate so visitors don't laugh at you when they find out there's more than one Eagles CD in the house? Actually, since you are no longer considered a marital rookie, are there any bits of advice you'd like to pass (guess I shouldn't say pass considering what you ate last night)......give me to make my life as happy and blissful as yours? (Boy I can't WAIT to hear this!)

Bad news, buddy Looks like I'm playing tennis again tomorrow. "I want YOU, Balboa!! I gots to have ya!! Come on Balboa!!" Perhaps, at this rate, I won't entirely embarrass myself in July. Know what they call Julie in Norway? The Great Vun (a little Uncle Chris smack for you). Anyway, time for me to go rustle up some chow. Have a great day.

Spending money on stuff you don't want to sucks, flan rules. OUT!!

Scrooge

Date: May 7
To: Lefty
From: Jeff
Subject: Marriage Tips

You will be proud, my boy, to note that we still have NO Eagles CDs in this house. Nossir. Never. Nada. Nadia. Comeneechie..sce...ah, hell. You know who I'm talking about. But I will tell you the secret to the music thing: Have plenty, and I do mean PLENTY of your own good music, so when guests look at your pile o' CDs, what they see is this: Dwight Yoakam, Los Lobos, Pearl Jam, The Replacements, The Indigo Girls, Los Lobos, Stevie Ray Vaughan, Buddy Guy, Chris Duarte, Tracy Chapman, Los Lobos, The Beat Farmers, Crash Test Dummies....You see? Just make sure that you have five times as many CDs or tapes or albums (STILL my preferred method of partaking) as she does, and then it'll look good. "Oh, yeah, that Mary Chapin Carpenter CD? The wife's." Actually, by the time the guests look at the top five CDs in the pile -- which, coincidentally, are always *your* CDs -- they will be so impressed by your incredibly diverse musical taste, they will stop looking; they will know you are one enriched and tasteful dude.

As far as my other tips for a happy marriage, I'll take a whack at that right here. Actually, I'm home alone tonight, because the wife is in Pueblo for some kinda "Business Meeting Type Thing," so I'll write these down as I'm wandering around the house bottling *La Cerveza De Fiesta De Matrimonio* and doing other assorted odd jobs. Here we go:

1. Establish a joint-checking account, while keeping a separate account for each of you. Have each of you contribute a certain amount to the joint account, to pay for such things as rent, groceries, Weekends at the Male Awareness Institute in Las Vegas, and other "shared" things. This way, you can never know exactly how much money she spends at Nordstrom's each month -- nor do you want to know -- and she can never know how much money you spend on your guitar habit or your beer-making frenzy. Although, at this point, with *mi esposa* making so much more *dinero* than me, I begin to wonder: Shouldn't we be contributing proportionate to our salaries? That means I put in $5.00 a month, and she puts in the other $1500.00.

2. If she owns any type of clothing that makes her resemble a green peanut M&M, make her get rid of it. I did this.

3. In the same vein, expect a full assault on your treasured T-shirt collection. If they start to disappear on you and you notice that every time the Amvets call your wife, she says, "Yeah, I've got some more junk for you," then, buddy, you are in trouble. Because, for some reason, women apparently don't like the raggedy T-shirts that say, "My buddies went houseboating on the Sacramento Delta and all they got me was this lousy T-shirt!!"

4. In the same vein, don't ever expect to get out of the house with her while you are wearing your "Replacements" T-shirt. Collared shirts, long a symbol of oppression, will be required. Hell, I've even bought a couple of collared "polo" type shirts to get through the summer, just so I can avoid the "Get back in that house and change or else you are NOT going to see Chris Duarte tonight" thing.

5) Make sure your wife can let a fart that is as smelly or smellier than yours. This is VERY important; because, and since you are a man I know you do this, after a splendid meal of enchiladas and Chilean wine, you are going to be walking around the house creating the nastiest, smelliest windstorm San Diego has ever seen; and she's gonna be doing the "Ooooh, gross!!!!" thing. And all you have to say at that point is, "It's not nearly as bad as one of your farts, Honey." This will shut her up faster than you can say "Phhhhhtttt!"

6. You must make her think that everything is her idea; when, as we men know, all of the good ideas actually come from the male side of the relationship. This is quite important. Whether through subliminal (buy beer) methods (buy beer) or otherwise, she must think that everything is her idea -- or else it won't happen. If you can get your wife to say to you, "Honey, don't you think it's high time I bought you a new guitar?" you've got it made. She won't have any idea why she's saying this to you, and that's the beauty of it.

7. It is your job -- and only your job -- to mow the lawn. Wives do not do this.

8. This is probably the most important tip I can give you about a successful marriage: Make SURE you have a Happy Place you can go to if she's having a meltdown about "the mud tracks all throughout the house that

obviously came from your boots" or "work," which happens much too often. So, you go to your Happy Place, which could be a basement, the computer room, any room with beer in it, or any room without your wife in it. This gives her time to sulk and eventually realize she is wrong and you are right.

9. Which leads to: Don't ever let Alden take herself or her work too seriously. This is a very dangerous thing in our generation. Julie and I try to reconcile this time and time again. She is always thinking about work and the stress and shit that comes with it, even at bedtime. I, on the other hand, as you probably know, could give a shit. Once I walk out the office door, I'm a free man. And I'm a different man. I'm no longer "El Jefe, the anal retentive perfectionist engineer." I become "Jeff, the laid-back tennis-playing, guitar-slinging, beer-quaffing dude who sees the world through rose-colored glasses." Julie is learning. I'll give her that. When she's freaking out about work, I simply ask, "Are you working now?" "Well, no." "Then KNOCK IT OFF!!!! I WANT MY WIFE BACK!!! I DIDN'T MARRY A JUNIOR EXECUTIVE ON THE FASTRACK TO SUCCESS (although it was a small consideration). I MARRIED YOU!!!" So, she's working on it, and getting better every day. In fact, we recently had the "Why do we work so hard? Why don't we just buy a mobile home, park it down by the river, and live off of the land?" conversation, which was interesting. And short.

10. Finally, surprises are good -- Especially when they involve roses, weekends away, or lingerie. Glow-in-the-dark condoms don't count. Nor does getting her name tattooed on your pecker. That only works for Tommy Lee. Surprise her. Always make time for just the two of you. Lots of weekends out of town, just lounging around at the pool or hiking or biking or throwing snowballs at each other. Make time for the occasional "Date Night," where you go out on a date with each other, just like the good ol' days B.M. (before matrimony). Dinner, dancing, maybe a movie, and maybe you'll get lucky.

Well, you asked for it. Those are my tips for a successful marriage. Not that I'm an expert. But the first year has been a blast. And I am looking forward to *muchos mas años con mi esposa*. I'll talk more about that tomorrow night. Tonight, I must return to work. Yes, I'm working at home. Because now my butt is bruised and bloody and blistery, and I have to make the corrections to the school drawings. What does not kill you only makes you stronger. Correct? Whoever said that ought to be shot. Anyway, the *cerveza* is bottled and now carbonating in the "Evil Tub Of Carbonation" right here in my guest room. It smells and tastes pretty good, let me tell you. As the "Official Taster of the Sacred Brew," I have to check it, of course. You will love it in Vegas, I guar-an-tee. Nine more days.....

Junior Executives SUCK, Marriage rules. God, did I actually type that? Five years ago, I would have pulled the plug on myself right now just for typing that. What a difference a good woman makes, no?

-Dr. Jeff Brothers

See, I knew if I prodded enough you'd lead us to greener pastures. And there was actually some pretty sound advice in there. So, here's my REACTION to your various views on marriage as a whole:

-Uh, I like Mary Chapin Carpenter.

-We'd been talking about separate accounts, and I wasn't too sure it was such a great idea, but, based on your recommendation, I now feel more comfortable with it. Congratulations, you have more influence on my finances than my future wife (due, mostly, to the fact that I don't trust dames with money).

-I agree. Contributions to the joint account should be proportional to the individual salaries. Spoken like a guy who knows his woman will make more than he one day.

-Do not encourage her to dress like a green M&M, but do encourage their consumption. I can't imagine anything making Julie look like a green M&M except maybe a garbage bag.

-If she does want to throw out your T-shirts, suggest that you look at her wardrobe which takes up 75% of the closet and see what else the poor might look good in. Rule of thumb: if it hasn't been worn in two years or was bought more than ten years ago, OUT!! You'll be surprised at the size of the pile.

-Yeah, I get a lot of that, "You look so good in polo shirts" crap. Translated: "God, I hate that orange shirt with the number 7 on it."

-How does one influence the smell of someone else's farts? "Look honey, I made you some extra spicy Polish sausage and cabbage soup. And there's some generic beer in the cupboard. Me? No, I'm just going to eat this celery stick."

-How about if I compromise and let her think all the crappy ideas are hers?

-We're going to live in an apartment, so we got no stinkin' lawn.

-Does the Happy Place have to be a real place? I mean, Homer has his land of chocolate and Dorothy flew over the rainbow. Can't you just tune-out for a minute, then wake up and say, "Good idea, Honey"? This would also fulfill the rule about letting her think all the ideas are hers. I ask this because she has a tendency to follow me while giving me hell. She says it's to keep my ass accessible for kicking, chewing out, and general abuse. Problem with a surreal Happy Place is that sometimes she realizes she's wrong while you're still there and you say shit like, "That's okay, Shania."

-And a big nod of approval regarding not letting her take work too seriously. Alden's outlook on life is this: "I have a million things to do, I have ten minutes to do them all, and if I don't get them all done the world will implode." This, of course, is much guano. At some point, these women have to understand that, contrary to what any boss might tell them, sometimes the answer is, "No."

-Yes, it is always good to plan a "special surprise."

So, I feel pretty good about this marriage thing. I figure with all the wonderful advice I've gotten from you and Country Dick Montana, how can I go wrong? Anyway, that's all for today. Talk to you tomorrow.

Polo shirts suck, green M&M's rule. OUT!!

Grasshopper

Date: May 8
To: Lefty
From: Jeff
Subject: Where everybody knows your name

I realized something very important on the way to work this morning: Even if you tattooed "Alden Kidd, the most lovable, beautiful, intelligent, vivacious, babelicious babe in this whole gigantic world whom I love with all of my heart" on your pecker, what would you do with the other 14 inches? "This space for rent?"

Forgive me, maybe I'm missing something, but Mary Chapin Carpenter? Isn't that like the female version of Sting for the Nursing Home Generation? Nap time Muzak? What?

Yes, the Green Peanut M&M outfit WAS real. It was like this green cloth-like substance that was literally shaped into a circular-like shape. Julie donned it when she felt like getting "comfortable," but it really just made her mother and me cry with laughter. It is probably the funniest thing I have ever seen my lovely wife wear, *my* underwear notwithstanding.

And speaking of underwear, I'd like to add one more Marriage "Tip:" Choose one day a month, preferably on a weekend, when both of you can go commando. Yes, both of you. It's kind of a cool thing to be out running errands or sipping brew at your local pub and realize that neither of you has any 'ders on. Especially if you can find a quiet place in the corner where you can be alone with her, 'derless. Quite a romantic thing, this is -- until your pecker starts to chafe your thighs, of course; or it dangles out from your pant cuff, and as the world passes by, all wearing 'ders, you realize that nothing stands between you and a quickie except her jeans and your jeans. And the fact that you are in the middle of a public library......

You know, there are a few truly beautiful things about this life. Beer, Julie, Guitars. You know the routine. But there is something I have been noticing about life that really gives me a kick. It's when people know who you are. I call up the Tennis Center anymore, and Trevor says, "Yeah, is this Jeff?" I call up Sabor Latino and ask specifically for José, who then calls me at home when our table is ready. Yes, at home. The casting director from the

Northwest Denver Playhouse calls me at work and says, "Yeah, I've been checking out your resume, and we're having auditions for *Kids at Play,* a kids show, on Tuesday. We would like you to audition for us." These things are very cool to me. It makes me feel like I'm somebody, you know? Like I'm important or something.

Have an excellent Thursday, won't you? *Ocho mas dias*!!!!!
Nap time Muzak sucks, commando-ness rules!

-This Space For Rent

Chapter 13
There's No Place Like Vegas,
There's No Place Like Vegas....

Date: May 9
To: Jeff
From: Anthony
Subject: That boy's crazy

You are FAR too kind. If I were to tattoo that extensive message on my tallywhacker, there sure as hell wouldn't be no 14 inches left over; 12, maybe, but never 14. I'm going to overlook your nasty little smack comparing Mary Chapin Carpenter to Sting. What can I say? I happen to dig chicks that can rock with an acoustic guitar and have a little of that country 'tude about 'em. Yes, it does seem like every woman out there has a "green M&M outfit." Alden's was this turquoise cotton jumpsuit with a white belt that screamed, "I'd really love to see Berlin open for Duran Duran." Can't do the commando thing, dude. It rubs. And rubbing creates friction (not to mention pain). And friction creates sparks. Next thing you know, you're the guest of honor at a weenie roast. You realize, of course, that from now on whenever I see you and Julie, I'll be wondering if it's a "'derless day." Concur, it's great when people know who you are. I get that from my bookie, bail bondsman, the guy at the free clinic. Sort of gives you that warm, tingly feeling all over. Either that or it's time to call the guy at the free clinic again. Just please tell me that when you call Sabor Latino, you say, "José, can you see...if you have a table for Julie and me?"

I'm starting to get the, "I don't know if I like you going to Vegas and hangin' out with nasty sluts" spiel. In the first place, she shouldn't be calling my buddies "sluts." In the second place, isn't it a little early for me to have to endure this? By my way of thinking, I shouldn't have to hear about this until two days before the actual event; because this conversation inevitably escalates into, "Well, wait until my bachelorette party" yadda, yadda, yadda. So juvenile. By the way, did you know that her bachelorette party is going to be the same night as the gig?

Oh, one more thing about the trip. I've been asked to write an article about it in the next company newspaper. Yeah, one of the ladies who works here went to Laughlin last month for her bachelorette party and they wrote it up in the paper, so they thought it'd be fun to get the male perspective. So, I'll write it and, if they don't print it, I'll send it in to Penthouse Forum.

I'm sure there's something in the Farmer's Almanac that says the next eight days are going to be the longest in the history of the world, followed by the two shortest. But it IS only a little more than a week away. So, with that in mind, I say to you have a great day and we'll talk tomorrow.

Bachelorette party smack sucks, free clinics rule. OUT!!

Weenie Roaster

Date: May 10
To: Lefty
From: Jeff
Subject: 1984

Berlin opening for Duran Duran? It could be 1984, or it could be the 1990s. I wouldn't be surprised if this bill is coming to Red Rocks this summer, with "most of the original members" or something. Which really means that the original drummer for the group somehow got hold of the name and decided that he ran out of money and any real opportunities to make more, so he decided to hire 4 or 5 new people to be Berlin. Hell, it'd probably be a guy singing.

Aldiente is holding her bachelorette party the same night as the gig? What up with that? I don't really have a problem with it, I suppose, but who's gonna come and see us? All guys? Great, everybody in the audience will be undressing Carol with their eyes instead of me. And you, of course. I can just see it: "Let the babe sing. LET THE BABE SING!!! YOU GUYS SUCK!!! LET THE BABE SING!!!" "Hey, wired guy in the back. Don't you think you've had enough coffee? We're gonna cut you off. Maybe you better call somebody to come and pick you up."

As far as the "hanging out with nasty sluts" bit, I am not nasty. She gets to have a bachelorette party, so *you* get to have a bachelor party. 'Nuff said. The Great One (not to brag, but I will) just lets me go to these things, because she knows that I love her extensively and would do nothing to compromise her trust. Besides, while I'm gone she gets to shop all weekend.

So, I've already worked 45 hours this week, and I haven't even gone in for Friday yet. But I guess I must, and I'll probably work yet another in a long-ass line of weekends. But this all makes the trip to the Male Finishing School in Las Vegas next weekend loom larger and larger and larger. I saw an artist's rendering of that Stratosphere thing, and the roller coaster on top of it, and the other freefall-type ride up there. The freefall-type ride looks kind of like it's at the top of a tall giant....uh, member, the tallest....member west of the Mississippi as a matter-of-fact, and it kind of spurts you out the end of it......

Well, off to work. I'm late, but fuck it. I work late, I go in late. Fuck it. Fuck. Have an excellent weekend.

Bachelor Party Smack sucks, undressing people with your eyes rules!!!

-One Fourth of The Original Snipehunters

Date: May 10
To: Jeff
From: Anthony
Subject: Sin and how to worship it

Hey, check this out. I had a brainstorm regarding the article I'm supposed to write for the paper about the bachelor party. Now you and I both know that I'm not going to be able to truly disclose the events of the weekend, so I decided to take a different approach. Here's what I got:

"Like you, I was appalled last month to read about the sin and frivolity that occurred during Mary's bachelorette party in Laughlin. I haven't known these women very long, but I never thought they were capable of such animalistic behavior. So when I was asked to chronicle the events of my own bachelor party in Las Vegas, I jumped at the opportunity to prove that all the moral fiber hasn't been pooped out of American society.

There were no vans of coolers and God knows what. We flew into Vegas late on Friday, May 17, got a cab to the hotel, and immediately went to sleep. Hey, it was almost 11:30! Refreshed after a good night's rest, we were all up at 6:00 a.m. for calisthenics, followed by a 12-mile run, and meditation. Breakfast was a lively repast of fresh fruit and grain (we pride ourselves on being "regular" guys). Fully invigorated and fed, it was off to the city to "see what kind of trouble we could get ourselves into."

I never realized it before, but there's an awful lot of, well, "that element" in Las Vegas. I was beginning to wish we'd been able to book that trip to Disney World, but it's just too far for a weekend trip. We continued on through the city, keeping our eyes firmly glued to the ground so as not to be tempted by the trappings of sin. We browsed through the bookstore at UNLV and took a wonderful sightseeing tour of all the art museums in the area. Las Vegas is known to be quite warm, so it was back to the hotel for a tall iced tea by the pool. Unfortunately, a few young, nubile ladies dressed in next-to-nothing showed up and spoiled a good time for everyone (I AM engaged after all). So, we were forced to retreat back to the hotel for a nap.

We were hoping to catch one of those fabulous Las Vegas shows while in town, but, as luck would have it, we missed Wayne Newton by ONE week. We could've gone to see Tom Jones, but we figured there'd be nothing but rowdy women there, so we decided to proceed to the seminar early to get a good seat. While we were too late to catch "Mr. Danke Shoen," we were fortunate to be on hand for a seminar entitled, "Women and How to Worship Them." What an opening of the mind! We returned back to the hotel and had a lively

131

discussion about the changing roles of men in the 1990s and how we could be better partners in a relationship (respecting her individuality and "lifting the lid" seemed to be the rules of choice). We had such a good time that we didn't even notice it was 9:30 p.m. Off to bed!

I couldn't sleep, however (I attribute this to all the iced tea I drank before turning in), so I quietly got up, dressed, and left the room and my sleeping comrades. I will admit to you that I'm not exactly proud of what happened next. I had found a quarter in the lobby earlier, so now I decided I was going to put it in a slot machine and find out what all the excitement was about (I had brought an extra ten dollars for gambling purposes, but I gave it all away to the various charities collecting at the airport). I dropped the quarter in the machine, pulled the arm, and promptly won $1000. I then realized that I had become one of Satan's own agents of evil. I was no longer a man, I was a thing, a creature of the night. I threw the money down in disgust and went screaming into the night in search of a church or a Gamblers Anonymous meeting. Forty five minutes of confession and I was cleansed. I returned to the hotel, woke my friends, bared my soul, and was relieved to find that they welcomed me back with open arms. What a great bunch of guys. And what a wonderful weekend of fun and fulfillment through spiritual awareness and male awakening. That's my story and I'm sticking to it."

So whaddya think? An accurate representation of the weekend's events? Speaking of weekends, this is the weekend I put an end to Uncle Chris. Gonna miss the old boy to some extent. We're supposed to be taping tonight so, if it comes out fairly well, I'll see about getting a copy to you at some point. Alden's home for her final dress-fitting this weekend. Yeah, it's kind of a bummer that she's going to miss the gig in July. She feels terribly guilty about it, so, in a way, I guess I've accomplished something. Hopefully, her guilt wrecks her bachelorette party, but I'm not counting on it.

You, my friend, have an excellent weekend with your lovely *esposa*. And if things get rough just tap your heels together three times and say, "There's no place like Vegas, there's no place like Vegas....." ONE WEEK!

Creatures of the night rule. OUT!!

-Regular

Date: May 13
To: Lefty
From: Jeff
Subject: Death of the Pile

asadkjl;uoiukamcmnaklj;ljkaandI'm just a little too groggy this morning.

This morning's top stories: A couple of deaths this weekend still have the world reeling from shock. First, on Sunday, Uncle Chris of San Diego passed away. Uncle Chris, a constantly cranky Norwegian dude, was most famous for putting lighting boys through hell during his long three-week acting career. Also on Sunday, The Largest Pile Of Dirty Laundry In The Whole World was found dead in Denver, Colorado. When questioned about the death of The Pile, Jeffrey C. Chacon, the purveyor of The Pile, was heard replying, "I ran out of clothes to wear about two months ago; the smell of the dirty clothes I keep wearing over and over has had a profound effect on my social life. Also, I've been commando since March, and the rash on the inside of my thighs was killing me. Besides, I finally blew off work for half a day, so I could do all this laundry. And what are all you reporters doing in my living room?" Mr. Chacon's wife was seen enjoying the furniture and the carpet in their bedroom, since both have been covered by dirty laundry for the last few months.

In other news, the Osceola Street Brewery announced today that they will be premiering their *Fiesta De Matrimonio Y Bailar* beer on Friday night in Las Vegas, Nevada. Mr. Jeffrey C. Chacon, brewmaster at the Brewery, tasted a *Fiesta* beer on Sunday, and had this to say: "Thith ith beer. Yeth, thith ith beer. Theee boyth are gonna love ith. Hey, what are all you reporterth doin' in myyy living room?"

Pathetic (paw-thet-ic) -- When having a half a day off on the weekend is something to look forward to (See Jeff Chacon).

So, they entered the week of The Trip, and they all knew that somehow life would never be the same again.

You know what's funny? Most people I know here hate Las Vegas. I call this the "Taking yourself too seriously" syndrome. Most people think it is "disgusting" or "vile." "All they want is your money." All of these things are true; but, if you understand what Vegas is and why you are going there (more often than not, to attend seminars and conferences, heehee), then it can be a lot of fun. Vegas is mostly cheese, in the millions of lights and signs and the schemes to get you into a particular place, but it has value as well. We know what that value is (wink, wink). And we will get our full worth of it this weekend.

Well, time to jump into the shower. You have an excellent Monday now. And don't think too much about Vegas, makes it hard to walk.

Reporters in your living room suck, Vegas Rules!!!!

-Laundry Boy

Date: May 13
To: Jeff
From: Anthony
Subject: Monday the 13th

What government agency is in charge of weekends? I want to lodge a formal complaint, and I want a Senate investigation into what the hell happened to this past weekend that it went from a scheduled 48 hours to 3 hours, 24 minutes. All this leading up to Monday, the 13th. Now, I know everyone thinks Friday the 13th is unlucky, but imagine how pissed Jason would've been if he'd gone on all his killing sprees on Monday morning. Especially after an incredibly short weekend.

A moment of silence, please, for our dear, departed Uncle Chris, and for the daunting sight that was Mt. Chacon. So, being a structural engineer, can you tell me how deep a mountain of soiled clothing can cause a house to sink into the ground? As far as Uncle Chris goes, I'm going to miss the ol' boy, but it's good to have my life back. This play had its problems, but, overall, it turned out fairly well and I'm going to miss the cast members a great deal, most of them anyway. Scuttlebutt going around now is that I may possibly be nominated for one of those awards I wrote about some time ago. One of the girls in the play said she has a very strong feeling I'll be nominated, and she's psychic. It must be true, she works for a psychic hotline. You always meet the most interesting people when doing community theater. Can you imagine? Li'l ol' me receiving an award nomination for acting? This kind of thing could cause a terminal case of "wood," and Bertha would be totally out of control.

As far as the weekend goes, Alden and I had as much fun as you can possibly have in such a short amount of time. If you haven't figured it out by now, I really feel like I've been cheated out of a weekend. We spent some time talking about the wedding plans and the honeymoon, and she disclosed the fact that she wants "to do some snorking in Hawaii." Can't you just see it? You go downstairs to check out the various activities available to the hotel guests and you see that "Snorking Lessons" are available at 1:00 p.m. on the patio. And at 1:00 o'saka a bunch of tourists are all standing around going "Snork!" All the while, there's some dude with a whistle, wearing shorts and a white polo, going, "Make sure you follow-through. SNOR-KKK!" We haven't exactly figured out what snorking is, but I'm sure it'll eventually come to mean something sexual.

Yes, we are now within one week of going to Vegas. A matter of days now before we get to sample the latest batch o' Jeffbrew. Ya know, I know a lot of people with that "Vegas sucks" syndrome. I agree; there are just some things in this world that simply must be accepted for what they are. Vegas makes no bones about the fact that it wants all our money. As long as we know that going in, I say let the exploitation begin! Because one thing's for sure, Vegas ain't gonna change and neither are we.

Okay, Monotonous Monday is just about in the books. Terrible Tuesday, Weak Wednesday, This-sucks Thursday, and then it's Fly-to-Vegas Friday. Talk to you tomorrow.

Short weekends suck, snorking rules. OUT!!

Scuttlebutt

Date: May 14
To: Lefty
From: Jeff
Subject: Son of Rambo

We have Son of Rambo sightings in our neighborhood. This little kid, whom we think is visiting his Grandmama two doors down, has been riding his bicycle (complete with training wheels) up and down the sidewalk for three days. He grunts all the time while he's riding, he's got a bandanna wrapped around his head, and he carries around these two plastic little knives in his waistband or in his mouth. He doesn't say much, just grunts and rides, grunts and rides. The future of America is in this kid's hands, bro.

I just got done watching the first overtime of the Avalanche playoff game on the television. They look pretty good, I tell you. Ya know, with a little coaching from you, I could become a hockey fan, like the other two million band-wagon-ers in this town. Oh, wise one, oh understander of difficult sporting games, won't you please sit down with me this weekend in some nondescript sports book and explaineth the gameth for me-eth? I'd like to know what all the whistles are for, when do they get a face off, what the blue line is, and why he is called Patrick Wah.

Congratulations on the nomination. Of course, in my mind, it wasn't unexpected. You are The Man. And you *will* win. And, one day, maybe you can leave me some guest passes at the door for the Academy Awards Show where you are presented "Best Actor Ever For Anything At Anytime" award by Elizabeth Shue, who naturally will be wearing something that reveals the smooth shape of her breasts and the precise ovals that are her nipples.

Maybe you could get Alden to give you a "Snorkjob." Or you could perform "Snorkdiving" or "Snorkilingus" on her. Or you could of course do it "Snorkystyle."

Well, have a bitchin' Tuesday. I believe I'll go watch some more hockey, which will about double my total intake of hockey for my lifetime (yeah, I'm a bandwagon jumper-on-er-type-dude, don't knock it). Tonight, in my precious slumber, I'll dream of Art and *Bailar* and *Canciones* and *Cerveza* and *Chicas Bonitas Desnudas*. Yeah, that's it. Tomorrow, look for my movie review of "Operation Calculation, An Engineer's Tale." It'll be epic.

The Son of Rambo RULES.

-Caballero De Las Vegas

Date: May 14
To: Jeff
From: Anthony
Subject: Penalty Shot

So, let me see if I got this straight. Some little kid is dressing up like Rambo and riding up and down the street, grunting? Why do the words Waco and Freemen keep popping up in my mind? What the hell is going on there in "the heartland"? Why don't you follow this kid home to the trailer park and go up and tell his 'neck parents, "Say listen, I don't mean to be rude, but do you think little Timothy McVeigh here could leave the plastic knives home when he terrorizes my block? Excuse me? Oh, they're REAL knives? Well, then, do you think maybe you can keep him from riding his bike while carrying knives? I can't afford to be sued for living on a negligent street after little Mark Fuhrman falls off his bike and turns himself into John Wayne Bobbitt."

Yeah, I noticed you guys moved on to the Western Conference Finals last night. I'm all for catching a game at a sports book, and I'd be happy to explain the rules and nuances of the...nuances? I don't think there are any nuances in hockey. Figure skating, yes; hockey, no. Thus, I will be happy to explain the rules and...uh...shit to you.

Let's start now shall we? I'll give you some hockey terminology and a little background on it. Actually, it's easiest to think of hockey in relation to the normal world. For instance, cross-checking. In hockey, cross-checking is holding the stick with both hands in front of you and hitting a player from the blind side. Result: two minutes in "the box." Now, in real life, cross-checking is when you steal an extra glance at some stocky chick to make sure she's not a guy in drag. Result: two-hours in therapy. Get it? Okay, let's get to it.

SLASHING -- This is like what Tonya Harding did to Nancy Kerrigan. It's basically using your stick as if you were an L.A. cop. Result: two minutes in the box. In real life, it's when you're playing Guns 'N Roses too loud. Result: two days of hearing loss.

HOOKING -- this is when you use your stick to pull another player down. Some of this can legally go on, but, once you yank a guy down, it's a penalty. Result: two minutes in the box. (See a trend developing here?) In real life, hooking is...well...I'll show you when we get to Vegas. Result: two-years probation, sexually transmitted diseases, bad rep, not good.

ICING -- Think of this as delay of game. It's when a team purposely shoots the puck down to the other end of the ice to get it out of their end. Result: face-off, back where we started. This is sort of like a chick going to the bathroom to escape some drunk dude at a bar. Result: the option of returning and telling him to go to hell or going out the window.

TWO-LINE PASS -- This one I'm not quite sure about in terms of hockey, but going back to the analogy of the drunk guy and the chick, it's when the guy says, "Hey, baby, you come here often? You look kinda familiar." And she still tells him to go to hell. Result: bruised Bertha easily rectified by convincing yourself she's probably a lesbian.

FIGHTING -- Basically, it means what it says. Your normal hockey fight results in both players going to the box for five minutes. Sometimes, however, the fight results in the more severe penalty of ten minutes. For those classic brawls you see on the news at night, the player gets a game misconduct and he's OUT!! More often than not, fights result in penalties to both parties.

THE BOX -- This is where players go to serve a penalty. It's sort of like jail or putting a kid on time-out. Here is an example of life being opposite of hockey. In hockey, guys want to stay out of "the box," whereas, in the real world, guys will do everything they can to get into "the box."

CHECKING -- This is basically defending by putting a body on a guy. Particularly useful when a guy's up against the boards and he doesn't see the other dude bearing down on him. Too many definitions in the real world.

Overall, if you can understand basketball, you can pretty much get the gist of hockey. But, yeah, if there's a playoff game on, I wouldn't mind kicking back in some sports book for a while. That way, I'll also be able to put some money down on next year's Super Bowl Champion -- The Denver Broncos (no chance in hell, but if the odds are astronomical then a $2 bet could be worth it in case the unthinkable happens). Of course, if they do win the Super Bowl, I won't be able to spend the money because the world will come to an end.

Just to clear the record, I haven't been nominated yet. People are of the opinion that I *might* be nominated. I wonder what the odds are? We'll have to check the boards in Vegas. Dude, is it just me, or has time slowed to a crawl? I swear to God, this week is never going to end! Oh, well, I guess the best things in life are worth waiting for. Anyway, I'm off. As our friend Pat DiNizio once said, have a "groovy Tuesday," won't you?

Lawsuits suck, "the box" rules. OUT!!

Wah

Chapter 14
Operation Calculation

Date: May 14
To: Lefty
From: Jeff
Subject: Summer Blockbuster!

Coming this summer to a cubicle near you: JeffBrew Productions Presents "Operation Calculation," the buddy-feel-good film of the year. Starring Robin Williams as Cindy, and Meryl Streep in her most challenging role yet as Structural Engineer Jeff Chacon. This is the gripping story of Cindy, a young college graduate on her way to Denver to begin her dream career as a structural engineer. Her outlook is blindly positive when she begins the journey; but, when she is placed in the same cubicle as the grizzled burned-out, bitter, sarcastic, too-much-coffee-drinking engineer Jeff Chacon ("Who's he?" "Oh, he's Jeff Chacon, former world famous structural engineer, now just a burned-out shell of a man; we keep him around to do the shitty projects."), her life and outlook are never the same again.

A mere 25 years from retirement, Jeff has been doing this job way too long and has seen way too many stupid architects to initially give a shit about the young, perky, peppy, always-wanting-to-do-a-good-job Cindy -- and he treats her like it. He's not wanting a new bunkmate, he's wanting retirement. To complicate things, Cindy's father (Tom Cruise, in a series of dreamy flashbacks directed by David Lynch) was a maverick structural engineer back in the '70s who was killed when a severely under-designed beam -- one of his own -- collapsed and fell on his head at a job-site, killing him instantly Or so everybody seems to believe.

But Cindy feels that maybe there was some kind of a cover-up, and, in a poignant scene halfway through the movie, she travels down to Guantanamo Bay, Cuba, to meet with the foreman (played by Jack Nicholson) of her father's construction site. The foreman is overseeing a different project in Cuba now, twenty years after her father's death. When she asks him about the incident and demands to know the truth, he does the old, "You can't handle the truth." So Cindy, is thrown in with the lions ("Up with Lions?"), so to speak, as Jeff treats her like dogcrap for much of the movie and tries to convince her what a mistake she's made and that architects really do suck, which, with her Pollyanna fresh-out-of-school attitude, she does not believe.

Eventually, however, the two are teamed up on a project with a ridiculous deadline and a stupid architect; a project of national security involving Russians, a train moving at 100 mph through the Colorado mountains, and Steven Segal as the draftsman. Through this relationship Jeff and Cindy become at least civil with each other. In a particularly moving scene near the end of the movie, Jeff is tells Cindy, "You can do my beam calculations anytime, buddy. You can also check my steel shop drawings. And will you get me some coffee while you're at it?" By the end of the movie, Cindy comes to the realization that, "Yes, oh wise Jeff, architects truly do suck," and both Cindy and Jeff are burned-out shells of formerly good engineers.

Yes, it's true. They are putting a GIRL in the other half of my office. Jeez. Personally, I think it's a mistake putting a green rookie in with a burned-out veteran like myself; because I'm gonna turn Cindy, who is more than likely "excited" and "thrilled" about her career at this point, into a burned-out veteran in...oh, let's say...about a week. Not only that, but think of the QUESTIONS!!!!

"Jeff, can I ask you something? Why do you say 'Fuck!' every time you hang up the phone?"

"Jeff, can I ask you something? Why is my paycheck so small?"

"Jeff, can I ask you something? Why do all of the guys look out the window at the bikinis sitting by the pool across the street and drool?"

"Jeff, can I ask you something? Why are you so excited about going to Las Vegas?"

"Jeff, can I ask you something? If you have a bigass boat, and the load to the rear axle is 3000 pounds, and the axle is supported by two tires, does that equal 1500 pounds per tire? 'Cuz this guy on the phone says it doesn't."

"Jeff, can I ask you something? Why did you only work 72 hours last week? I worked 97 hours!"

Oh, man. I had to condense my double-wide Cubicle of Doom into a single Cubicle of Doom, so the rookie will have a place to put all her stuff. And she's apparently going to get started either Thursday or Monday. I can just see Monday. I come in, about 9:30, and she's sitting there, all bright-eyed and bushy-tailed. Me? I've got the yearly Vegas I'mprobablystilldrunkbutit's hardtotell syndrome.

"Hi Jeff!!! My name's Cindy, and I wanna be an engineer!!!!!! I hear you're the greatest!!!"

"Yeah, kid, whatever. Look, do these beam calculations, and wake me up when you are done."

Thanks for the Hockey Tips. I appreciate it immensely. I'm trying to incur some penalties so The Great One will send me to The Box sometime soon......This is a slow week. Kind of. Actually, now that I have this green rookie girl thing to keep me entertained, it should go relatively quickly. I'm not sure how the office is going to handle this; most of these guys have never worked with a female engineer.

Have a wicked Wednesday, won't you? A mere 72 hours from right now (10:30 p.m. MST), I'll be swilling beer at the Museum, waiting for your plane to arrive in the City of Sin. Ah, yes. Once a year may not be often enough for this event, little buddy. Twice a year may not be often enough. Let's think about that.

Slow Weeks Suck, Turning Optimistic Little Graduates Into Real World Pessimists Rule!!!!

-A Burned-Out Shell Of A Formerly Good Engineer

Date: May 15
To: Jeff
From: Anthony
Subject: Good ol' boys

See, the problem is that you didn't answer the question of what happened to Cindy's father. Now, as I see it, you have two options:

You can have a scene where Cindy is perilously hanging by one hand from a beam (the other hand has been lopped-off by a particularly sharp ruler) and Jeff is standing over her (said ruler in hand) saying, "Come over to the dark side, Cindy. Surrender." And Cindy defiantly yells, "I'll never surrender to you." To which Jeff replies, "You do not know the mistake you're making hanging with architects. You're just beginning to understand your true feelings. No matter what you think, there is one thing college did not teach you. *I* am your Father."

Or you can go this route. Cut to Guantanamo Bay to where the sinister figure of Jack Nicholson is sitting alone at a desk, perusing an old scrapbook. Inside are pictures of a little girl who bears a striking resemblance to our heroine. He makes baby sounds as he turns the pages until he runs across an old newspaper article detailing the shocking death -- by flattening -- of a young engineer who looks strangely like Tom Cruise. Now, the screen becomes blurry and we flashback to a back alley in Guantanamo Bay where a young Cuban tattoo artist is performing his first plastic surgery. He slowly unwraps the bandages and he's pleading, "Señor, I hope ju will forgif me if I fucked up dee operation." He unwraps the last bandage and steps back in horror, exclaiming, "Jesus Christo!" The patient, who looked like Tom Cruise when he came in, picks up a mirror to discover that now he looks like Jack Nicholson, and he demonically laughs out the door. Flashback to the present where Jack is sitting at the desk. "The truth, huh? Wait'll you get a load o' me."

Why, Jeff Chacon, I do believe that you and your buddies are threatened by the appearance of a li'l ol' female in your midst. I'm surprised at you. I mean, I expect this kind of behavior from the rest of those 'necks you work with, but I thought you would at least give her a chance. Yeah, I don't think it's the idea of a green rookie that bothers you; I think it's the idea of a pink one that's causing all the problems. What's the big deal? Just means no fartin', scratchin', belchin', sexist remarks at the water cooler; and you'll have to put frilly little curtains on the windows and lift the lid in the bathroom.

Whoops, better ditch those girlie mags, too. But, then again, you are just obeying our own personal code of life: "Don't try it 'til you knock it." I'll tell you one thing, though, I'd gladly trade you your cubicle-mate for mine.

Ya know, it's getting so that there are two things you can always count on in sports: Greg Norman will choke the Masters, and Magic Johnson will retire once a year. I tell ya dude, Magic retires more than Goodyear. And, quite frankly, I'm just about tired of this schtick. New rule in sports: when a guy retires for the second time, he's OUT!! And if he does want to come back, he must come back at half the minimum salary. Then let's see how often we hear that "love of the game" shit. I tell ya, the way the guy leaves and comes back, they're starting to use Velcro to hang his jersey on the Forum wall.

Okay, we are now slowly edging towards Friday and the goodies therein. Let's see if we survive this weekend before we start planning the sequel, huh? Regardless, two more days, my friend. You have a good day, and say Hi to Cindy for me. HA HA!

Multiple retirement sucks, Jack Nicholson rules. OUT!!

Cuban Tattoo Artist

Date: May 15
To: Lefty
From: Jeff
Subject: It's a School!

Well, I'm having my baby tomorrow. I've been in labor for the last two months, and tomorrow it will be born, whether it wants to or not. I think I'll name it, "Middle and Elementary School." Then I'll wipe off, go home, take a nap, and prepare for THE weekend.

I don't think "threatened" is the correct term when it comes to describing my feelings for the young Cindy. I think "tired" is better. I really just think it's going to be fun to see how this thing develops. She's probably a fresh-out-of-college, optimistic idealist and, with the way things have been the last few months, I really am a burned-out engineer. One of two things will happen: (1) Either I will completely turn her off to the whole profession, or the more likely scenario, (2) she will improve my outlook immensely, by virtue of the fact that I'll be reminded constantly what it's like to have the whole world in front of you and not a clue what to do with it. It's like whenever I get a chance to show a beginner a little bit of my guitar playing. He/she sits there with his/her jaw on the floor, saying, "Wow. How'd you do that?" At that moment, appreciate who I am and what I can do with a guitar. This engineering thing may be similar. But, in the meantime, it sure is fun to write movie scripts for summer blockbusters. Maybe we're on to something, no?

Sadly, I must retire to bed now. It is around midnight, and I JUST got home from work -- because I was in labor all this time, of course. I probably will go in early, too. Don't get the wrong idea. Contrary to very popular belief, I DO NOT enjoy this slavery lifestyle. Nor does The Great One. If you were to hand me any amount of money over, say, $500,000 tomorrow, I would retire. If Village Inn were to call me with that wait position, I would retire. See where I'm getting? I merely do this because the project needs me, and I need the cash that the project gives me. So, there. I suck, I know.

Have a scrump-dilly-icious Thursday, won't you? In a mere *cuarenta y ocho horas, nosotros* will be lighting up the City Of Sin like nobody ever has. Until then, get some rest, O.K? You're gonna need it, bachelor boy.

Slumming for cash sucks, having baby schools sucks, The City Of Sin RULES!!!

-Position Wanted

Date: May 16
To: Jeff
From: Anthony
Subject: ONE MORE DAY

Congrats on the birth of your new school. I'll bet he looks just like his father, the Post Office. Glad to see you finally went home at some point. Hopefully, you'll be able to relax a bit more, now that the project is done. And, as far as Cindy goes, you now have the power to shape a mind and I have the feeling that the shape it's going to wind up taking could only be classified as modern art. Like you say, either that or she'll be instrumental in helping you find the spark that once lit the fire of your engineering career. If that's the case, let me caution you, "Don't play with matches."

Hey, I was watching a documentary last night on the Arctic. I think in my next life I'd like to come back as a polar bear. Sure, the living conditions ain't the greatest in the world, but your life is spent roaming the ice daily looking for a nice fat seal. No bosses, no traffic, clean air; you are the baddest dude around, and you don't have to worry about cutting the fat out of your diet. *Au contraire*, they eat the fat first. No beer, though, and that could be tough. I've also considered coming back as a pineapple, or as a shower in a women's fitness club. Yeah, I know, time for the inkblot test.

So, tell The Great One it was great (ha ha) talking to her on the phone last night. Yes, it's my job to cheer up the lives of poor neglected wives whose husbands live at the office; satisfy their needs and encourage the deeds that lead them to finally off his......yeah, you get the picture. This, THIS is what happens when I haven't had my coffee!! So, I think I'll go solve that little problem right now. Less than forty hours to Vegas, my friend. Oh, by the way, let's go over the ground rules:

142

1. Anthony will look, but he won't touch.
2. Let's not get so drunk that we get sick. What fun is that?
3. Don't give me back my ATM card until we're ready to go home.
Basically, that's it. So, I'll be talking to you again tomorrow, I guess. Either way, I'll see you tomorrow night in Vegas. WOO HOO!!
Day before vacation sucks, polar bears rule. OUT!!

Nanook of the North

Date: May 16
To: Lefty
From: Jeff
Subject: Viva, Viva, LAS VEGAAAAAAAAAAAAAASSSSSSSSSSSSSSS!!!!!

We've got a big problem, my friend. You see, when I was at the zoo with The Great One a month or so ago, trying desperately to dodge the little kiddies who were hell-bent on playing pinball with my body, I thought to myself, "Self, it sure would be cool to come back as a seal. Yeah, that's what I want to be in my next life. A seal. You just lay up there on the rocks, occasionally posing and clowning around for the humans, then once in a while dive into the pool, swimming down to pose and clown for the humans looking through the window in the side of the pool. For this, they bring you all the fish you can eat!!!" But, no, you want to be a big bad polar bear. And that would mean that you would spend your days looking for ME, although I wouldn't be the "nice fat seal" you so eloquently refer to, because I would play lots of seal tennis to stay in shape, thus rendering myself unattractive to the likes of you, you big bully. In fact, I bet that, as a seal, I could kick your polar bear butt in a game of tennis; because I would naturally use my nose as my racquet.
Let's go over the REAL ground rules:
1. Anthony will look, but he won't touch -- with his hands, anyway.
2. Define "Sick."
3. Anthony does NOT need any type of any currency on this trip, because, alas, he is the Guest of Honor, Señor Bachelor Boy. This only happens once to a young man, hopefully, and, as mine was last year, your money will be no good in Las Vegas this weekend. Unless, of course, you want to place bets exceeding two dollars on any one hand. In that case, I will be looking the other way. You know how it works: Your room, your drinks, your wo...nky (look it up!), your stri...ng quartet will all be paid for by one or more members of the gang. So, sit back, relax, enjoy yourself, and let us take care of you. Because we love you, man. Duke? You know, you're my Duke, and..............I LOVE YOU, MAN!
So, here we go on another of life's little adventures. A weekend in Vegas. We'll just add this to the list: A trip with hundreds of young ladies to Magic Mountain, many messy stupor-type weekends in San Luis Obispo, ditto for Los Angeles, the EPIC houseboating trip on the Suckramento Delta, the

first roommate experience in Little Tijuana, the writing of the many songs, the second roommate experience in La Jolla, the band thing, the inadvertent women sharing, last year's weekend in Vegas, my wedding, and now this. Yessir, we've seen it all. Almost. And I expect this weekend to rank right up there with the best of them.

It'll be interesting, actually, to try and have a conversation with you:
"How's it going, Jeff?"
"Shitty, been working too much."
"Yeah, I heard."
"How about you, Dukey?"
"Not much, just the play thing."
"Yeah, I read that somewhere."

Ah, I'm sure we'll find plenty to talk about, because that has never been a problem.

Tomorrow, we throw off the moral fabric that governs our pathetic little lives for a weekend of sin. Tomorrow, we forget about trying to live life as men in a modern culture, and we go back to whence we came. Tomorrow, we revel in the glitz, glamour and cheese that is Las Vegas. Tomorrow, we look for Elvis; because, contrary to popular belief, he roams around Vegas searching for The Lost Chord, which, incidentally, is a D minor. Tomorrow, our five basic food groups are condensed into three: Steak, eggs, and beer. Tomorrow, our wallets feel the emptiness that a long night of bad dealers can bring. Tomorrow, Lady Luck decides that she's taking the weekend off. Tomorrow, we hook our arms up to an intravenous beer feeder for the duration of the weekend. Yes, tomorrow we Vegas. See you there.

-Wonkyboy

Date: May 17
To: Jeff
From: Anthony
Subject: DIS BE IT!!!

Dude, you don't wanna come back as a seal. For one thing, you'll have everything in the sea with teeth after your ass and, with your luck, all your ex-girlfriends will come back as great white sharks. Besides, you would never beat me in tennis, because myself and the cute little polar bear in the next igloo would be using your head as the ball.

Elucidation on the REAL ground rules: "Sick" means any state of physical being in which I'm arched over any sort of plumbing receptacle, depositing my three food groups while you bitch-slap me on the head, telling me "You're all right, dude," while my brother tries to choke me to death by pouring sugar down my throat. Seriously, I am not going to drink to the point of puking, because it'll totally blow (no pun intended) a whole day. And I love YOU, man!

Ah, so much you leave out my friend. The concerts, the ballgames, Vanilla Stew, Groovy City, Isla Vista with Bette Midler and your *hermana*, my first bachelor party, cat shelters, "Toast," softball, managing your brother's Little League team for that one game, the movies, epic tennis battles, the Playboy Mansion visit, camping, and those GIRLS, GIRLS, GIRLS!!! Ah yes, DEES ees de good life. Hey, by the way, a slight diversion off the whole subject. I thought of a good joke last night. What does Uncle Chris get when he goes to Vegas? Norwegian wood. Back to our regularly scheduled drivel. Yes, from the time we ordered our first Smithereens tickets, to the time we went on a naked clam hunt in a hot tub, I knew we were on to something grand. This weekend will rank right up there with the best of 'em. We also must confront our biggest fear, something neither of us has ever quite conquered, something so insidiously evil that the mere mention of it alters flight plans. I speak, of course, of my brother. Made worse by the fact that he's going to have Mario with him. Oh, well, if worse comes to worse, we'll do what we always do: throw Randy at 'em and run.

You so eloquently put the weekend into perspective that I will not cheapen it by trying to add to it. I will say, however, that I am looking forward to this. And with that, I enthusiastically say: "I'll see you tonight!"

Depositing food groups sucks, Norwegian wood rules. OUT!!

Willie Wanka

Chapter 15
Vegas Hangover

Date: May 20
To: Jeff
From: Anthony
Subject: Home again

With the three working brain cells I have this morning, allow me to take a few minutes to thank you all once again for the EPIC weekend in Vegas. Dude, I gotta tell you, *that was a blast*. From the delicious homemade brew, all the way to the loss of the last Keno game, I had a great time. The problem is, as I attempt to write this, my eyelids feel as though they each weigh twenty pounds. I am pooped. As with other poop, I sit here on this toilet waiting for someone to send me on a journey once again to a happier place. That will happen this weekend, when my Western-states tour takes me to Santa Cruz where a lovely young lady awaits. And SHE won't demand money every time I see her nekkid. Just spoke to Damon and he said Mario won 300 bucks at Keno just after we left, so we didn't get skunked after all. Let me take a minute to tell you that your beer was some of the most easily drinkable stuff around. There was none of that bitter taste and it wasn't too powerful. It was great and I think you need to brew another batch for the "post-gig" and "post-tennis match" in July. Serious man, it was great. I'd love to write more, but the fact is I am truly wiped out and I'd much rather take a little more time to think about the whole thing before truly commenting. But, again, I want to thank all you guys; you, Damon, Randy, Gary, Mario, David, Michael, Artie, and Tommy for helping me celebrate my last few weeks as a single dude. You guys are great and I love you, man. Until tomorrow.

Keno sucks, Vegas rules. OUT!!

Left Las Vegas

Date: May 20
To: Lefty
From: Jeff
Subject: Reality Sucks.

Engineering is easily the most thankless job in the entire world. You pour your entire heart and soul into a project, 65 hours a week for two months, pretty much giving up all your personal life, and all they wanna talk about is how "the process didn't work exactly as we hoped." WHAT IS THAT? You give me a bigass project with a shitty schedule and a shitty architect and of

146

course "the process isn't going to work exactly as we hoped." If 100 degrees is the point at which I would walk out of a place of employment, never to return, then I hit 98 degrees today. Easily. And that's all I'm gonna say about that.

Welcome home. Yes, it was a great weekend. I had much fun. I learned to play craps! I didn't puke! We ate like pigs, drank like feesh, gambled like the small-time gamblers we are. I would write more today, but I'm a bitter, bitter man (see above paragraph), and would not be able to accurately convey my feelings about the trip. My career is always in the damn way. Besides, I too am pooped and hope to get sent to The Box by The Great One sometime tonight. So, you have an excellent Tuesday, won't you? And I will brew some more Osceola Street Brew for the festivities in July -- just for you. I am very happy that you enjoyed it. I know I did.

Processes suck, The Box Rules!

-Right Las Vegas.

Date: May 21
To: Jeff
From: Anthony
Subject: Too late to go back?

Yes, my friend, the real world outside the friendly confines of the casino and art museum is a harsh place with unreal expectations. You do sound extremely bitter, and I attribute this to bad timing on the part of your supervisors. I mean, really, how can they expect you to deal with such a generous serving of bullshit after you've just returned from the happiest place on Earth? Perhaps now is a good time to think about starting your own micro-brewery. Something like "Jeff's Badass Beer" or "Bachelor Brew." Then you can spin off new products by the simple matter of throwing some honey, raspberries, or food coloring into the vat. Then you will have "Jeff's Honey Amber Double-Stout Raspberry Seasonal Lager Ale;" and, of course, "Jeff's Honey Amber Double-Stout Raspberry Seasonal Lager Ale Light."

Dude, I just can't get back into the swing of things. I finally got some sleep last night, but my body has been fighting the urge to wake up all day. I wonder what's going on in Vegas today? I've never seen Vegas in the middle of the week. Is that when they change the light bulbs and hook up new kegs? That place is amazing! Apparently, there's always need for one more casino, judging by the fact that there was so much building going on....

A quick aside here. I'm reading this article in *Science* magazine which says that a combination of chemicals may be responsible for causing "Gulf War Disease," which is a collection of symptoms suffered by people who served in the Gulf War. The symptoms include headaches, fatigue, short attention spans, aches, and rashes; they discovered this fact because, when they exposed chickens to the chemicals, the chickens suffered the same

147

symptoms. Perhaps in pursuit of my Bachelor's Degree I missed this lecture, but how do you know when a chicken has a headache? I mean really, does it go scratching around the yard looking for an aspirin? Probably; but it never finds it, because it fatigues so easily. So, then, the chicken contemplates taking a nap, but can't keep its eyes closed long enough because it suffers short attention span. Naturally, the rash it gets is chicken pox.

Back to Vegas. Yeah, I wish. Wait a minute. My brain must be functioning again, because things are starting to confuse me. A girl at work today was saying that the reason she parks her car on the second level of the garage -- rather than on the first level, where it would be out of the sun -- is so that, in case of earthquakes, the car won't be damaged. HUH? So after the 8.3 hits, you're going to get in your Honda -- which has fallen more than ten feet onto other cars -- and drive off? I think this is more a question for you. Won't there be at least SOME damage? Anyway, in Las Vegas there sure are a lot of casinos. Geez, I think I'm suffering the civilian strain of Gulf War Disease.

Speaking of disease, my throat has been sore all day. You can imagine how bitter I'm going to be if I have to be sick for the three-day weekend. So, did you catch the hockey game last night? Remember, you are now a member of the sacred hockey society. You know you're a fan when you can sit and watch an entire hockey game when in Vegas. And you did.

Anyway, back to daily life. Please to not be getting too upset with your steenkeeng chob. Just mellow out and keep smiling. And, with that, I say good-bye.

Chickens with short attention spans suck, too many casinos rule.

Henny Penny

Date: May 21
To: Lefty
From: Jeff
Subject: Steak and Eggs Withdrawal

How about "Jeffbrew Take This Job and Your Stoopid Architects and Shove It Ale?" That would be cool. Or, "If you give me three hundred more dollars, I'll show you everything Stout." That might only work in Las Vegas. Or, how about "Steak and Eggs Lite Porter." Ah, yes, the sights and sounds of Lost Wages. Yes, my friend, there is always the need for one more casino; one bigger, taller, and faster than all the rest -- because there are always customers for those things. Eventually, all of the non-glamorous casinos will be shut down, due to their lack of glamour and customers, to be replaced by casinos that are fifty times as tall as the Stratosphere and have a billion rooms. We dub this "casino evolution."

You ask how Vegas is during the week, and I've done it, so let me fill you in. Vegas during the week is an extremely cheap place to be -- Because, basically, nobody is there. Rooms are about a twenty spot. But the reality is that nobody wins anything during the week. Although we just proved that nobody really wins anything during weekends either, didn't we? It seems that in Vegas they like to giveitaway giveitaway giveitawaynow on Saturday nights, to create the biggest hubbub possible. "Oh, look, honey, somebody just won fifty thousand bones!! See, people really do get lucky in Vegas!!!!! Let's withdraw our life savings and win fifty thousand for ourselves, shall we?"

During the week, Vegas is about one-eighth as crowded as it was on the weekend, which makes it a lot of fun. Two dollar craps and blackjack tables are easy to find, as is the Cocktail Lady. Buffets are easy to get into, Siegfried and Roy are accessible, Elvis can walk around virtually unnoticed. You get the picture. You and I really need to go to Vegas during the week.

As far as your little paranoid friend is concerned, tell her this: If there ever is an earthquake in San Diego that takes down a concrete parking garage, there will be no need for her to drive, nor will any of the proper authorities allow her to do so.

The Avalanche rule. I can't watch the game, because I have no cable; but I can listen to the game whilst I am running around the house preparing for the Sacred Arrival of The Parents of The Wife. Tonight, the Avalanche smoked 'em. It sounds like the Red Wings lost this game on the way to the hospital, because that's where most of their players ended up. The greatest thing about this -- well, the first greatest thing -- is that I can listen to the game and know almost always what they are talking about -- icing, offsides, spearing with the stick. Thanks to you, I am in the know. I am officially a hockey fan. All of a sudden, my team is headed back home with a 2-0 lead. This brings up the second greatest thing about hockey: The little cowtown of Denver, Colorado, is hockey crazy. Everywhere you go, it's, "Did you see the game last night?" or "How about that Sakic guy?" or "Ju wanna buy an Abalanche T-chirt?" This weekend will be epic, not only because of my five days off, but because the 'Lanche are playing on Thursday night and again on Saturday, here, for the right to represent the....the....the.....whatever conference they are in, in the Stanley Cup Finals. Yessir, I like it. And maybe, just maybe, I can find a television with the ESPN, so that I may partake of another thrilling game of my new obsession -- hockey. Although that seems highly unlikely because of the impending arrival of said Parents of The Wife. Oh well, I'll be sure to watch The Finals -- assuming we make it, of course.

As far as the job goes, you say "mellow out." You know that normally I am the most "mellow" guy around, typically. But, for some reason, this has really gotten to me and turned me into exactly what I never wanted to be: a perennially cranky pissed-off grumpy engineer. I think this is affecting me more than usual because of the time, sweat, blood, and love I put into this project -- and the fact that all I'm getting out of it thus far is "The Process." This truly truly sucks, because my attitude lately has been terrible. In fact, Cindy asked me yesterday (her first day), "Do you like working here?" I had to say, "Yes." But I really meant, "If I have to work at all in this business, I'd work here. But I'd really rather not be working with or near or even in the same state as any architects, my dear." So, my approach is this: In the "Project Post-Mortem" coming up in a week or so, which is where everybody is supposed to "check your titles at the door" and come out swinging, I will have my entire case prepared and, as soon as somebody sends a big pile of dogshit my way, I will stand up, give everybody a copy of my "Exhibit A," and heap my own massive piles of dogshit on everybody else. That will be my way of dealing with "the criticism." And they will be blown away, guaranteed. Because, most of the time, people just sit there and go "Yeah, you're right, I suck."

Well, it's time to go. The Parents have officially arrived, and I should go play Official Host. Have an Excellent Wednesday, won't you? And call me should you decide to go back to Vegas; because I could easily be persuaded to join you.

Earthquake paranoia sucks, Abalanche T-chirts RULE!

-Official Tourguide of the Osceola Street Brewery, home of Jeffbrew Bachelor Brew

Date: May 23
To: Lefty
From: Jeff
Subject: Cyberspace: The Final Frontier

HELLLLLLLLLLLOOOOOOOOOOOOOOOOOOOOOO!!! Is anybody out there?.................Man, it sure can be lonely here in cyberspace all by myself.

Obviously, I didn't receive the usual belly-chuckling e-mail from my lee'l friend yesterday, so I am feeling a bit lost. It's like the fifty times I tried to quit smoking, you know, the feeling in my body like something is missing, perhaps my brain. My body starts to shake, mildly at first, until it turns into a full scale temblor, rocking and rolling. It's eerily similar to how I felt last Saturday in Lost Wages. My head was light and airy, with lots of nooks and crannies, all day long. My feet were detached from my body; and my stomach was on the barf-line (the thin line between barf and belch) all day long. Joyous. So, uh, where is my e-mail? I can't handle this, you know! I feel like I'm down at the clinic and the methadone supply has run out and ohnoohnoohnoohno..........

It seems I can't escape my theatrical tendencies, or my "obvious" talent for it. One of the writers for the "Colorado Dramatists" called and offered me the lead in a public reading of a Children's Musical. Yes, it involves singing. The truly incredible thing about this is that the writer saw my last performance as Jeff, the under-paid over-worked wise-cracking beer-swilling woman-chasing guitar-slinging janitor in *Low Budget, the musical that never stops sucking.* And she wants to give me the lead in this new thing. Although I can't do it -- because it's going to be on July 22; which, incidentally, is our post-wedding vacation time -- I am sporting a major performing wood right about now. YOU LIKE ME!!!! YOU REALLY LIKE ME!!!!

So, I am currently embarking on the beginning of my Glorious Five-Day Weekend. Although I will be hanging out with an architect, which normally would be considered a capital offense, the architect is The Dad Of The Great One, which makes it okay. So, The Great One -- who turned 29 yesterday -- and I will be playing Official Tour Guides of the City of Denver and taking these much needed days off. Needless to say, I am looking forward to it. So, I will leave you now with these words of wisdom: "E-mail, it's not just for breakfast anymore." Have a nice Thursday, if you ever come back from the E-mail Black Hole that you appear to be in.

-Mandy Patinkin Wannabe

Date: May 22
To: Jeff
From: Anthony
Subject: My hero...

Ya know, it is so reassuring to have a structural engineer for a friend. The way you threw out that line, "If there ever is an earthquake in San Diego that takes down a concrete parking garage..." just has a way of making me feel safe as a Southern Californian. And the way you were giving us all the details about the new buildings in Vegas, it made me proud just to know you and even prouder that I was responsible for bringing you into the lives of the others who never would've had the opportunity to meet you -- if not for me. In a nutshell, dude, you are my hero. You're everything I wish I could be. You brew beer, you play guitar, you know what structures will and won't fall on my head. The only problem with you is you don't have cable, which means you didn't see the Avalanche take down the Detroit Buffalo Wings. But, then again, I didn't see it either -- because I was out with our mighty softball team, getting squashed by a superior squad. 'Twasn't pretty, my friend. When I stopped wondering about the score, it was 22-2 and the 4th inning. The myopia must be overwhelming in Denver today. I can just see all the 'necks in the pawn shop saying, "Look, I'll swap you this here Bronco jersey for that there Abalone T-shirt straight up; but don't sell it because I'll be back in September if the Broncos win their first game." Or: "Hey, I want one of them there Patrick Wah jerseys, cuz he's my favorite. Whoa, not this one, this one belongs to some guy named Roy." Yes, my friend, the Abalanche may pull this thing off yet.

Wow, that's pretty cool that you guys have a "leave your title at the door" meeting. Wasn't that the format for USA For Africa? "We're engin-eers. We are the thank-less. We are the ones who keep beams overhead, and we are bank-less. It's a chance we're taking, we're selling out our lives. It's true we make a lot of cash for the com-pan-y."

Well, anyway, I'll let you go now. Sorry there isn't much to report on this end, but I'm just now starting to realize that this is actually a computer I'm looking at and it will not pay me off no matter how many quarters I feed it. Hi to The Great One and The Parents of the Great One. Have fun.

Computers that don't pay off suck, The Abalone rule. OUT!!

Jeffbrew Fan Club President

Date: May 24
To: Jeff
From: Anthony
Subject: Miss me?

Modern communication has one very serious flaw; we have to rely on a communications company to deliver our messages. Now, every once in a while, said company gets rather uppity with us lowlings who have the gall to pay our bills on time, and they send some corporate mouthpiece to give us some line: "Backlog. Too many calls. Big mess. Shutdown necessary. OUT!!" And we have no service for a while. Sorry, buddy, THE MAN felt it was necessary to shut down for a day. Hope that means we get a discount on our services.

Ah, yes, it is hard to resist when your lesb...thespian tendencies take over. Congrats on receiving the offer to play the lead; but you're right, can't give up vacation time for it. Speaking of vacations, I'm leaving early this afternoon to fly up and see Alden who currently is in the process of finishing her Master's thesis. So, I'm flying up there so she can chew my ass out in person. Dude, let me give you a little piece of advice: if The Great One ever decides to go back and further her education, do yourself a favor and move out. Not that you shouldn't be totally behind the decision, but staying around under those conditions is bad for your health. I ask you, why is HER Master's thesis giving ME an ulcer? Jou don't know? Den I tell ju. Ees because chee calls me every night and tells me how hard it is to write dis ting and den I try to help and BOOM!! Chee goes fuckeen' nuts. This is a strange pheno..m..e thing about women. Sometimes when they bitch and whine, they truly don't want you to make it better; they just want you to be there. It's like that song by Sheryl Crow, the one where she nasalizes, "Are you strong enough to be my man?" Now, I always thought this song was about some totally insecure woman with low self-esteem -- and I'm still not convinced I was totally wrong -- but this one chick explained to me that it's about how a woman doesn't necessarily need a guy to solve her problems but to be there and listen. Ahh, ain't that sweet! I don't know, man. It's a vicious circle; when she's hurting, I want to put a stop to it; but the best thing I can do is shut up and listen. But the more I listen, the more I want to help, so then I try to and then I'm protecting my jugular. STOO-PID!! Anyway, that's how I'm spending my weekend, protecting my jugular.

What up with you, dude? Why didn't you tell me it was dee Great One's birthday? Go play, Jeff, I have to talk to Julie now. Hi, Julie. Happy 29th (uh huh) B-day, you Gretzky-quoting, Jeff-marrying, washboard-stomach-lusting, cell-phone-having, big-money-making, "I can never tell you guys apart"-complaining, Railyard sippin', honey of a gal!! And may I say that you don't look a day over 28. Of course, after you live with Jeff for a while it all sort of sneaks up on you, then one day you'll wake up and realize that a startling metamorphosis is taking place and your hairline is apparently sprinting to the top of Mt. Baldy. Trust me, I know. But I'm glad to hear that you guys are taking some time off to show your parents around and enjoy your B-day. So, hap-hap-happy birthday to our favorite Great One. But you still have to buy because you make all the money.

Okay, bro, ju guys have a good time hangin' with The Parents d'Great One in the fine city of Denver. When you get to the Wynkoop today, have a cold Railyard for me. Enjoy the rest of your weekend.

Not ending e-mail with a "sucks/rules" line sucks, The Wynkoop rules. OUT!!

Backlog

Date: May 27
To: Lefty
From: Jeff
Subject: Reverse Work Week

PRESS RELEASE:

DENVER (UPI): Local weirdo Jeffrey C. Chacon, Esq., today announced that he was "throwing in his hat" and becoming a candidate for The Presidency of these United States of America. Chacon, who is well known for his bad attitudes about architects and bosses and for his penchant for sleep, announced that he would be running for the "Nap Party" and that he would be advocating a radical new idea: the "Reverse Work Week and Daily Nap Policy." This policy, according to Chacon, would entail, "a two-day work week and a five-day weekend every week, plus a mandatory two-hour nap for all Americans every day of the week." This announcement was greeted by exuberant applause and deafening cheers by the huge crowd of three people who attended the announcement. It is not yet known just how this might affect the policies and campaigns of the other candidates.....

I feel like I'm back at full strength, dude. My other four teammates -- Arturo, Poindexter, Leroy, and Cesar, who is my optimism -- are back on the ice and we're ready to go score some goals. I've got a five-day napping streak going, and I feel ready to rejoin the fray, because this is exactly what the doctor ordered: five days off, napping opportunities each of those days, and no architects or bosses bothering me. Talk about reju..v..en..you know, the batteries are recharged. It pretty much rained the whole time, which is quite unusual -- although I'm not sure l'Parents d'Great One believe that at this point -- and which kept us indoors, and pretty much forced the napping to commence. I loves me some napping, dude. I swear to you that I would nap each and every day if I could. And I have -- for five days in a row now. Tomorrow might be a problem. I can see it. Around 2 o'saka in the afternoon, here's Jeff in a meeting: "And we need a column here, and the bee...the bee...the beam......zzzzzzzzzzzzzzzzzzzzzzzzzz." THAT might be a problem. But I'll deal with it. Coffee is a cure-all in that situation.

The truly great thing about having guests in town is that we get to show them our favorite local restaurants. In the last five days, we've had Seabass at the Fourth Story Restaurant, which is on the fourth floor (thus, the name) of the Tattered Cover Bookstore in Cherry Creek; they also have Railyard. We've had *chile rellenos* and *Concha Y Toro* wine at Sabor Latino; Gumbo and Railyard at the Wynkoop, and *sopa y ensalada* at the Baldpate Inn in Estes Park. Yummmmmmmmmmmy. I need to play an awful lot of tennis to work this off. We SCARFED!!! When you have guests, you always order alcohol, hor's d' ovaries, and dessert, adding around 4 billion calories and 73 kazillion grams de fat to every meal. So I'm looking very Homer Simpson-ish right about now. But that's okay, because I the tennis playoffs begin this week. Because it rained all weekend, and none of my league buddies had a chance to play either, there is a strong possibility I am going into the playoffs ranked either number one or number two. I have no problem with that -- I'll be ready. The next league starts this week, too; I'm actually signing up for the 3.5 level, which is a tougher level than the last one. Maybe this way I can avoid the "what are you wearing?" guy for good.

Another benefit to having the ma-in-law in town is learning all the things we are supposed to know, but don't, about gardening and drapes. We -- Julie's family and I -- bought The Great One a sewing machine for her birthday, and Julie and The Mom of Julie wasted no time making some beautimous drapes for the living room. Of course, I had to go to Target, buy the rods, and put them up. So, now we have tremendous drapes in the living room that, no kidding, are gorgeous. Even I like 'em and I'm not sure guys are supposed to like drapes at.

The garden is now planted beyond capacity. Since Julie and have both been so frickin' busy, *el jardin* has been neglected -- Until now. Now, we've got marigolds, corn, lot of peppers, peas, beans, zukes (lots of zukes, because I like 'em), black-eyed susans, and lots and lots of tomatoes. *El jardin* is literally planted to the rim. Maybe now we can find the time to keep it up. This means that every day when I get home from work, I get to go out and feed the little plant life with water and nourish it with love and pull out the bad bad weeds; then, in the fall, we will be rewarded with more good-for-you food than we know what to do with. That's where stir-fry comes in handy. Stir-fry is a great tool for a young married couple, let me tell you. Just get yourself some chicken or beef (although chicken is really better), marinate in some soy sauce mixed with a bit o'honey, then stir-fry in a wok with a bunch of veggies -- whatever you like. Of course, if I know you, you'll just want catsup on your chicken, because that's how you like your burgers. Anyway, it was a great looooong weekend. I am feeling 458% better about life, and we have drapes and a garden. It's a beautiful thing. Tomorrow, I won't take myself or my projects, or my architects quite so seriously -- because it's not worth it.

I am NOT a hero, O.K? I'm not a role model! Sure, I play guitar, brew beer, and design buildings. Playing guitar is in my blood, brewing beer is a cheaper way of continuing my weekend beer-schlepping habits -- not to mention I can search for a taste that only I can -- and designing buildings is my job. You are the real the hero here. You are a le.....uh, thespian; you write with a wit and a timing that is unmatched anywhere; and, if we were stranded in a rain forest somewhere, with no food or water or cell phone, you could probably tell me which of the animals and plant life I can eat, and which of the animals and plant life are going to eat me.

Jeez, there are a lot of topics on my list for this week. So many topics, so little time. How about you? How was your weekend? I hope everything is cool and that Alden realizes that it's only a thesis and that two months from now she'll be laying on a beach in Hawaii sipping some nondescript alcoholic tropical drink with a straw and little umbrella in it, having some tall, dark, and handsome dude (you, duh!) lather sunblock 98 all over her smooth silky flesh and that none of this thesis crap will matter. That's the problem with our women. They don't see the jungle for the trees. Or maybe that should read, "They can't see the kegger for the beer." Have an excellent Tuesday, won't you?

Thesis anxiety SUCKS, Nap Party RULES!!!!

-Señor Sleepy

Date: May 28
To: Jeff
From: Anthony
Subject: Sick days

"I am not a role model. I play tennis. I act on occasion. But I am not responsible for raising your kids. That's your job. Therefore, I absolve myself from blame in the event that your son or daughter tries to emulate me or my lifestyle. That said, let me tell you why you should buy this brand of shoes, eat this brand of hamburgers, and wear this brand of deodorant." I thought about this concept not long ago while watching a basketball game on TV. Interesting, no? Regardless, you are still my hero.

Yes, my friend, sounds like you had a great weekend of rest and hangin' out with the in-laws, not to mention the food and drink. I had a pretty decent weekend myself. Actually, I could've very easily had a great weekend if not for the fact that my cold came to life Saturday and Sunday. There is but one occasion when I don't feel like naps are good things, and that's when I'm forced to take one. Saturday and Sunday my cold beat on me to the point that I had to take a nap and -- while I did feel much better for it -- I'd much rather take naps on my own accord. Still, though, we managed to have a very good time. Alden took me shopping and bought me a bunch of new clothes with Hawaii in mind, so I'll be styling on the islands. Naturally, this means I now have two new polos and one more collared shirt. We also found time to see the movie *Twister* which is Oscar material in my mind; not because of the storyline (which was as thin as Shawn Bradley on a diet) or the special effects -- which were outstanding -- but because Helen Hunt runs around in a white tank-top the whole movie. Tight, too. How tight? Well, she's caught in the middle of a tornado and the damn thing still wouldn't blow up or, better yet, off.

Like you, Alden and I went to dinner and breakfast, and I'm definitely the walrus today, so it's back to some hard-core running this week. I'm not too worried about it though; I am confident that I can lose the weight in a reasonable amount of time. I think a lot of what was happening with Alden's thesis was merely a manifestation of the frustration she feels in her life at not being able to finish said paper plus her feelings of loneliness and isolation. You start talking like this when you hang with a psychologist for any length of time. So, Alden and I talked, had sex -- and she's all better now.

Today, for lunch , my co-workers and I took my boss to lunch at a fancy place that serves *dim sum*. Ever done this? My first mistake was thinking that it was a type of food; actually, it's a style of serving. They constantly roll carts of food by your table, you take what you want, and some lady marks it down on a card that looks surprisingly like a Keno slip. As a matter of fact, the whole concept made me think a lot of Vegas; not just because there was food everywhere and little Keno slips, but because they'd bring these carts by and say, "You rike chicken?" and you go for it if you want it. Now, where else do the employees of an establishment walk up to you as individuals and ask if you'd like to sample their wares? Rike I said, same concept as Vegas minus a two-drink minimum and a marked difference in the "wares" of the employees. Also, the food was far too exotic for my "catsup-only" palate (that really hurt, by the way) so I spent twelve bucks and I'm starving. Anyway, that was runch.

Time is quickly approaching for me to move into our new apartment. This weekend, I will begin the task of moving my few paltry possessions, then next week I will take up residence....This means that for the first time in my life, I actually will be living alone in my own place. Thees prospect fills me with much anticipation; but, realistically, it ain't no big thang. I mean, I'm engaged, so what good will it do me to have my own place? It's not like I can have chicks over to "check out my etchings." But the apartment will provide me with some form of escape and plenty of peace and quiet, which I will immediately wreck by practicing for the upcoming gig in July. Then I fly back to Santa Cruz the weekend of June 14th to see Alden graduate. So, as you can see, things are starting to happen at a very quick pace. That's it for me, and I'll be talking at ya tomorrow.

Getting sick on vacations thoroughly sucks, white tank-tops rule. OUT!!

Little Penny

Chapter 16
Inner Slob

Date: May 29
To: Lefty
From: Jeff
Subject: Nylonathon

"Jeff, how can you be completely relaxed when you still have your work socks on? That's like me wearing my nylons all night long." "No, it's not, honey. These socks don't cover my crotch."

I don't understand nylons. Why would a woman choose to wear a man-made material, albeit with a "cotton crotch panel" (quote courtesy of The Great One) that covers both legs and waist? Why? To change the appearance of what are already two of the most beautiful parts of a woman's body, the legs? To appear to have some kind of suntan? The Great One tells me she wears nylons because they are "the socially acceptable leg-covering apparatus of the workplace." Now, if she were working in Boulder, I bet she wouldn't wear nylons; she would also be peer-pressured into never shaving her armpits. There's an attractive thought. Why do women shave their armpits and men don't? Why why why?

Yeah, I've been in your boat before. Living alone is truly a great experience; you get to eat all the macaroni and cheese you want right out of the saucepan; you get to hang your dirty underwear as "art" all over the apartment walls; you can fart and belch and pick your nose endlessly; you can let the dirty dishes pile up in the sink, until you run out of dishes and are forced to buy new ones; and eventually you get a "girlfriend" or a "wife" who wants to spend lots of time at your pad to screw the whole utopia up. In my case, I had a "friend" who wanted to sleep on my couch forever. Just kidding, dude.

In our relationship, however, I was the slob and you were mister clean jeans. The Odd Couple didn't have jack on us. Anyway, enjoy your living alone experience and try to make the most of it, because very soon it will be over. Forever. This is the time when you should allow Timmy (who is your inner slob), to come out and play and go on a rampage; because from here on out, he will be behind closed doors -- forever.

Well, catsup boy, I take it you didn't like *dim sum*. You and my wife. I, however, have had *dim sum* in the capital of *dim sum*, namely China Town in San Francisco, and found it to be a very enjoyable experience. Of course, I was sitting at a table with seven other hung-over slobs at the time, which may have influenced my feelings about the place, but I really liked it. We tried lots and lots and lots of different morsels of food; some yummy, some disgustingly horrific, which, for the most part, were obvious to the eye. You know, we

158

didn't try the pieces that resembled octopus, worm, dirty boots, spiders, dirty underwear, or anything having to do with architecture. I really enjoyed it. Of course, I took my future wife (who, at that time, was The Pretty Good One) to a *dim sum* place in San Diego, and she didn't like it. But the ambiance wasn't half that of the one in 'Frisco. Chinatown rules, dude. Someday, I'll take you to the capital of *dim sum,* Chinatown. There you can spend twelve bucks and fill up, so it takes three hours to get hungry again instead of the one hour you experienced yesterday. Twelve bucks? Expensive, my man, expensive.

By virtue of the rain and the fact that none of the other jokers got a chance to play the last two weeks, yours truly is entering the playoffs in the *numero uno posición.* Yessir, I am The Man. I play the number eight guy this week, and, barring any unforeseen circumcisions..uh, stances, I will meet my nemesis, Netboy, in round two next week. Of course, these playoffs are so weak that even the "what are you wearing" guy made it to *numero siete posición*, and I don't think he won a game all season long. Kind of like the NBA, huh?

I suppose it's time to head to *la oficina.* They must have known about the 458% improvement in attitude yesterday; when I got to work, there were a kazillion efforts to try to awaken Oscar -- who, as you recall, is my temper -- and to reduce my optimism to a pile of leftover *dim sum.* But no. The pile of work that stands before me right now me resembles The Empire State Building in size, but I am undaunted. -- because I no longer work weekends, and I no longer work past 6:00 on any given weekday. When The Great One picked up her raise, RETROACTIVE even, last week, I realized -- AGAIN -- that I am SO underpaid. So I'll go to work, work my 40 hours, and that's it. And I shall retain my good attitude and feelings about gardening, drapes, *dim sum*, and tennis, and not let anything get me down. I am man, hear me belch.

Covering up parts of the female anatomy sucks, Timmy RULES!!

-Cotton Crotch Panel

Date: May 29
To: Jeff
From: Anthony
Subject: Inner slob

I don't know that most women *choose* to wear nylons. Being that I am not a woman, cross-dresser, or Joe Namath, I can't really say if they are truly an optional piece of clothing or, if under certain circumstances, it's more or less required. However, I must point out that while a woman's legs are generally beautiful, the sight of even an average pair of legs in nylons turns me into a lusting, slathering creature prone to howling. Therefore, I ask that you refrain from bad-mouthing nylons, because you may actually influence women to stop wearing them and return to those days of the thick, baggy leg-warmers, then myself and the rest of "the pack" will be obliged to kick yo' ass.

What have I said that would make you think that I'd even be willing to give *dim sum* a second chance? Look, from here on out, if I'm going to spend 12 bucks for lunch, I'm calling the shots. Plus, I'm ordering alcohol. Dude, you can put me on a plane and fly me first-class to China itself and I still won't eat the shit. Seriously, we went in for some pretty low-key stuff and I still didn't like it, so you can imagine how I'd do if I was forced to gnaw on fried chicken feet; from what I've been told, this is actually a dish you can get at *dim sum* joints. Sorry, bro, but anything used to propel an animal through chicken shit will not soon find itself on any plate of mine. And I'm sure that holds for The Great One.

Oh, sure, you talk smack now, but I'll bet that there are times in the deepest, darkest, most inaccessible parts of your brain right next to the part where you harbor (cool word, hope I spelled it right) fond feelings for all architects that you wish you were back in that one-bedroom asylum. Yes, I am looking forward to the freedom living by oneself affords, but there is one little difference; I am looking forward to the freedom to be neat and tidy. I cannot stress to you how nice it will feel to have a clean house and a clear conscience. I know this sounds goofy but let me explain. You see, most of my roommates over the years have been people who don't put a premium on keeping things orderly and, any time I tried to clean things up, I felt guilty. I guess I was worried that somehow I'd offend them because of my obvious desire to keep things clean. It was kinda the same way when I was living with you, only I knew you wouldn't mind if I cleaned up the joint; and I knew that if I actually did offend you, you would tell me to knock it off and I'd continue doing it anyway. So you see, dear boy, my inner slob has been running rampant for a long time and it's now time for him to get back in the closet.

All right Sampras, you're going in at Number 1, so let's not play like Number 2, okay? By the way, how are you going in at Number 1 if the Number 2 guy beat you? Did he lose to someone else? And if the "what are you wearing" guy came in at Number 7, what the hell is Number 8 like? He must be the "what are we playing" guy. Regardless, don't overlook any other opponents in anticipation of your big rematch with "Netboy."

Thus, I must now get ready to hopefully watch the Abalone munch on some Buffalo Wings. Let's hope they get 'em tonight, because I really don't think it would be in their best interest to play a Game 7 in Detroit. So, I will call it a day. You have a nice evening and enjoy the game.

Fried chicken feet suck, ordering alcohol rules. OUT!!

Abalone Bandwagon

Date: May 29
To: Lefty
From: Jeff
Subject: SCOOOOOOOOOOOOOOORRRRRRRRRE!!!!

Because I'm too lame to have cable, I'm sitting in my living room, complete with new drapes, eating pasta, listening to the Abalone dismantle the Bed Springs. Every time the Avalanche score, the announcer guy goes a little more ballistic: "Sakic steals, down the lane, SCOOOOOOORRRRRRRRRE!! Forsberg in front of the net, SCOOOOOOOOOOORRRRRRRRRRRRRE!!!" And, on the fourth goal, which put the Avalanche up 4-1, he practically blows out his voice: "SCCCCCCOOOOOOOOOOOOOOOOOORRRRRRRRRE!!!!!!" I'm sitting here crying because this guy is sooooo funny. He sounds like I might sound if I were to win the lottery. He's classic. He's like the Mexican dude who does the *Goalgoalgoalgoalgoalgoalgoalgoalgoal* thing at soccer tournaments. And Big Mac (McNichols Arena, soon to be replaced by the brand spankin' new Pepsi Center) is rockin' tonight.

Here, sit here, yeah, right here, there's plenty of room on this bandwagon for you and for me. Maybe even for The Great One, who has declared several times in the past that she (say this in your best female snotty voice) "Hates hockey." All of a sudden, hockey is my favorite sport. To watch and listen to, anyway. Just think, just a few short weeks ago I didn't know the rules, nor did I know that Valeri Kamensky is a player, not one of the cheerleaders. Thanks, dude, for turning me on to this game. Actually, thanks to the great city of Quebec for introducing this great game to me and all of the other hicks in our great city. Methinks that next winter I may have to have some cable, as opposed to laying some cable, to keep up with this team.

The other night I had a couple of dreams that really disturbed me: I dreamt I was playing basketball for the University of Kansas Jayhawks in some kind of tournament. When the dream started, I had decided I had to go to the bathroom. So, I took off in the middle of the game to go find a bathroom; after draining Mister Happy, I started trying to find my way back. I was running all over the building -- which, for some reason unknown to me, had several hundred basketball games going on -- looking for my Kansas teammates. I ran and I ran, but I never found them. At some point in the dream, I realized that I wouldn't recognize my teammates if I did see them.

Then, in dream #2, I was making love to my beautimous wife. We were going at it when she had to go do something, possibly answer the phone or something, never to return. Naturally, I was left with a hard-on for the ages that would not be rectified. What up with these dreams? I know what any amateur psychologist would tell me: "You have tremendous feelings of unfulfillment." Yeah, but they must be deep down inside. Just thought I'd share.

I'll finish this e-mail in about 14 minutes, hockey time, at which point the Avalanche game will be over and we can discuss the results; or at least I can discuss the results and you can listen........

Well, I guess I'm watching hockey next week!!!!!!!!!!!!!!!!!!!! Stanley Cup, here we come!!!!!!!!! Let me see if I got this straight: For winning the Western Conference, we get some kind of Bowl. And then there is the Stanley Cup. When do we get a plate? Or better yet, when do we get the honorary beer mug? That's what we'll do. The worst team in the league will be annually awarded with the Chacon Beer Mug, full of Jeffbrew. I'll call the NHL and talk to them about this idea.

Manohman, this town is going hockey crazy right about now. You gotta feel for the Rox, the Broncs, and the basketball team. I mean, none of them matter right now. HOCKEY is what matters. You gotta love it. I'll keep you posted on how the 'necks are dealing with this, and how all the hard-core Broncos fans are dealing with it. Can you imagine? All these years, and the first professional sports championship to come to this town might be a HOCKEY championship? Gonna piss some people off, yessir. Bring on Jagr, bring on Mario Lemie..you..xx, hell, bring 'em all on. I'm CUUUUUPPPPPP CRAAAAAAAAAAAAAAAAAAAAAZZZZZZZZZYYYYYYYY!!!!!!!!
HOCKEY RULES!!!!!!!!!!

-Jeff Lemi..e...you.

Date: May 30
To: Jeff
From: Anthony
Subject: Lord Stanley's Cup

Dude, never say *hard-on* and *rectumfied* in the same sentence. Oh, sorry, that says *rectified*. Still too close. Try *denied*. Seems to me, your Freudian use of a term that sounds like another term that conjures up visions of butts could mean that your subconscious is a Homersexual. Let's see, tall muscular men in shorts, then your wife is gone? Nah, you probably just brewed a bad batch o' beer.

The Rox? The Broncs? What the hell are you talking about, dude? There is but one sports team in all of Denver and that's the almighty *ABALONE!!*

Now let me tell you all about wedding invitations. I pretty much had all the invitations addressed already, so I thought I'd put an end to the whole process and stuff the envelopes while I watched the game last night. However, I soon learned that stuffing envelopes is not the easiest thing in the world to do, especially when you would rather focus on a hockey game. I did manage to get through the whole thing, however; but it cost me -- every time I turned my attention away from the game, the Abalone scored. They kept showing different places in town where people were watching the game, so I was looking for you; but I guess you pussed-out and stayed home. Gotta be there for the Finals, dude.

At work, we are now in the process of employee evaluations . This I hate. Today, I had to fill out the "goals and objectives" portion of the interrogation. So I had to sit around and think of wonderful bullshit idealisms, because I can't write that three main goals for the year are:

1. Retain employment until I no longer need it.
2. Work less, make more.
3. Win lottery so I can quit.

No, can't tell 'em that. Instead, I have to dazzle them with tripe like, "Become more independent and self-reliant," which, as we all know, means "avoid boss."

It IS now official: the Master's thesis has been turned in, and it is powerless to ruin my life anymore. Yes, at noon today, the last changes were made and the final draft handed in. Alden is now looking forward to an evening of champagne, chocolate, and a bubble bath. Me, I'm looking forward to the fact that I no longer have to spend my evenings thinking up new and exciting ways to "talk her down," so to speak. Now I know how the Munchkins felt when a well-placed house fell to the ground.

Remember back in February when I made a phone call with the intent of getting my teeth cleaned, and the phone call resulted in another call to my doctor to verify that I wouldn't croak during cleaning? Then the consultation with the endodontist led to a root canal and countless return visits to rid myself of a recurring infection? Well, today, three months later, I finally got my teeth cleaned, and I feel like I've gone ten rounds with Freddy Kruger. My hygienist, "Captain Hook," gaffed me twice. Now I know how a fish feels. But once you clear away the blood and the torn flesh, the teeth look pretty good.

Thus, I will take leave of you for a Thursday. Get your Abalone gear ready as we make a run for the Cup. I think tonight we will know for sure that we will be opposed by the Pittsburgh Penguins. Doo-bee-doo-bee-doo...

Goals and objectives suck, well-placed houses rule. OUT!!

John El-Wah

Date: May 31
To: Lefty
From: Jeff
Subject: Enter The Court.

Master, today I enter the court to play the first round of the Denver Open (actually the playoffs for my tennis ladder). I guess I never really explained how I got to be the *numero uno* guy in the playoffs. The rules are thus: During the regular season, if you don't play during a given two-week period, you drop down, below at least all of the people who played during that

163

period. The last two-week period was so Seattle-like and rainy that I and the guy I beat were the only ones who played. Get it? So I enter the playoffs number one; the guy I beat enters number two; and "Netboy" enters number three. That's is how it works. So, today at 3 o'saka (MST) I "Enter The Court" to begin my playoff run. Master, won't you please send me some good vibes and wisdom at that time?

So, when does your little love-interest actually come home? I'm glad to hear that her thesis pieces is done. Now, she can join the real world and get an underpaying overworking job like the rest of us -- except for The Great One of course. I'm sure Alden would have filled out that question and answer thing yesterday with all kinds of flowery idealisms and optimistical observations; but that's because she's just getting out of school. You, on the other hand, are much like me; we've seen the real business world, we know how quickly a boss can decide that "Hmmm, you suck. OUT!" Once Alden has spent a few years out here, she'll become a realist, too. Just ask The Great One. She was optimistic and idealistic when I met her. Now, she pines for the day when I can play my guitar for a living and she can bake cookies and work in the garden and make wreaths all day.

More work smack: Yesterday, Boss #1 (the boss with whom we're purchasing lofts), came into my office and was ranting and raving and pretty much bowing in front of me about something I did for him. I was taken aback, because I haven't worked for him in a while; I've been working for Boss #2, who is more negative. Let's compare, shall we? This metaphorical rant is about appearance. Boss #1: "Jeff, you have holey jeans on, a ripped T-shirt, your socks don't match, your shoes are dirty, you smell like a pile of burning tractor tires, your hair is approaching dreadlock status, but you're wearing a tie. You're the greatest, Jeff." Boss #2: "Jeff, you have on a beautifully tailored Armani suit, you smell like a dozen roses, your hair is perfect, your shoes impeccable, and you have on a gorgeous Calvin Klein tie. But, Jeff, you have a nose hair sticking out of one nostril. You suck, Jeff." This is known as the "almost perfect but not close enough" myopia. I hate it, obviously. And I get it all too often, obviously. But it's not nearly as bad as my last job, where I must have had way too many nose hairs because I got fired.

Well, I suppose it's time to go to the office and try to figure out if I'm going to get ripped or praised today. Kinda fucks with the mind, ya know? It's extremely difficult to prepare for this. Anyway, have a great Friday, think of me at 2:00 your time, and I'll e-talk at you on Monday.

"Almost Perfect" sucks, Love Interests RULE!!!

-Jekyll/Hyde

Date: May 31
To: Jeff
From: Anthony
Subject: Concentwate

Look, boy, the only real piece of advice I can bestow upon you going into today's tennis match with the eighth seed is to never underestimate your opponent. In case you haven't heard, Andre Gag-assi (once rumored to be a pretty fair tennis player) was ousted in the first round of the French Open; which, I guess, since he immediately jumped into a limousine with Brooke Shields probably didn't give a fart about the $2000 fine he'll have to pay for dodging the mandatory post-match press conference. YOU, on the other hand, will have to limp over to your truck and bear the harsh reality of being a big tank. While The Great One may be on par with Brooke, Julie doesn't have near the money, regardless of what you think. Thus, I will tell you to take the Chicago Bulls' approach to competition: put him down fast, and keep him there.

Let me tell you the story about a true champion and a low-life, yellow-bellied, pompous, "our-shit-don't-stink-but-we-ordinarily-smell-so-bad-you-couldn't-tell-anyway" governing body. Unless you've been living under one of those many tall rocks your state boasts, you know that the Olympics are coming this summer. Well, apparently, our best hope for the gold in the 400m swim (which I guess is like butterfly, backstroke, breaststroke, buttstroke, thighstroke, etc.) was disqualified during the Olympic trials for an illegal turn. Okay, here's the catch. During the Olympic trials there are rules and regulations regarding turns; but, in the actual Olympics, there are none. This means the swimmer was disqualified from the Olympics for making a turn that would've been perfectly legal in Olympic competition. So, she then was encouraged to sue to regain her spot on the team, but decided not to, because, "The only way for me to win was for someone else to lose. I couldn't live with myself." In short, our best swimmer isn't going because of some stupid rule, and she won't fight it because she doesn't want to bump someone else. Now, is this or is this not the stankiest piece of thistle-infested horseshit you've ever heard? I mean, the level of stupidity incorporated into laws, rules, regs, etcetera, never ceases to amaze me

Hey, got my evaluation today. To put it plainly, my boss loves me, but it won't keep me from quitting in the event that I become independently wealthy. It is nice to know, however, that my efforts are recognized. Either that or I do a particularly good job of keeping my nasal passages groomed.

Boy, it's amazing the transformation that comes over someone the day after turning in her Master's thesis. Alden's sending me cheerful e-mails, the phone's ringing off the hook, and she's leaving enticing messages on my voice mail. I just wish she was around for me to take full advantage of the situation. Soon though. Like I said, I'm moving my stuff into the apartment this weekend, and Alden'll be returning to San Diego sometime around June 22. Prior to that, however, she will begin networking the many leads she has regarding possible employment.

Yeah, I'd love to hear a green rookie's reply to questions such as, "So, why do you want to work here?" "Well, because I feel that this is a dynamic, forward-thinking company that puts integrity and reputation ahead of profit. As such, I feel that my chances for advancement within this type of aggressive setting would provide me with both the challenges and rewards that I seek." This is what we all say; but, as you pointed out, the rookies usually mean it. Those of us cynical realists may say it, but we're really thinking, "Well, I don't really want to work anywhere, but I need money and you have an opening."

All right, enough cynicism heading into the weekend. So, anyway, I'll talk to you Monday.

Governing bodies suck, breaststroke rules. OUT!!

Booger

Date: Jun 3
To: La Cucaracha
From: Jeff
Subject: Reverse tank..........

Reverse Tank: When the Number One seed finds himself down to the Number Eight seed 6-2 (in a best of ten series) and comes scratching back to defeat the underdog 12-11. Aye yie yie yie yie. I played like dogshit, master. I do not deserve to continue, but since I somehow found a way to win, I will join the Final Four of the Tennis World, or at least that part of the world concerning the men's 3.0 tennis ladder at the Denver Tennis Center. Eet was ugly. My biggest problem, and this happens every single time I play, is I forget to keep my eye on the frickin' ball! Or I get a little cocky, like, "Yeah, I'm only down 3-6, now I'm coming back," and I totally forget to keep my eye on the ball! What is that? Ever since Little League, they've been telling me to keep my eye on the ball, and I still forget to do it! *Hijole.* I am not proud of my accomplishment. But a win is a win is a win. And maybe next time I will do better. I'm not sure, but there is a great chance that I will have to play Netboy this week. I think I'll try to schedule an hour with the ball machine before I get on the court with him; 'cuz if I screw around like I did today, he'll kick my ass and be home taking a nap before I wake up and realize what the heck's going on.

Yeah, we played today. My opponent called me Friday at 2:50 and said, "I took my car in to get it fixed and I took the bus back to my house and I realize that I forgot my house keys. I'll gladly forfeit, but I'd really like to play you sometime." Being the gentleman that I am, I said, "No, that's okay. Let's play Sunday," which led to the problems described above. Of course, if I had been the Olympic Committee, I would have said "A rule is a rule is a rule, no matter how stupid and unfounded in logic it may be." What's up with them?

So, after the tennis war today, I came home, showered, and threw on a polo (read: collared shirt), some neutral-colored nice shorts, and my Prince tennis shoes, and The Great One and I went to the Sanitarium to experience the Grand Opening of the model of our investments. We were late, so I had to

166

say, "Sorry we're late; I got into a tennis game which ran long (It did, two hours!!)." So, now, The Great One has started calling me "Country Club Boy," because that's what I look like in this outfit. I told her it's my Shrewd-Investor-on-a-Sunday-Afternoon look. But "Country Club Boy" works just fine.

In fact, I think it's going to become my alter-ego: "Country Club Boy;" born into wealth, he spends his days playing tennis and guitars; shops only at the finest men's stores in La Jolla and Cherry Creek; has his own jet parked at DIA, has his own boat docked at the Cherry Creek Reservoir. His beautiful wife, The Snobby One, spends her days eating bon-bons and having tea at 3:00 o'saka at the Brown Palace with the society ladies. They have their own staff of cooks, maids, guitar technicians, and mechanics, who keep their 23 classic cars in tip-top shape. Country Club Boy has never worked with architects, so his life and his soul are at peace. The Snobby One has never had to fire anybody, so she knows no pain.

A question for you, mister biological genius: How can a squirrel fall 20 feet out of a tree, PLOP, right on his back onto the ground, and not die? These two squirrels were warring in our front yard, no doubt over the squirrel babe sitting nearby; one squirrel was up in the tree, and the other was chasing him around. Twice, I noticed this small rodent-like shape falling from the tree, SPLAT, right on the ground; twice, the squirrel got up, dusted himself off, and went back up into the tree. SPLAT!! THUD!! KA-ZOWIE!! (I should write for "Batman") We had to duck for cover. The neighbors came out of their houses to go somewhere and I warned them, "Hey watch out for falling squirrels!!" But no dead squirrels anywhere!! How does this work, oh knower of everything? How?

Well, it's that time again. Time to prepare for the week. I think tomorrow I'll cross-check an architect hard into the boards and see if I can get a two-project suspension. Have a good one, won't you? And, remember, Tuesday night on Fox, our Colorado Avocados begin the dismantling of the Florida Pantless on the road to the STANLEY CUP!!!!

2-6 sucks, Reverse Tank RULES!!!

-The evil opposite of Greg Norman

Chapter 17
Pliability and the Theatrical Wood

Date: Jun 3
To: Jeff
From: Anthony
Subject: Numb

Jess, my fren, a win is a win is a win. So, you had to struggle against the Number 8 dude; you still were able to pull out the win under adverse conditions, so you're not a total tank. However, should Netboy pin you 6-2, you may be in trouble. So, get your chit together and KEEP YOUR EYE ON THE BALL.

Ya know, I really can't give you a definitive physiological or anatomical reason why squirrels can survive falls of twenty feet. I will tell you this, however. Any creature that makes its life in a tree is very nimble and has a very long back. Now, as an engineer, you understand that the longer something is, the more pliable it becomes. Also, you have to do some pretty drastic shit to break it. Ah yes, but what if said creature falls on its head? In the case of little Sammy Squirrel, it probably wouldn't matter much, because squirrels ain't too bright (hence the name). My guess is that it probably has something to do with the way animals turn and contort their bodies when they fall. Animals don't just fall, they wriggle on their way to the ground, as if getting themselves into position to withstand the impact. Either that or they're trying to kiss their ass good-bye. Thus, until next week, enjoy our wild America.

Had quite the weekend. Most of the time I spent moving stuff into the apartment. While it's true that I don't have much stuff, it does take a while when I'm using a two-door Toyota Tercel, I'm alone, and I'm lugging stuff up two sets of stairs (one set to get up to the building, and ANOTHER to get to the apartment). But, for the most part, it's over, except for the few items that are coming down from Santa Maria this evening. Hopefully I'll be taking up residence in the apartment tomorrow night.

Saturday night, there was a party to celebrate our old friend Linda's 30th B-day party. Same ol' shit; BBQ, booze, male stripper...yeah, I saw the first male stripper of my life Saturday night. Actually, stripper isn't the right word, considering he never actually got nekkid (thank God for small favors, HA HA). And, let me tell you something about women in the presence of strippers, does the term "feeding frenzy" mean anything to you? Jeez, they were groping and mauling this guy! How come WE aren't allowed to handle the works of art when WE go to art museums? I guess the common thinking is that WE would be unable to maintain control, but whoever came up with that concept (probably a chick) obviously has never seen a bunch of horny, drunk dames revert back twelve evolutionary steps. Scary, my man.

So, last night the Associated Community Theaters had a reception to announce the nominees for the Aubrey Awards. You remember these. I told you that our little production was too concerned about awards and shit and not doing the work required to win said awards. So, anyway, they begin the process of announcing the nominees, and a certain production about a Norwegian family is getting shut out. Then they come to the category of "Best Actor in a Major Supporting Role," and I'm thinking that if I'm going to be nominated, this is where it'll happen. Nada. So, now, our little group is panicked that we ain't gonna get shit and we're looking for ways to slip out of the reception without being seen. Then, suddenly, they announce the nominees for "Best Lead Actress in a Drama" and the woman who played "Mama" gets nominated, which is cool -- because there goes the shutout. Then the next category is "Best Lead Actor in a Drama" and they call my name. Needless to say, I am damn near in shock. Mostly because I never considered my role as a lead. But, anyway, I got it, and I must say I am very excited about it. Okay, it is community theater in one city in one state in America, but what the hell? I'm going to feel justified in feeling proud of myself, and I will not repress the big theatrical wood I'm still sporting today. I do feel kinda guilty though, because I talked so badly about the production. Whaddya think? Was I justified in talking smack about the whole thing? Anyway, I would like to take a moment to thank you for always being a very supportive friend with regards to my thespian tendencies. I don't know that I'll win the actual award, but I feel great for being nominated; and the thing that makes that worthwhile is knowing that I have the support of great friends such as yourself. So thanks again, buddy.

So it seems that I should call it a day before I give us both a mouthful of cavities with all this sweetness. Prepare yourself for the start of the Stanley Cup Finals, my friend. It's gonna be a helluva ride. Have a good one, and we'll see ya tomorrow.

Belligerent drunks suck, award nominations rule. OUT!!

Sammy Squirrel

Date: Jun 4
To: La Cucaracha
From: Jeff
Subject: Barbecue Fever

And now, to present the award for Best Lead Actor in a Drama, here's Miss Shania Twain....

"......the longer something is the more pliable it becomes. Also, you have to do some pretty drastic shit to break it." Yeah, just ask my wife. She's tried and tried to break it, to no avail......

Congratulations on the new apartment and nomination. You are quickly becoming a real boy, aren't you? All you need now is a real barbecue. We just bought one, a "Super Duper Max-Out Grill Everything At The Same Time Queue-Zilla," or something. It's pretty incredible -- I think it'll even balance my checkbook. It's a gas BBQ, so we don't have to deal with that messy charcoal anymore; and it's got an ignition switch so I don't have to light it manually. We threw out our old rusty "Patio Buddy" Saturday (complete with burial ceremony); I think it's going to be my next rock 'n roll blockbuster opus-"Good-bye Little Buddy." Whaddya think? Then we grilled shitloads of Shish-shish-shish-ka-bobs and corn-on-the-cob on the new *barbacoa que moderna*. YUMMMMMMMMMMYYYYYYY!!!

I'm really sorry I wasn't there to help you move. I feel like I still owe you one after that "My arm is broken, but I still came down to help you move" episode in Los Angeles in 1987. That was pretty incredible of you. Remember that? Those were the good ol' days, when it took just a couple of trips with a couple of cars to move everything I owned. In fact, in college, I could move everything I owned in one trip in my Volvo, a.k.a. "The Mountain Mobile." Those really were the days. Now, it would take a full army of government transport vehicles. But no tanks, please. I have a big enough problem with those.....

Well, it's morning, and I gotta go find something to iron, ironically, and get to work. Tonight, however, I'll be lounging on my couch, a homebrew in hand, watching the teli as the Colorado Avalanche begin the dismantling of the Florida Panthers. Will you be watching? Until tomorrow, have a great Tuesday.

Rude drunken people puck, Pliability Rules!!!

-Plastic Man

Date: Jun 4
To: Jeff
From: Anthony
Subject: Fodder

Hey, a little breakfast humor for ya. What city do you get when you drop a waffle at the beach? Sandy Eggo. HA HA HA!

See, you probably don't think that's funny, but you totally get off when I talk about pliability. I am detecting an air of sauciness about you, boy. And I think I know what it is. You're feeling pretty good about your new "cue." Yep, I've seen it before. For some guys it's different. For rednecks it's a gun; for geeks, it's being the first to own "Mortal Kombat Version 28"; for acting wanna-bes, it's being nominated for some obscure award; but for you social-climbing, polo-shirt-wearing, country-club-belonging, sanitarium-turned-luxury-condo-owning suburbanites, the "cue" is an extension of your dick, thus making it even longer and more pliable than ever. HOWEVER, I

170

would caution you that as something grows longer and more pliable it becomes increasingly more difficult to achieve and maintain rigidity. At this point, you fall into The Trap. Yes, you start believing that you'll be able to get by without rigidity as long as you can boast of having ultimate pliability, so you seek to be judged by what you have instead of what you can do with it. Think of it as bringing a bowl of plastic fruit to a party; it looks good but you can't eat it, and everybody thinks you're an "object of male pliability." Where the hell am I going with all this? Good question, let me go back and read. Ah yes, just remember, I know the real Jeff Chacon and, if I ever catch you barbecuing veggie burgers while wearing a Ralph Lauren polo and an apron that says "slumming it" as you sip liqueur from a funny-shaped glass, I'll shove my foot so far up your ass that you'll be able to see the dogshit on the bottom of my shoe. That said, congrats on the new BBQ and I'm confident that soon your T-shirts will be covered with grease spatterings and your hands will have many scars where you've accidentally burned yourself on the grill because you had too many beers and forgot the damn thing was hot.

Ah, don't feel bad that you weren't here to help me move. After all, you provided a place to stay when I had nothing, so, in my eyes, that makes us at least even and I think I still owe you. For the sake of prosperity though, I will tell you that it was my leg that was in a cast when I helped you move to that apartment in Los Angeles that we so eloquently dubbed "The Curson Street Cat Shelter," and it was no big thang. The foot wasn't even broken, it just had to be immobilized because I sprained it so bad and the doctor knew I wouldn't stay off it. Actually, the only difficult thing you owned were those records which, admittedly, were incredibly heavy. So, see, if you'd gone to CDs that year it would've been no trouble at all, except for the ultra-skinny staircase. Like I said, don't worry about it; I know you would've been there if you could.

Well, so glad I was able to provide you with e-mail fodder thanks to my pliable comment. The only problem is I'm still a little early for Fodder's Day. HA HA. Ah, you probably don't think that's funny either. Oh, well, it's always better to go down swinging. Have a great time watching the game, and I'll talk to you tomorrow.

Sandy Eggo rules. OUT!!

Pepe Lemieux

Date: Jun 4
To: La Cucaracha
From: Jeff
Subject: Role Reversal

The other day, actually Sunday, The Great One and I were out in the front yard. In a weird twist of reality or something, I was pruning the rose bush -- I am quickly becoming RoseBoy -- and *she* was painting some trim on

171

the house. I looked at her and said, "Look at us, Li'l Darlin'. We've got complete role reversal goin' on here." And she replied, "Yeah, and maybe you can be on top tonight." Every once in a while, she blows me away with a comment like that.

All this talk about being on top and blowing leads quite eloquently into my next topic: Pliability. Lest you forget, my friend, I am a structural engineer, and there are very few people in the world who know more about pliability and rigidity than a structural engineer. Therefore, my pliable-y-challenged friend, I assure you that I can balance the social ladder, the polo shirts, the sanitarium, the plastic fruit, AND the barbecue on Mister Happy and still maintain both pliability and rigidity to the degree required to satisfy both myself and a certain woman friend of mine. Don't you worry about me, nossir. Because I know what happens when a male exceeds reasonable pliability. And I'll let you in on it, because you're a good guy. Of all the people who know about this, I'd say 95% of 'em are structural engineers. It's kinda our little secret. It's what makes those bumper stickers that say "Structural Engineers make better lovers" or "Structural Engineers do it with Pliability" soooo true. Ready?

They call it The Plastic Range. When a pliable (in books, called "elastic") structural material, such as steel or Mister Happy, exceeds its maximum Pliability, it goes into The Plastic Range. This is the point of no return. Nothing is broken, mind you; but when a material such as steel is in the Elastic Range, it always returns to its original shape after it's through being used. In The Plastic Range, however, a big strong piece of hardened steel becomes a piece of overcooked spaghetti, know what I mean? In effect, a stretched-out limp dick, forever. No going back. No getting up. HA! Being an engineer, I am familiar with this phenom...eno...n...thing, and acutely aware of the pliability limits of Mister Happy and the dangers of exceeding them. This gives me an advantage over commoners like yourself; although, now that you are enlightened, you can experiment and get comfortable with your own limits. In fact, with exercise and a LOT of practice -- which, since you are soon going to be a newlywed, you should be getting -- you can increase the limits of your own pliability and rigidity and pretty soon you, too, can balance the whole world on your own Mister Happy and still satisfy your little love thing. Any questions? Good. Now read Chapters 68 and 69 for the next class.....

Au contraire, mon frere, I think all of your jokes are punny. And I still have all of those vinyl records that you helped move. In fact, I've increased my collection substantially in the nine years since. Nine years? Say it ain't so! God, I feel old. Not really. My pliability and rigidity keep me young. There are those who say I'm a thirty-one-year-old man with a sixteen-year-old pecker.

Well, Pepe, I gotta go move the sprinkler. I must tell you again, thanks for enlightening me on the rules of the fabulous game known as Hockey. I thoroughly enjoy watching our Colorado Avant Garde beat up on the Florida Pantaloons; I owe my vast hockey knowledge to you.   I'm a believer.

Plastic Range sucks, Elastic Range RULES!!!

-On top, finally

Date: Jun 5
To: Jeff
From: Anthony
Subject: None

"Yeah, and maybe you can be on top tonight." Uh, on top of what?

Boy, nothing would make me happier than to talk a little Abalone hockey, but I only saw the last five minutes of the game. I had to wait at the apartment for the cable guy; then, once he finished, I took Alden's Mom to dinner for her birthday. By the time that was done, so was the game. So, while I'm upset that I missed Game One, I take comfort in the knowledge that I'll be watching Game Two on my brand new 25-inch TV. OF COURSE, I'll be sitting on the floor, since that's where the TV's sitting at the moment. I gotta get an entertainment center. With the TV and the stereo on the floor it looks like a couple of Munchkins live here. So, while waiting for the cable guy, I unpacked some shit and began the task of assigning shelf space. Alden is really lucky I didn't talk to her BEFORE I put shit away, or I would've put stuff on the very top shelf out of the little runt's reach.

Have you ever heard this sentence: "You're not listening to me anyway"? This naturally is followed up with, "I'm listening to you." Now the strange part of all this occurs when she replies, "Then why aren't you saying anything?" "I was taught that it's rude to interrupt when someone else is talking." There's a certain beer commercial that illustrates this situation perfectly; and I have found myself slamming my beer on the table, hoping against hope that Alden will turn into Vin Scully and I'll catch the end of the Dodgers game. Yeah, she'd better shape up or she's going to be cut off from sex for a while. Oops, wait. On second thought, that's more of a punishment to me, isn't it? Hmm, well then, if she doesn't knock it off, I'll put all the shit out of reach AND stop lifting the lid for a month. HA!!

Interesting comments about The Plastic Range, although to me it kinda sounds like the maximum amount you can charge on your credit cards or the extent to which cosmetic surgery actually will help. You gave me a good idea for a bumper sticker though: "Structural Engineers Get It Up and Keep It Up." Hey, it's better than "Biologists Do It Naturally."

Feeling kinda old today. Saw Paul Westerberg's new video last night, for his song, "Love Untold." Catchy little tune. Anyway, in the video, Paul's hair is well-groomed and he's wearing glasses, a jacket, and a tie. The most tell-tale sign of aging, however, is that I saw it on VH-1. Also, this morning, I decided I need a haircut, because the back and sides are bushy and out of control. Naturally, this means that the front is somewhere down below my eyeballs. Not necessarily. In fact, not even close. I would like to think this is because I cut my hair significantly shorter in front; but the ugly truth is that, these days, the front starts about an inch further back than it used to. Thus, I think it's time, my friend:

> "If you wanna grow hair, you have to take the dare, Rogaine
> (de de da daa, da daa)
> If your head is a dome, you better take it home, Rogaine
> (de de da daa, da daa)
> Hope it works, hope it works, hope it wooorks, Rogaine."

So, I'm outta here, to prepare for the big basketball finals tonight. Bulls in a sweep, I figure. You have a great day, and I'll talk to you later. Feeling old sucks, Vin Scully rules. OUT!!

Gulliver

Date: Jun 6
To: La Cucaracha
From: Jeff
Subject: No pain, no Rogaine

Mister Phelps,

The man you see in this photo is one Tom Cruise. As you probably know, he is a Hollywood "movie star." Your mission, Mister Phelps, is to stop him and his kind from making any more movies out of television series from the past, and to force them to come up with some new ideas for the movie-going public. This e-mail will self-destruct in 5 seconds.....~poof~

The Great One has to see every single "blockbuster" movie that comes out every year; so, if I am to remain on her "good" side, or if her friend Tina is busy and can't take my place, or if The Great One insists on Date Night and her choice of movie, well, then, I have to go see them, too. I don't mean to complain, but you know my taste in movies, and it doesn't run in the "I can name that plot in three minutes" type, which most "big" movies are. But I have to placate her, so I find myself going to movies that normally I wouldn't go to. Funny how it doesn't work the other way. She doesn't like movies that are "scary" or "disturbing"; but I say if a movie actually "disturbs" you, then you are taking it way too seriously and should always remember it's just a movie. So, we never (I better say "hardly ever" for fear of reprisal) go to the movies that I particularly want to see. Anyway, enough of that.

Mission Impossible was decent, except for the fact that I was confused about what was going on in three or four significant places. Some of

174

the action was downright impossible, which is why I didn't particularly enjoy that last Ahnold/Jamie Lee flick, save for the dancing. But *La Misión Imposible* was at least entertaining, and it had me on the edge of my seat a couple of times. I just wish I coulda reviewed the script before it was shot. That's what I should be doing with my life. Reviewing scripts for bigass movie-making companies, so the general movie-going public will be entertained at all times. Nah, that wouldn't work. I would want to introduce characters that act like Elvis or sound like Andre The Giant or have seventeen naked women in their hot tub.

Besides, what will they think of next? How long before we see big screen versions of *Happy Days, Mork and Mindy* (with Robin Williams as Mork's long lost grandfather), or *Charlie's Angels*. Oh, there it is. A big screen version of *Charlie's Angels* (with an "R" rating) back in the '70s woulda sold a gazillion tickets, mostly to shy crater-faced young men like myself who would have killed to see Farrah, Kate and Cheryl naked. Okay, mostly just Farrah.

I understand your plight, I feel your pain. I've probably not had the "Are you listening to me?" experience. Instead, I get the, "Are you in a bad mood?" which comes right out of nowhere. To which I naturally respond, "Hell no, what the hell gave you that idea?" To which I receive a passing shot of "See, you are in a bad mood." To which I lob, "No, I'm NOT!!!!" Which, of course, puts me in a bad mood, and the wife doesn't talk to me for the rest of the night, and I just don't get it. What makes her think I'm in a bad mood? The Abacus just won; I've been vegged out on the couch all night; I'm in a great mood. Have you had this experience? And that commercial that you reference sure must be offensive to the feminist quadrant of our society. I've seen it, and I think it's pretty funny and accurate; but I wonder how the women feel about it. Say this in your best high-pitched whiny-girlie voice: "You'd rather listen to some sport-talking guy than me? You PIG!!"

How could you? How could you miss Game One? HOW COULD YOU? I was sitting there watching it, all the while thinking, "Oh, Duke's gonna love this. He's lovin' it right now, as a matter of fact." But nooooooo. You took your mother-in-law-to-be out for her birthday? You suck, dude. In-laws over the Finals. Jeez, I thought I taught you better. You gotta find a way to get out of these things on important nights like that. You gotta come up with an excuse to blow off your in-laws on important nights, even if you call her during the day and say, "I think I've got food poisoning from that cheeseburger with catsup that I had for lunch; I better stay home tonight and ride this out." Or "Tonight's flossing night. Can we do this tomorrow?"

Alrighty then. It's apparently time for me to head to the old hellhole for the day's work. Have a great Thursday, won't you? And WATCH THE GAME TONIGHT!!!!

Missing Game One sucks, Rogaine rules!!!

-The Fonz

Date: Jun 6
To: Jeff
From: Anthony
Subject: Excuses, excuses...

My friend, I know you won't believe this, but I felt I had no choice but to miss the game. Let me explain. Monday afternoon was Mom-in-law's B-day, but that also was the day my Dad was bringing my stuff down from up north. This led Alden's Mom to suggest that the three of us all go out to dinner. Now, I don't see any reason why I should have to endure parental meetings alone while my dear little fiancé is elsewhere; so, faced with the possibility of going to dinner so that her Mother could meet my Father -- who is not Mr. Conversationalist -- I desperately searched for some way out of it and came up with the suggestion of going the next night. Yeah, I wasn't happy about missing the game, but in a moment of crisis it was the best I could devise.

Yeah, I haven't heard great things about *Mission Implausible,* but it makes no difference to me, because this weekend *The Rock* comes out and THIS is the one I've been waiting to see. I know what you mean about different tastes in movies. Alden's tastes tend to run toward these ultra-chick movies like *The Piano* and *Nell;* but, strangely enough, she absolutely loves Ah-nold. Weird, huh?

Oh, boy. We got some very bad news about one of our two top products last night, and everyone's walking around work wondering if (and where) the ax is going to fall. My boss said this shouldn't affect us, but I've heard this song and dance before. I'm not really worried, but I figure I'll take some time this weekend and update the old resume. What's the job market like in Colorado, and do you have enough room for two on your couch?

Anyway, tonight is the first night I'm going to stay at the apartment. I may miss the first period of the game, because I'll be bringing stuff over. But I'll be settled in with a couple of cold ones for the final two periods. I'm hoping by next week I can start taking advantage of the facilities (namely the lighted tennis courts), but that'll depend on whether or not I can find a partner.

Boy, this e-mail has all the creativity of vanilla ice cream. About the only thing going on is the move. I guess I'll stop here and hope for better things tomorrow. Have a great evening watching the Out-to-lunch mess up the Panfries, and we'll talk at ya *mañana.*

Lame excuses suck, Ah-nold rules. OUT!!

Vanilla Ice

Date: Jun 6
To: La Cucaracha
From: Jeff
Subject: Superman never made any money.....

176

Uh, sorry, dude, our couch is barely big enough to fit The Great One and myself while we lounge and watch reruns of *The Simpsons*. No more room. OUT!!

Weirdly similar wavelengths department: Ya know, I was giving some thought to updating my own resume today. Weird, isn't it? I bet we both thought the exact same thing at the exact same time. Say, I wonder if this has always been true...Hate architects? Feeling a little persecuted and under-appreciated, not to mention underpaid, by The Man? Making love to the most beautiful woman on the planet every now and then? DUDE, I'M YOU, AND YOU ARE ME!!!! WE ARE THE SAME!!! It's no wonder women can't tell us apart. It's because we aren't apart. If this is the case, then you are your own hero. Wow, that's deep. Were you also thinking about beer and walking out of your job today? WOW!!!!

Why would I be updating my resume, you ask. Well, tomorrow is my official A.C.T. (Ass Chewing Time) concerning the last project I turned out -- the school. The rumor is that some of my co-workers, a couple of bad-attitude Night-Ranger-lovin' punks, are "unhappy" with me and are coming after me with some verbal knives at this little meeting. I'm not necessarily unhappy about the fact that a couple of punks are coming after me; it's more the fact that they had the gonads, or actually lack of 'nads, to tell everybody in the office that they are unhappy with me, except for me. Chickens. Also, Boss #2, seems to be coddling these *pendejoes* and is seemingly actually going to let this little farce come to fruition. This does not make Jeffrey a very happy boy, because I do not like to be made to look bad in public, valid or not. So The Great One and I prepared a little speech for me so that I can be on the defense tomorrow. I will not get personal, because then I'll look like the stoopid one; but I will say something like "We work under tight pressure, tremendous deadlines, and with a variety of difficult clients. The key to our success is operating as a team amidst these variables. In retrospect, I see that we were not operating as a team in this instance, because it took two weeks to sit down in this forum, and in that two weeks I have heard rumors from other members of the team that I would be the focus of the problems brought to light at this meeting. If, in fact, we are a team, then why aren't we bringing these problems to light with the people who are apparently causing them at the time that they are being caused?"

Whaddya think? I've also prepared a calendar showing the chain of events that led to "the problem" and a list of constraints under which I had to operate. I realize it all sounds New Age-ish, but you know how it is. You gotta be politically correct in the work environment these days in order to keep your job. Of course, if I could really do it *my* way, I would just say, "Fuck you guys. If you can't stand the fuckin' heat, stay out of the fuckin' kitchen." But in this age of Political Correctness, I'll try to be nice about it.

One more funny work story. At a meeting on Monday, Boss #1 stood up and said, "We've got a new award for the hardest worker in the office, and we're gonna pass it around based on whoever deserves of it." Great, we're all thinking. Cash. Cars. Vacations. Nope. It's a red cape with a Superman logo on the back. Yes, you read that right. So, he gave this cape to the *pendejoes* described above, whom everybody seems to love these days -- except for me, of course -- and said that *I* was a close second. ~shudder~ I was thinking that if I actually received this joke of an incentive, I would have to stand up and say, "Thanks, but can I just take what's behind Door #2, or cash, or a couple of days off?" What up with bosses, dude? Don't they realize who is making their salaries for them? (Me!) Don't they realize what a real incentive is? (Money!!) Don't they realize that a bad incentive (a Superman cape), is much more damaging to office moral than no incentive at all? (No!!!) Jeez....I tell The Great One all these stories so she'll know what not to do with her staff.

O.K. I gotta get some sleep to prep for my thrashing tomorrow. Wish me luck, and have a nice weekend. I sure hope The Village Inn is in need of a fabulous waiter.....

Stupid "Incentives" suck, Fighting Back RULES!!!!!

-Bobby Shapiro

Date: Jun 7
To: Jeff
From: Anthony
Subject: Born to lose, destined to fail

So, I finally manage to drag the very last load up the stairs and put it in the closet. I slowly turn and try to contort my back into something slightly resembling a straight line, while the sweat pours forth from the ever-increasing expanse of my forehead. "Now I will rest," I say, "and it will be good." Slowly, I stagger over to the refrigerator and open the door The contents: a jar of mayo, a bottle of mustard, and four beers. I relieve the fridge of the burden of one of the beers and throw the cap in the garbage. I slam the cold bottle to my lips and begin to suck the icy, life-giving contents with the urgency of a starved animal over a fresh kill. I look at the clock: 6:15. Surely, I couldn't have missed more than the first period and nothing ever happens in the first period anyway. I turn on my new, beautiful 25-inch TV and search the 60-some channels for ESPN, only to discover they have gone to commercial. Cool, I now have time to settle in. The music begins and the announcer bellows, "The Avalanche, behind Peter Forsberg's first period hat trick, are all over the Florida Panthers 4-1." Instantly, my beer goes sour, my back tightens up, and my sigh of relief becomes a cry of disbelief. "Oh, well, it's only three goals. They can still make a game of it." Shortly thereafter: "Okay, four goal leads don't guarantee anything." Ten minutes later, after the five-goal lead has been established, I'm in the bedroom putting things away as the "Massacre at McNichols" is officially on. The only question remaining is, how did *you* watch the game since it was on ESPN? After the verbal thrashing

I received yesterday about missing Game One, I know there's no way in HELL you'd miss a game, because that would make you a serious hypocrite. So, like I said, I'd be interested to know where you watched the game.

Diggin' this "my own pad" lifestyle. What are the chances that Alden will continue to help pay the rent, but stay at her parents'?

Sorry to hear that you're headed for such a serious ass-whompin'. While I agree that getting personal is not the recommended course of action for this meeting, I do have a little problem believing such phrases as, "The key to our success is operating as a team amidst these variables," ever enter your mind let alone come out of your mouth. I dunno, maybe I'm wrong, but you sound like you're standing before a Senate subcommittee. While I know that my message won't reach you until after the fact, I would like to say I think Jeff Chacon is perfectly capable of handling this situation without doing his Oliver North impersonation. But you are "The Man" so I know you'll smooth-talk your way outta this.

Anyway, it's getting late. You have a great weekend and we'll be talking at you Monday.

Ass-whompins suck, weekends rule. OUT!!

Bachelor Boy

Chapter 18
Fireballs and the Stanley Cup

Date: Jun 10
To: Jeff
From: Anthony
Subject: Sweeps

Did you know that there were 935 rats thrown on the ice in Saturday's game? Boy, I bet they need a big BROOM to SWEEP all those rats away!!

It looks as though the city of Denver finally will have a sports champion to boast about. I didn't know Denver never won a title in anything, until I saw the graphic on TV the other night. My guess is that Denverites are totally enjoying this, and I hope you're having a blast with it. I remember when the Kings went to the Stanley Cup Finals and, even though they lost, it was so much fun to be in Southern California while it was happening.

Pretty uneventful weekend. On second thought, a pretty bad weekend. I went into it feeling pretty good, but the whole thing was caca. Friday night was shot because of that doubleheader that went about as expected; the company team lost, the Friday-night team won, and I was a wreck afterwards. Saturday, I had grand aspirations for a fat-laden dinner, excessive alcohol, hockey, live rock music, and scoping out trashy women. I got the meal, the hockey, and some alcohol; but the place we usually go for rock music and trashy women decided to feature a funk band and, contrary to one of their cover songs, it was not "Ladies' Night." So, we decided to try out the new redneck bar over where I live, and the crowd there gave rednecks a bad name: very subdued, no hats, no Confederate flags; as a matter of fact, the eight people there were all watching the Padres game. It was a scary situation when you consider that the biggest redneck in the place was me, despite the fact I was wearing my "Jeff shirt." That's is what Alden calls it. Last time she took me shopping, she bought me a shirt and a pair of shorts that she says looks like something you'd wear. Now now, don't get your undies in a bunch, they're just a little to the left of my normally conservative taste in clothes. The shirt is a powder-blue polo, but it has two white areas that extend from under the arms into the middle and back. To me, it kinda looks like something my father used to wear in the '50s when he was kickin' it down at the pool hall. Very Ricky Ricardo. The shorts are a blue-and-white checkered pattern and give the appearance of an Italian tablecloth. But, like I said, the actual events of the evening fell woefully short of what I'd hoped.

"Oh where, oh where has my lee'l fren gone? Oh where, oh where can he beee?" It's starting to get late in the day and I still haven't heard from you. I hope this is in no way indicative of bad news. Perhaps they've got you working the breakfast shift down at the Village Inn. I say this only because you had your confrontational meeting with those underground-dwelling co-workers and I'm hoping you didn't take your own advice and tell the whole place to kiss your ass. But if you did and you're looking for ways to spend a little extra time, how about going down and getting measured for your tuxedo? Look, I know this sucks and you don't want to do it, but if I gotta wear one, so do you. Of course, if you don't send me the correct numbers, I shall be forced to guess. Let's see, I'm guessing 6'-4", 225 pounds, chest 48 inches, waist 30 inches, neck 20 inches, and..uh.."inseam" 13 inches. Let me know if I'm anywhere close.

The first drawback to the upcoming Hawaiian honeymoon has surfaced. The other day, I was talking to one of the women I work with just after she returned from her honeymoon in Kauai. She told me stories of white sand beaches, tall drinks, waterfalls, snorking, and an abundance of food. However, on the flight over, they were forced to watch the latest effort by Ashley and Mary Kate Olsen, the twins from that show *Full House* which also stars those other talent banks Bob Saget and John Stamos. Knowing that something like this could happen, I am taking the necessary precautions and bringing a parachute and a can of shark repellent. Face it, dude, there's only one Olsen out there with any kind of talent and, no, it's not Merlin. I'm speaking of Ashley and Mary Kate's older sister, Carol, who was forced to toil in obscurity for many years to further the acting careers of her baby sisters. But, as the twins got older, Carol felt the cold chill of a sibling's shadow, so, armed only with her bass guitar, she caught a Greyhound to California, and the rest is San Diego rock history. Now, you know the REST of the story.

Well, doesn't look like I'm going to hear from you today, so, if you'll excuse me, I must go call my therapist. Just a little insecure when I don't hear from so-called "friends" who gain my friendship and trust, then turn around and thrust the knife in me, laying me open for all the vultures of society to come in and pick my bones clean. But, as I say, I find that I cope much better with this sort of thing now. So you have a good day and go to hell.

Bad weekends suck, Ricky Ricardo rules. OUT!!

Cybill

Date: Jun 10
To: La Cucaracha
From: Jeff
Subject: WHOOOOOOOOOOSHHHHH!

Well, the ass-whompin' was postponed until Tuesday. Isn't it funny how a person can gear him/herself up for something and be totally ready for it, then when it doesn't happen experience kind of a letdown and feelings of aimlessness? After the postponement, I was thinking "Jeez, I was so geared up for this. What do I do with all of this energy now?" So I went out and hit tennis balls for an hour at 3:00 o'saka in the afternoon. That's a great way to spend a Friday afternoon, let me tell you. Just me and the ball machine Once I figured out how to stop it from hitting all of the balls over the fence, and once I figured out how *I* could stop hitting all of the balls over the fence, it was a lot of fun. I set the machine for a forehand, backhand, and repeat combination; and I whacked the balls for an hour. Quite a workout. I hope it did something for my game, because Netboy beat his opponent 10-1 and will be calling me any day now to play the semifinals. You should try this ball-machine thing. They have a contraption that you push around the court after you've whacked all the balls; it actually picks up the balls for you and puts them in a wire-tray-type-thing which you then empty into the ball machine. And repeat. I pushed the contraption backwards to see if it would spit all the balls out, but I guess it doesn't work that way....

"Mister Barbecue Makes A Mistake," Part One: Have you ever enjoyed the delightful scent of burnt human hair? Just last night, The Great One and I were getting ready to grill up some Chops d'Pork on the new Q. I went out to light it, and noticed that it didn't want to light. So, I tried again, but no. So I went and I got the ol' owner's manual, because I needed some direction. It said that "If it doesn't light initially, but it lights with a match, then the ignition switch is out of whack for one of the following reasons." O.K. So I got some matches, headed out to the 'cue, and opened the propane. Then I did perhaps the stupidest thing that I have ever done, save for the time I spilled hot chocolate all over that dude at the baseball game. I stood there, lit the match, and dropped it in the thing. WHOOOOOOSSSSSSHHHHHHH!!!! The fire was fast and furious. It flashed out at me like a Claude Lemieux hit. I jumped back, wanna kiss myself, but the fire still got to me a little bit. I now have very little hair on my right arm, some charring on my right eyelash, some hair that is now stringy instead of its normal silky smooth, and I smell like burnt human hair. Yeah, yeah, yeah, I'm an idiot, first and foremost. But, man oh man, this does make a guy realize his own mortality faster than just about anything. I mean, all I wanted to do was eat some succulent porkchops, and I almost became a human funeral pyre. So, I think when work gets me down, I'll just have to remember this little incident as a symbol of the things that are really important in life, like living.

Time to go to work. ~Ugh~ So you have a great Monday, won't you? And tonight, it's STANLEY CUP TIME!!!!!!!

Mistakes that involve fire suck, Ball machines RULE!!!

-Firewalker

Date: Jun 10
To: La Cucaracha
From: Jeff
Subject: Stanley

STANLEY CUP!!!!! STANLEY CUP!!!!! STANLEY CUP!!!!! STANLEY
CUP!!!!! STANLEY CUP!!!!! STANLEY CUP!!!!! STANLEY CUP!!!!!
STANLEY CUP!!!!! STANLEY CUP!!!!! STANLEY CUP!!!!!

Okay, I've got a confession to make, and I'm only gonna do this once, so here goes: I....I....I....I'm a hockey fanatic. That game tonight was the most intensely nail-biting hair-pulling-out wiping-the-poop-out-of-my-pants hockey game that I have ever seen. I LOVED IT!!!! And now that OUR TEAM has the Stanley Cup and the Steven Bowl and the Scotty Saucer, it's braggin' time. BRAGGIN' TIME, BABY!. Shall I pick up a "Stanley Cup Souvenir" for you, my fellow bandwagon-er jump-er on-er? Perhaps a delightful pair of Avalanche Stanley Cup Champion Underwear? Or a full pair of Avalanche Stanley Cup Champion Bed sheets, featuring the lovely mug of Claude Lemieux on one pillow case and the beautiful face of Mike Ricci on the other? Alrighty then. It'll be interesting to see how Denver handles its newfound fame. I think there'll probably be a parade to honor our boys; then what? All summer long, we'll be seeing the boys on the television trying to sell us various goodies. "Hi, I'm Claude Lemieux for Rock 'em Sock 'em Robots...." "Hi, I'm Patrick Roy for the Acme Broom Company, where every chore is a clean sweep...." "Hi, I'm Mike Ricci for Doctor Jones' Cosmetic Surgery...." Ah, yes, the joys of stardom.

But now what do we have to look forward to? Another Bulls championship -- then a long hot summer of nothing but baseball. Boo hoo....Baseball is incredibly boring compared to hockey. In fact, a bad game of hockey is better than a good game of baseball. In fact, we went to the Rox 19-8 drubbing of the Braves last Friday night, and I could barely pay attention But hockey rules!!!

Jeez, talk about an overreaction: I have not left you for another cyberlover. I am not writing you a "Dear Juan" e-mail. I am not deliberately ignoring you in hopes that you'll go away like so many pesky girlfriends in the past. On the contrary, I *did* write you an e-mail yesterday. I tried and tried to send it out, but my Internet Provider, which should be called "The Company That Takes My Money, But Sends My E-Mail Only When They Feel Like It," was apparently under the weather or something. So, tonight I sent *that* e-mail first. Enjoy, won't you?

Let me see if I got this straight: Your little love-muffin is buying you "Jeffshirts" that are powder blue? Hmmm...nossir, I don't like it. I don't know where she ever got that idea, *amigo*; but I do not do powder blue. First, because that is a weak-ass excuse for a *real* color; second, isn't that a UCLA color? We all know that UCLA, only on a clear day. Weak joke, I know. Maybe Alden and I need to spend a little time together so she knows exactly what a "Jeffshirt" is. A "Jeffshirt," much like an "Anthonyshirt," typically is a white T-shirt with a snappy saying or cool character or logo for an excellent pub plastered on either the front or the back. Is this not true? Ricky Ricardo and I have never ever ever been on the same fashion plate. Unless, of course,

I have been completely fooling myself this whole time, and I *do* dress like Ricky. WOW!. Hang on, I'll be right back, I've got to go check my closet .... Nossir, I do not dress like Ricky Ricardo. Don't scare me like that.

As far as the old Inquisition goes, I'll be heading into that witch hunt tomorrow at 1:30 o'saka. And you are right, that little speech I have prepared does sound like I am standing in front of the Whitewater Hearings trying to muck everything up with big words. "If you can't something something, baffle 'em with bullshit." The Great One helped me with that little speech, because, as you know by now, my vocabulary consists of words no bigger than "fuck you" and "fuck you, too." So, "the meeting" should be interesting. I've got a better attitude about the whole thing today, but I'll keep you posted.

Well, time for beddy-bye. Have a nice Tuesday, *amigo*, and don't wear anything powder blue. I wouldn't.

Powder blue sucks, STANLEY CUP STANLEY CUP STANLEY CUP STANLEY CUP.......

-Lord Stanley

Date: Jun 11
To: Jeff
From: Anthony
Subject: Human torch

"If your head is in flames you know it takes the blame, propane..." So, I'm reading your account of the BBQ and I'm in hysterics. Sorry, dude, I don't mean to imply that you catching on fire is in any way funny, but your description of the whole thing is. I know it's not a good idea to kick a guy when he's down (although I understand it's not a bad idea if he's on fire), but, yeah, you're an idiot. Quick chemistry lesson, Smokey: propane is extremely flammable, matches produces flames. Get the message? At least now we have another addition to the list of celebrity Zippos: Richard Pryor, Michael Jackson, Jeff Chacon. (Congratulations for being the first white boy)

I'm going to tell you a wonderful story now. It's called, "One Minute is a Lifetime." Once upon a time there was a young man named Anthony. Nice enough young man with chiseled good looks, black silky hair, rippling muscles, and a vivid imagination. But Anthony had extremely bad luck. How bad? One night Anthony was watching the Stanley Cup Finals. It was Game Four and the Colorado Avalanche were up on the Florida Panthers 3-0 in their best of seven series. "Oh joy," thought Anthony, "I get to sit here and watch the whole game tonight." And so, he did. Anthony watched the pre-game, he watched the first period, the second, the third. Then his Mother-in-law-to-be called. "Can't talk," Anthony said. "Stanley Cup Finals. OUT!!" Anthony watched the first overtime. "My, it's starting to get late," he thought. "I hope this ends soon." The first overtime ended. Anthony watched the second

184

overtime. He was starting to get very sleepy. "Goodness," he yawned, "I hope I don't fall asleep." At the start of the third overtime he was very sleepy, but this wasn't the real problem. "Heavens, I really have to piss," he said out loud. So, unable to control his bladder any longer, Anthony dashed to the bathroom to heed nature's call. As relief came to him (or flowed forth from), Anthony heard an evil cry from the living room. "Krup shoots, SCORES!!" Bewildered, distraught -- and wet -- our hero dashed into the living room to see a mass of elated humanity laying on the ice. He hung his head low. His other head hung low. Anthony missed the game-winning goal, because he ducked-out of a five hour game for *one* minute. So, let this be a lesson to you kiddies out there. Always keep a little Stanley Cup handy so you don't have to leave the room. The end.

Yeah, in that fleeting instant when I ducked into the head, the Avalanche won the Cup. Congratulations to the city of Denver, the state of Colorado, and to you, my friend; for you now realize that hockey is a true spectacle, and I hope you continue to enjoy it through the years.

Can you do me a favor? My brother wants to get a championship T-shirt, so will you let me know how much they are, so I can get him one for his B-day? *Muchas gracias.* By the way; separated at birth, Mike Ricci...and Ringo Starr?

So, I guess today was ass-whompin' day, huh? Never any fun, but it doesn't surprise me that this is happening to you today, because I'm having one of those days where lots of irritating shit constantly happens to me. I banged my elbow on a counter, I picked up the phone just in time to hear "click," I discovered that I used an expired chemical in a very touchy assay, shit like that. Must be that cosmic thing again. Like spiritual twins or something. So, which one do you want to be, Ashley or Mary Kate?

I do not think it was the color powder blue that made her think it was a "Jeffshirt." Rather, it was the air of uniqueness, the delicate balance of being different without being bizarre. A lot like you, my friend. But do not kid yourself, Ricky Ricardo dressed very well; besides, he was the closest thing to a Hispanic on television for the better part of thirty years. Then there was Ricardo Mont...a...l....that guy who starred in that show with that very short other guy. Then Freddy Prinze. Now, we have Jimmy Smits who may not even BE Mexican for all we know. Smits? How many Smits can there possibly be in Mexico?

Glad to hear all is well and that your Provider is back on the job. No hockey tonight, no basketball. Good night to play guitar, so I think I will. Have a good one, and I'll talk to you tomorrow.

Untimely pisses suck, Joe Sakic rules. OUT!!

The Beezer

Date: Jun 11
To: La Cucaracha
From: Jeff
Subject: Just win, baby.

Jeff's Rules for Winning Dogfights and Influencing People:

1. Always make sure the biggest dog in the room (i.e, the bossdog) is on your side, even as he's placating the runtdogs as they try to throw tons o'shit your way.

2. Always play a vicious winning set of tennis just before the dogfight. This calms the nerves and helps you focus not on the bullshit, but on the real task at hand (i.e., the demolishing of the runtdogs who are trying to wreak havoc on your peaceful little existence).

3. Let the runtdogs know from the get-go that they are completely out of their league and have no idea that the level of crap you put up with is inconceivable compared to the level of crap they're complaining about.

4. Lose your temper, but only once. This lets all of the other dogs know that you can and will get personal if and only if it's necessary.

5. When the smallest runtdog in the room continuously says things like, "I don't mean to pick on Jeff, but...." then starts laughing as if to take some of the seriousness off the remark, stare at him coldly, as if to say "I know where you live, fucker. And I know where your dogdish is. So, don't fuck with me."

6. Spring at least one surprise on all of the dogs gathered. This surprise should consist of evidence as to why this dogfight shouldn't ever have started, and evidence that you are the biggest and smartest dog of all. They'll never expect it.

7. After the runtdogs have left the fight, sit with the bossdogs and talk a LOT of shit about the runtdogs.

8. Just before you leave the room, make sure that you get a "We think you did a GREAT job, Jeff" from the bossdogs. This is good for Arturo and for Mr. Happy.

Well, my A.C.T. today wasn't too bad. In fact, it was almost exactly as described above. I wowed 'em with evidence. I threw 'em off guard with my comment, "I really can't respond to that remark objectively." Afterwards, Boss #2 let me know he still likes me. It was good, but not fun. I hate having to defend myself -- realistically, I shouldn't have to. But there's always some little jerkoff trying to steal my thunder and make me look bad.

Oh, and, uh, I'll be Mary Kate. She's the cute one.

I'm so happy you experienced so much joy from my "Human Melting Yellow Peep" affair. I realize I'm an idiot, I should have known better, and if you had been here, you'd still be laughing; but, in this instance, I'd rather be almost-burned than The Guy Who Had To Take A Piss and Missed The Winning Stanley Cup Shot By The Guy They Said Wouldn't Play Again This Season. You gotta time your urinations better, my friend. I only pissed during

186

commercials and between periods, because *I* don't get up in the triple overtime of a Stanley Cup Finals! Oh, by the way, if it was yellow, that means you are dehydrated and probably should have a couple more beers. And, yes, Uwe Krup had his knee blown out in Game One of the season by the Detwoit Wed Wings and was not supposed to return; but he defied the odds and his doctors, and came back for a couple of regular season games and the playoffs. Now this. Can you say *NBC Movie of the Week,* starring Richard Chamberlain as Uwe Krup, the hockey player who said "Never say die"; Cheryl Ladd as his wife, Helda Krup, the woman behind the man; and Michael J. Fox as Marc Crawford, the coach who gave Uwe his chance to play in the Stanley Cup Finals. What a story!

So I wake up this morning, still dreaming of hoisting a large silver cup over my head and laying a few smackers on it, while being adored by billions of fans. Then I hear on the radio, "The Avalanche are landing at DIA right now." I've heard about this kind of city-wide nutso reaction to national sports championships, so I turn on the TV to see if anybody is covering this historic event. Keep in mind that it's 6:15 o'saka in the morning. And, yes, all three major television stations are running "All Avalanche, All The Time" coverage of the Avalanche landing at Denver International Airport, as well as the few hundred nuts who went straight from LoDo to the airport after partying all night; plus endless replays of Krup's Goal last night. I tell you, this place is nuts! I guess all of LoDo went streaming into the streets last night after the game and starting partying all over downtown. Then, as it always seems to happen, things got a little ugly. People started building bonfires in the middle of the streets, and the cops showed up The "fans," who were probably 99% blitzed on alcohol, started throwing bottles at the coppers. End of story. Around twenty people got arrested and some store windows got busted, but the real issue here is this: Why the hell does this always happen? Why, I ask you, WHY? Why can't people just celebrate in a good clean way? Why does celebration have to mean "Yeah!!! Let's destroy something!!!!!" I do not get it. I'm glad The Great One and I decided against going downtown last night to watch l'game. That would have been almost as stupid as trying to light myself on fire.

Well, *amigo,* I'll address some of the other topics on the table, such as the Ricky Ricardo thing, in tomorrow's missive. Until then, STANLEY CUP!!! STANLEY CUP!!! STANLEY CUP!!! STANLEY CUP!!! STANLEY CUP!!!

Runtdogs suck, Uwe Krupcake RULES!!!

-Mary Kate

Date: Jun 12
To: Jeff
From: Anthony
Subject: Hermit boy

Before I forget, do you remember when we were in Vegas (think hard) and I put that ten-dollar bet down on that horse to win the Preakness? Well, the dumb nag won the Belmont instead. Yet another 30-second synopsis of my life.

Typing with one hand is not an easy thing to do. My fingers are shredded and aching because I've been playing guitar for the last hour or so. I also played during my lunch hour. Yes, there is nothing like finding a cozy little corner of the parking garage where you can make yourself at home and strum your instrument to your heart's content. Makes me feel very Boxcar Willie.

Well, glad to see you took down all those bottom feeders in your office. Face it buddy, some dogs are destined to yap at you from inside a car and, since they won't come out, all you can do is strut on by and occasionally piss on their tires. Just make sure the Stanley Cup Finals aren't on when you do.

Look, don't try to make me feel guilty about laughing at you for doing your tiki torch impersonation. You wrote it so that I would laugh, so don't give me the "Glad you find my pain so entertaining" schtick. As far as timing my peeses better, I invoke the ol' "when ya gotta go, ya gotta go" philosophy. Yeah, like I WANTED to take a piss during triple overtime!! So, I'm watching the news last night and they're showing the Avalanche escorting the Cup off the plane; then they cut away to downtown Denver and show a crowd standing around this huge fire and the guy says, "There is rioting in the streets of Denver." My response was, "Either that or Jeff's barbecuing again." Like you, I am highly perplexed as to why, after all these years of waiting for a championship, the people of Denver would celebrate by destroying shit. So senseless. Anyway, besides Richard Chamberlain, Cheryl Ladd, and Michael J. Fox, don't forget Ringo Starr as Mike Ricci and Dolph Lundgren as Claude Lemieux; co-starring the Mormon Tabernacle Choir as the Detroit Red Wings.

Dumb horses that win the wrong race suck, tiki torches rule. OUT!!

Ashley (so why are you always the cute one?)

Date: Jun 13
To: La Cucaracha
From: Jeff
Subject: Hey, Lucy!! Ju have some 'splaining todo!!!

I'm always the cute one because that's just the way things worked out when we were separated at birth, Okay? Nothing I can do about it now....

Ya know, playing your instrument in the corner of the parking garage is a good idea. Do the people coming out to the garage ever look at you as if to say, "If you touch me, you bad man, I'll spray you with mace and knee you so hard you'll be doubled over in pain for the next decade?" That happened to me. I was assigned to go look at an underground parking garage; you know, walk around, look at the cracks, check out the water damage, make sure the thing needed only minor repairs and wasn't going to fall down go boom. So, I dressed in my grubbies, as engineers are want to do, and headed down to the garage. I spent three days down there just walking around, looking at the cracks, etcetera. I carried a flashlight, clipboard, and tape measure. Still, the women who came down to their cars during the day looked at me as if though I might be a close relative of Ted Bundy. Of course, they might not have seen me until they got right close to their cars, and I'd be standing there with my flashlight pointed at the ceiling and my neck strained to look at said ceiling. So, I believe they thought either (A) I was there to commit bad crimes against the office building inhabitants, (B) I was breaking into all of their cars and stealing lots o'goodies, or (C) the parking garage was about to fall down go boom and I was there confirming that fact. It was an interesting experience about the human psyche and how it feels to be in parking garages.

I've reconsidered the Ricky Ricardo thing, and....and.....nossir, I don't like it. Don't get me wrong, Ricky was a man. And he was and really still is the closest thing to having a real live Mexican on television; for that I am respectful. I just don't wanna dress like him.

There were 450,000 people downtown last night to worship the Avalanche at the parade and rally. 450,000 people. That's like every man, woman, child and dog in the entire state of Colorado and the nearby states of Wyoming and Kansas combined!!! This has been an amazing thing. Abalone tickets are going to be harder to come by next season than tickets to a Pearl Jam show. On the news last night, it was "Avalanche this, Avalanche that.....And in sports, the Avalanche had a parade and blahblahblah...oh yeah, and the baseball team, the....the....what is their name, the....oh yeah, the Big Mountains to the West, well they played, and....ah, hell, who gives a shit? Avalanche, Avalanche....."

Well, I gotta go to work. I've got a "useless 8:00 o'saka meeting" that I need to be at, so I will go and let you try to figure out how to become the Cute One. Have a *bueno* weekend with your *señorita* up there in Santa Cruz Hippieville. And tell her congratulations on the degree and welcome to the *real* world. *Adios!*

Parking Garage Suspicion sucks, STANLEY CUP!!! STANLEY CUP!!! STANLEY CUP!!!

-Don't mind me. I'm just trying to make sure that this thing isn't going to fall down and kill anybody.

Date: Jun 13
To: Jeff
From: Anthony
Subject: Canciones de mi parking garage

I think when they built my car, they installed a powerful magnet in the front bumper that attracts big, smelly, smog-spewing trucks. Whenever I get on the freeway, inevitably I wind up behind one of these behemoths, and I'm bloody well tired of it. I'm actually now forced to take the freeway to work since moving into my...uh, OUR new apartment. This too, is getting to be a problem. Perhaps I can interest Alden in some kind of a time-share. She can come over anytime I want. See, ya just know she's not going to agree to this. Women aren't very cool, are they?

Okay, fine, you don't dress like Ricky Ricardo. You dress like Fred Mertz. Happy now?

Actually, our parking garage is not what one would consider "standard." It's two stories, above ground, and open to the sunshine between the stories, just like most mall parking lots. There's a sawhorse at one end, so I take it out into the sunshine and sit there and play. It's nice because it's our company's private lot, so everyone who sees me there knows me. Nothing I do surprises these people, anyway. In a world of scientists, I come from the Island of Misfit Toys. I'm far too right-brained for these people and I'm more a source of entertainment to them than anything else. Have you ever noticed that people don't approach you when you're playing a guitar? Or maybe it's just because I suck. I always kind of thought that the minstrel was sort of a revered person but, in the electronic age, I guess people are more apt to get their tunes from the highly polished faire available on radio or wherever. In all honesty, playing guitar doesn't hold the same attraction for me that it once did. You're in Denver and my brother's up north. It's no fun playing by myself. I don't even write in my journal anymore. This actually is Alden's fault. Once I get happy, my ability to write poetically goes right in the tank. Boy, she's got a lot of nerve making me happy, doesn't she?

Here's a little sample of some of the scientific discussion that takes · place in the break room of this major pharmaceutical research corporation where I work. Today's topic: between Buck Owens and Roy Clark, who was "a-pickin'" and who was "a-grinnin'"? I voted Buck for "a-pickin'" and Roy for "a-grinnin.'" Speaking of Buck, the dog who played Buck on *Married With Children* died recently. The guy who plays Al looks like he's about to. But he still rules! Too bad about Buck though.

Okay, as you know, I'll be in Santa Cruz this weekend. I'll be sure to extend your congrats to Alden, but I think I'll spring the real world on her AFTER the honeymoon. Might as well let her have some fun. Have a good one, buddy.

Big, smelly, smog-spewing trucks suck, Al Bundy rules. OUT!!

Bud

Date: Jun 17
To: Jeff
From: Anthony
Subject: Penguins in modeling school

Hey, new name for a band -- Gringo Starr.

Yes, I have returned from the wilds of Northern California, where, on the front page of the San Jose newspaper, it says the "Affects of (something) felt on (something else)." Point is, major newspaper and they don't know the difference between "affect" and "effect." Such is NoCal. Elvis may or may not be alive, but Jerry Garcia is alive and well and he received his graduate degree from the University of California at Santa Cruz this weekend as did my little Alden in a very nice (thankfully it was also short) ceremony held downtown. Along with getting her degree, we also found time to go buy Alden a business suit for all the interviews she'll soon be going on. Yes, my little meal ticket is finally primed. But let me expound a little on the ceremony. I dropped Alden off at the Civic Center and went to pick up her parents at the hotel. When I returned, it was still kinda early, so I went to see if I could find her and get some pre-game comments on camera. I walked around the corner of the building and there, right before my eyes, I saw a sea of graduates milling about. And I swear, they looked like a bunch of penguins balancing books on their heads. I dove into the squawking masses, looking for my little Chilly Willy, but I couldn't find her. Then, this one Emperor penguin told them all to get in line and they started to waddle into place, so I rushed into the auditorium to get a seat.

I gotta hand it to Santa Cruz. They said the thing was going to start at 5:00, and they started it at 5:00. Not only that, but the ceremony lasted only a little more than an hour. True to form, however, there were a few gentle reminders that this, indeed, was Santa Cruz. An old guy with long white hair and a matching beard went up to get his degree, sporting sandals and showing off wrinkled, hairless legs. Also, one of the professors looked EXACTLY like Charles Manson; and, forty years from now, will probably look like the old guy in the sandals. But this all represents the culmination of two years' worth of very hard work for Alden and I'm extremely proud of her. The only problem is she kept insisting that I call her "Master." Finally I told her that if I did, then she'd have to call me "Bachelor." Thus endeth the discussion. So, hopefully, now Alden will be able to find a job in a timely manner and in a few years will make enough money so I can retire.

Checked out *The Rock* yesterday before leaving Santa Cruz. Good but not great, though one aspect of it did leave me with a lot of hope; much as I hate to admit it, Nicolas Cage is losing his hair faster than I am. However, it is good to see that he's not taking the Burt Reynolds approach to the problem by buying the "toupee of the week." No, Cage is losing hair but he's still Nicolas and he's still THE MAN. Thus, I am no longer going to let the prospect of baldness worry me. I'll fight it as long as I can but it doesn't make me any more or any less of a man. I'll just let nature take its course; I refuse to help it along with the aid of a propane BBQ.

Looks like your Provider isn't providing today, so I'll quit here. Have yourself a wonderful day and hopefully I'll hear from you later. If not, then tomorrow. Take it easy.

Squawking masses suck, wives with Master's degrees rule. OUT!!

Wildlife photographer

Date: Jun 16
To: La Cucaracha
From: Jeff
Subject: I'm a pickin'.....

Roy was DEFINITELY "a-pickin," and Buck, the younger, good lookin' one, just like you, was DEFINITELY "a-grinnin." As an avid fan of *Hee-Haw*, I know this to be fact. The only reason I ever watched *Hee-Haw* was to get a look at the fine, exposed young flesh therein. At the tender age of twelve, it was the best flesh to which I had ever been exposed. And you know what else? I never ever understood that song about "You found another and *phhhhtt* you was gone..." Now I do, thanks to a certain young lady of my past; but, back then, it was just another catchy tune. How many of those catchy tunes did I hear but not understand when I was at that tender young age? "Witchy Woman," by The Eagles. "Wildfire," that song about the horse, by somebody, Glen Campbell? "Shake Your Booty," by K.C. and the Sunshine Band, the funkiest white boys around. "The Electric Boob" song by Elton John. What exactly are Electric Boobs? I'd really like to know, now that I am intimately familiar with The World's Only Perfect Pair Of Non-Electric Boobs. The "Wrecked Up Like A Douche" song by Manfred Mann, a song that actually was written by Bruce Springsteen. I'll have to think about this list. There was a time in my life when I was twelve, thirteen, and fourteen, with a face full of zits that resembled the Rocky Mountain Range. I was shy, unpopular, and afraid of that new feeling in my groin. All I had was my little hand-held A.M. radio. That radio was the world to me. I listened it station KCBQ out of San Diego, because "Shotgun Tom Kelly" was the coolest deejay, with his "Booorrrrrrrraaaaaaaaaaaaaahhhhhh" shout that was supposed to sound like a shotgun -- thus, the name -- and his ability to play the coolest songs over and over. I'm sure that, with a little thought, I can come up with a staggering list of songs that affected me at that age, even though I had no idea what the songs were actually about. How about "The Night Chicago Died?" Now there's a song. I'll think about this and get back to you.

I heard a vicious rumor recently -- about you. I heard that you call your little love interest "Pookie." "Pookie?" What is that?!! Is that *her* choice, or, gulp, your choice? I'm not really sure I want to know. Let's examine this nickname thing, shall we? First of all, just so you don't think I'm

192

hiding anything, here are the other nicknames for The Great One: Beautimous, Lover, Sa-weetie, Cutie, and Sweet Thing. That's really about it. Seriously. Although sometimes in the middle of fooling around, and with a little coercion, I've been known to scream out "Queen of All Things!!!!" Let's examine now the nicknames that possibly are worse ~gulp~ than "Pookie," shall we? How about "Snookums?" That's pretty bad. Or maybe "Bunny." "Muffin." "Kitten." They all suck. Is it true? Do you really call her "Pookie?" Say it ain't so, Joe.

Well, enough of my ranting and raving for today. After a complete rain out yesterday, complete with a little hail ("Aah, hail. It ain't no hail!!"), we enjoyed a spectacular Colorado day -- 80s, sunny, then a late afternoon thunderstorm to satisfy the yardly requirements for photosynthesis, (with which I'm sure you're intimately familiar) it was gorgeous. After checking my calendar, I realize that it's only five weeks until your fabulous matrimonial-type thing. With that in mind, I've finished the audio tape of the songs for the gig, and will be send it out Monday or Tuesday, so that you may listen to the songs whilst driving around losing your mind over trivial things like napkins, cummerbunds, and "boot-in-ears." Enjoy it, my friend. There is no type of stress like pre-wedding stress. Eventually (usually after it's all over), you realize how silly the whole thing is and how next time you're DEFINITELY going to Vegas to get it done.

Oh, and, uh, happy Father's Day. Someday your five little Anthonys will be running to join you and Pookie in bed early in the morning on this day, and they'll bring you burnt toast and undercooked eggs and little crayon-drawings that don't resemble anything recognizable to your eye; and they'll be scream "Happy Father's Day, Daddy!!!! Look what we brought you!!!!" For now, it is only I -- without breakfast, without drawings of Mommy -- it is only I who wishes you Happy Father's Day.

Oh, wait, one more thing. Julie is yelling at me from *la cocina*, something about a "scorpion on the window." Since she is typically overly-paranoid about bugs, I'm laughing. But, no, she is serious. So I will now take leave from my mindflow that is this e-mail, and go take a look.......At a bug, no bigger than my fingernail. Scorpions. Aren't they those big giant ugly things found mostly in South America? Or are they an aging German rock band on tour with Alice Cooper as part of the "Never to Old To Rock You Like A Hurricane Tour?" Just wondering. Have a great Monday

Bug paranoia sucks, Electric Boobs RULE!!!!

-K.C.

Chapter 19
A Death In The Family

Date: Jun 17
To: La Cucaracha
From: Jeff
Subject: A Death In The Family

Oh, man. A brother-in-spirit of mine (a co-worker) passed away Friday, and I'm struggling to come to terms with it. Jimmy didn't show up at work this morning, and our ever-alert receptionist called his apartment building to see if they would go and check on him. They got to his door, noticed that the Saturday and Sunday editions of the *Denver Post* were laying undisturbed on the Welcome mat, then they went in. Once inside, they found Jimmy dead in his bed.

He died in his sleep on Friday night -- as deduced by the *Posts* that were on the mat. Then our boss had the solemn task of telling us all this had happened. This sucks. I didn't know Jimmy well, because he was a very keep-to-himself kind of guy, but I knew him. I knew him in Los Angeles, where he was an intimidating presence to a just-out-of-Califonia-Polytechnic-State-University-at-San-Luis-Obispo-green-as-they-come engineer-wannabe at my very first job. I knew him at Oktoberfest a couple of years back here in Denver, where he recognized me but couldn't remember my name. I knew him in my cover letter to the place where I work now, where he already worked, when I slyly dropped his name into my begging and groveling for a job. I knew him when his bosses asked him about this "Jeff Chacon character who wants to work here," and he replied "he's a lot like me -- quiet, smart, damn good looking, you know. Hire him." I knew him when I started this job and discovered that he was still an intimidating presence ten years later.

But lately, I knew him as a brother-in-spirit. That's because he very recently discovered an intense love of the guitar. After the death of our office manager's husband last year, Jimmy decided that he needed to try something new that he always wanted to do, so he bought a guitar. He learned by himself for a while, then I noticed that he began to ask me questions about the guitar and it's magic. I shared with him some things I know, and I encouraged him. After just a short period of time, he had it. He had the love for the guitar that I have. And this made us brothers. It changed our relationship dramatically. We were no longer Jimmy the Intimidating and Jeff the Meek; instead, we were Brothers In Music.

I brought my guitar to the office a couple of times to show him some things, because I am always encouraged and excited by people who are interested in the guitar. He shared with me of the things he was learning -- the Chuck Berry riffs, the 12-bar blues, the Crosby, Stills and Nash songs. In turn

I showed him "Blackbird" and some blues shuffles he could easily sing over. Eventually, Jimmy decided that he wanted to buy an electric guitar and asked if I knew anything about them. I, of course, became very excited about this and brought in both of my electric guitars (complete with a practice amp) on separate days so Jimmy could plug in and see what it's like to play two very different styles of electric guitars. The next Monday, when Jimmy came in to work, he proudly proclaimed, "I went a little crazy this weekend." I replied, "All right, what did you buy?" He'd bought a Gibson Les Paul, which was one of the guitars I'd shown him. I felt proud that I could help with his decision.

What was most impressive about Jimmy was his passion for the guitar, a passion that is rare. Every day, Jimmy and I and another a co-worker who is also learning guitar would talk about guitar playing, and it seemed that Jimmy practiced whenever he could. He always had a song as a "project" he was working on. Just last week, I brought in the music for "Riviera Paradise" by Stevie Ray Vaughan, because Jimmy thought that would be a great song to learn. We kept talking about getting together on the electric guitars and having a little jam session, but he always said "it'll be a while before I'm ready for that." Now, it's too late.

Death has never been this close to me. I was shocked. I stood there thinking about things for a good ten minutes before I finally went out and sat in the grass and thought about some more things. Life kind of passed before my eyes -- all the things I still have to do, all the things Jimmy still had to do. How does one get the absolute most out of each and every day? For the rest of the day I threw myself into my work, which made my emotions kind of go away, or so I thought.

Then, at 5:00 o'clock, after most everybody else had gone home, our receptionist came in to my cubicle and said that Jimmy's friend called and wanted us to know that, "Jimmy really loved to play that guitar, and he really loved to play with you guys." That's when I had to go home. Because I was bawling like a baby. In a trying time like this, Jimmy's love for the guitar seemed as important to somebody else as it was for me. This notion completely overwhelmed me and drove me to sobbing for minutes on end. Jimmy's passion was my passion, and that makes his that much more difficult for me. So long, brother. See you in the next life, where you can be the Meek and I can be the Intimidating.

Not much left to say about anything. I guess coming to grips with one's own mortality is not an easy task. We can take from this so many lessons, the most valuable being that life is too short to put up with bad television or bad bosses or racism or anything that is not worthwhile. We must live each moment to its fullest. We must go for the gusto, we must live on the edge, we must not tell ourselves "No."

Love ya man,

Jeff

Every day, I open my e-mail knowing that I'm going to find something that will keep my day from being a total loss. This morning, I found a rather somber message from the guy I count on to provide at least one smile on the darkest day, and I still find it in me to smile; not because of the circumstances leading to the writing of the message -- far from -- but because it's good to know there are still people out there who revere life, like you. I can't tell you how sorry I am to hear about the passing of Jimmy. Indeed, it's easy to sit back and become embittered wondering why the world is populated with low-lifes who will live to a ripe old age and continue to be a burden on the rest of us who ask no more than to be able to enjoy life on our own terms. But to go that route is to hand the world over to the low-lifes for it kills the only thing that stands in their way -- love, the love of life.

I wish I could say that I know how you feel, but, thankfully, I don't. I have never lost anyone even somewhat close to me. I don't know if you remember this, but shortly after Alden and I started dating a friend of hers was murdered. I accompanied Alden to the funeral; and to see her young, beautiful woman friend lying there dead filled me with an unexpected rage. I really wanted to vent my anger; but, at the same time, I realized that, while Alden felt the same rage over the senselessness and cruelty of the act, she was consumed by sorrow, and my first priority was to be there for her. The point of this is that death is an inescapable, necessary conclusion to life and, while we may mourn the tragedy of it, it should always serve as a reminder to cherish the time we have with those we love and continue to make room for more loved ones. Knowing you as I do, I know how very much you love life and I'm sure that Jimmy's passing, while it may hurt for a while, will only make you even more firm in your resolve to get as much out of life as you can. You have to, because the whole purpose of death is to ensure life. I suggest that you consider playing a song for your friend in July. I think he would've liked that. And remember, if you need someone to talk to, I'm never more than a phone call or a keyboard away.

Since I didn't get your Monday e-mail until late in the day, I didn't have a chance to respond to it. so let me do so now. Like you, I always thought it was "electric boobs," but now I know it's "electric BOOTS," because the next line mentions suits. But who the hell wears suits made out of "mule hair"?

I do NOT refer to Alden as "Pookie." That was an exaggerated comment flippantly tossed-out to someone who decided to make it an issue. I understand tabloids work in this manner and, to deny it only means that in the next issue you'll see, "Antonio Denies Wife's Nickname--So Who's The Mysterious 'Pookie'?". This is great. Already I've learned to blame the media.

See, this is good training for me should I ever become famous. Truthfully, I pretty much have the standard nicknames for Alden: "Babe," "Sweetie," "Tower of Estrogen," ya know.

While it is true that impending weddings produce undue amounts of stress, they also can produce unbridled elation when members of the bride's family start kicking down thousand dollar checks as wedding presents. Yes, Aunt Mary is now my favorite aunt. Problem is, she won't be able to attend the wedding. Guess I'll have to fix up a plate for her and send her some beer.

Take care buddy and I'll talk to you soon.

Gossip sucks, Jimmy rules. OUT!!

Longfellow

Date: Jun 19
To: Duke
From: Jeff
Subject: Netboy strikes again.

In a world full of people who don't have any idea what to say in difficult times, you, my friend, are a godsend. Thanks for the support and, most of all, the understanding. Are you sure we weren't once connected at the brain and had to be separated? Oh no, wait, it was a connection at the testicles, that's right.

After the initial shock of this whole thing, I don't think it's really hit any of us yet. I did get my first phone call yesterday from a client who said, "I just heard about Jimmy." Finding something to say in this situation is difficult. "Yeah, he was a good guy, blahblahblah...." Our boss had to go to a meeting yesterday for one of Jimmy's projects that he was in the middle of and had to tell them. That would be difficult as well. Then there's all the weird stuff you never thought would be close to you: They have to clean out his office and set aside his personal effects; his brother has to come here from Nebraska to clean out his apartment; and we're gonna have some kind of a local service for the guy. And life goes on.

I AM NOT A TANK!!! I AM NOT A TANK!!!!!!!!!!!!!!!!! Netboy finally called me Monday to play the semifinals of our little tournament. He wanted to play that night, but I was a little broken up by the day's events and agreed to play him last night instead. I showed up, played picture-perfect tennis, went up 6-1 in a "first to ten" series, then Netboy just took the thing over. This guy is a great tennis player. I didn't tank, he just kicked my ass all over the place. Needless to say, I lost 10-7. I'm not happy about it, but Netboy did gush about my "improvement" and said he'd play me any time. He also is signing up for the next level, the 3.5 Summer Ladder, which I am on as well. Do you get the feeling Netboy is to me what Michael Jordan is to the rest of the NBA? What the Super Bowl is to the Broncos? This guy is my

Achilles Heel. Maybe someday I will beat him. I would have yesterday, if he hadn't awaken like Godzilla after a long winter's nap.

I'm glad you've got this media thing figured out. We're gonna need it when we become rich and famous. I'm also impressed that you know exactly who to feed the rumors to in order to get them out of your city and all the way to Colorado. Very impressive, my dear boy. Very impressive indeed. I guess I should have realized I was being set up when said "rumor-passer-on-er" called me. I really should know better. We've been through all of this before, with both the current "rumor-passer-on-er" and with Patty. Hell, at one point back then, you and I were gay and had a little "love-child" named Norman.

My Internet Provider sucks. I tried and tried to get on last night, but no. So, I've sent them a nasty e-mail telling them I am shopping for a new Provider because I'm sick of it. I'll lob you a phone call and let you know when it happens, so your e-mails go to the right place.

Well, *amigo*, it's time to head to the office, which, needless to say, is quite a somber place right about now. We'll be fine. Have a great Wednesday, and thanks for the right words.

Rumors suck, Jimmy Rules!!!

-I am not a tank, I am a Hum-Vee

Date: Jun 19
To: Jeff
From: Anthony
Subject: YES YOU ARE! YES YOU ARE!

You know what song still gets my blood pumpin' like no other? "New Year's Day." Sometimes, I really miss those guys.

Your e-mail wreaks of denial, my friend. You know that when you have your opponent down by a substantial margin, you should finish him off. Do not let him become the unattainable goal, make him your fiercest rival. In other words, don't let him be the Super Bowl and you be the Broncos -- you be the '80s Lakers and let him be the '80s Celtics. That way, you'll finally beat him, and continue to win over the years.

Also, it makes it easier to beat the snot out of him if you think of him as one of the four most-hated teams in history (the other three being Notre Dame, the SF Giants, and the Oakland/Los Angeles Raiders). Hmm, interesting, I seem to hate northern California teams and teams whose mascot is a little Irish guy. Uh oh, you know what that means.

"Mr. Reynoso. Mr. Reynoso. We've heard you have an intense hatred for the Irish. Where does this hatred come from?"

"That is not true, I have no prejudices against the Irish. In fact, a good friend of mine, Jim O'saka, is Irish. So's my other friend, Carol O'lsen. We were in a band that used to perform U2 songs. Gimme a big break, huh?"

And, thus, the next day the headlines read, "Antonio Reveals Identity of Mystery 'Pookie'--Irish Bombshell Carol O'lsen." Then one day on Geraldo: "Anthony, you've dispelled any prejudices against the Irish, but it has since come to light that Jim O'saka is from northern California. Why the intense hatred for northern California?"

By the way, Norman was asking about his "Mommy" again the other day. Got any suggestions?

Yeah, I can imagine that people are still shaken up over Jimmy. But, you are correct when you say "life goes on." It'll take some time, so allow yourself the time necessary. Glad I can be of some small use.

Looks like we're going to take our new windfall de Aunt Mary and buy ourselves a real couch. Alden has a futon, but it's too small for both of us to lounge on. Considering the size of our apartment, it looks like we're going to try for a sectional since it doesn't look like a sofa and love-seat-thang will work too well. This, of course, is fine with me, since you know my affinity for sectional couches. I'm still enjoying the bachelor pad, but starting to yearn for a little more furniture than a chair and a bed. So it'll be good to get Alden in there and let her "fill in the blanks," so to speak.

Yes, time to get a new Provider; but, when you get it, don't "lob" me a call, send it via overhead smash. Perhaps you lack the killer instinct necessary for winning. I have that problem. I never have trouble getting the lead, but I have difficulty closing the thing out. I call this condition "involuntary larynx constriction." Choking, to the layman.

Well, man, guess I'll hang it up for the day. Having dinner at Tony Roma's tonight. Gonna gets me some o' them ribs. CHOMP! You have a good one and we'll talk to you tomorrow.

Involuntary larynx constriction sucks, ribs rule. OUT!!

"How much for the ribs?"

Date: Jun 20
To: Duke
From: Jeff
Subject: Queenie Weenie

Thanks for the advice on The Instinct d'Killer. It is something I definitely don't have a lot of. I get up on a guy, and I start to dilly-dally (now there's a phrase you don't hear much after you leave home) and think about the great victory party and the prizes, cars, and cash ahead; which makes me lazy, which makes me hit the ball flat-footed or take my eye off of the ball (I HATE that); which makes me lose. Then I just get mad at myself, which makes me play even worse. Aah, yes, the psychology of tennis. Did Alden study this in Penguin School?

Ya know, a couple of weeks ago, when Jim and Barb were here, we went to Estes Park for the day. In Estes Park, there's a shop. And in this particular shop, they have Big Beltbuckles of every design you can imagine. Big ol' silver buckles that say "Elvis Lives" or "Broncos Rule" or "Skoal Is Life" or "If You Ain't Drivin' A Monster Truck You Ain't Drivin' Shit." So, I got to thinking, does a huge beltbuckle cover up for deficiencies in other areas?

Then, I remembered that at one time -- now sit down before you read this, so that you don't fall over from laughter -- I used to wear a big ol' beltbuckle, back in high school. I had a beltbuckle that said "Queen" (the rock group, you butthead) and had a weird logo from their *Bicycle Race* album. Of course, I was a pretty big Queen fan back then and was merely supporting my favorite rock-and-roll group. Now, I'm wondering, was I a dork back then? Not that there was ever really a question; I knew by the way the Cool Kids treated me that I was not merely a dork. I was Superdork. But I was trying to be cool. Did other kids have beltbuckles that said "K.C. and the Sunshine Band" or "Disco RULES"? I think they probably did. But I was the only one who had "Queen" on his beltbuckle. Just another example of being different without being bizarre -- back then, anyway.

Come to think of it, I also had the "Steve Miller Band" mirror-logo in my bedroom. And I had the "Cars World Tour" softball-style shirt that was so popular. Remember that? The Cool Kids would show up to school probably once every couple of weeks with souvenirs on their torsos from the previous night's performance by the hottest rock-and-roll bands around. All of us Superdorks would stand around, staring at the Cool Kids, wondering what it would be like to be a Cool Kid, and we would say, "Wow -- you went and saw who?"

"The Who."

"Yeah, Who?"

"The Who, Superdork. Don't you know the Who?"

"Who?"

Eventually, I developed a different taste in music and moved on. I started to wear my "Devolution by Devo" T-shirts to school, which I'm now sure charmed the hell out of everybody. That may have gone over the fine line of bizarre. No wonder I never got laid in high school.

Just thought you'd like to know about the belt-buckle shop. I've been meaning to write the above diatribe for weeks. Norman is actually sleeping through my morning e-mail today, so I can get something done. As far as his "Mommy" goes, tell him she's Alden, and Julie. Yeah, we can scar the kid pretty good with a few mind games. Just like we've done to so many girlfriends. Have an Excellent Thursday, won't you?

Cool Kids Suck, Superdorks RULE!!!!

-Who?

Date: Jun 20
To: Jeff
From: Anthony
Subject: Chaconian Rhapsody

Boy, ya think you know a guy. Before I get too far into this, allow me to answer your question. Yes, my friend, you were a severe dork. But, then again, we all were. I gotta tell you, in a way I'm kinda proud of you, because I think Queen was just a little too "much" for most high school kids to handle; so I applaud you for showing a bit more musical discriminatory taste at such a tender age. I don't know that I'd go so far as to position what amounts to a shield that says "Queen" over the area of my wanka, but it's your world, buddy. I'm just here on vacation.

Truth be known, you were probably the coolest kid around, but that's relative to one's point of view. Let me explain. As we grow older, we view individuality and a willingness to express our views as "cool" traits; as teenagers, we just strive to be part of the group. You seemed to be the weed growing on the outskirts of the garden, which makes you cool in the eyes of adults but a dork in the eyes of your high school brethren. Not only that, they probably thought you were a fag.

But since you've given me the best laugh I've had in weeks, allow me to tell you MY belt buckle story. Basically, I didn't have one. I didn't wear belts, because my corduroy pants fit pretty well and I didn't tuck in my OP and Lightning Bolt shirts. I had a belt, but I only used it when I worked down at the food court in the mall. In high school, I walked that very thin line between being one of the "in" crowd and dorkdom. Realistically, I belonged in the dork category; but I let enough of the jocks and cheerleaders cheat off my tests to where they accepted me as some sort of unusual pet. Yes, each day was a constant struggle for me as I tried to answer the question, "Am I happy as supreme ruler of the dorks, or do I want to be the cool kids' doormat?" Never really answered that question.

Anyway, when it came time for senior pictures, my belt broke and I didn't have another, so I called my cousin to ask if I could borrow his. On the way to the photographer's studio, I picked up the belt only to discover that it had a big buckle with the cover of Van Halen's second album on it. So, even though it never made the yearbook, I actually have a senior photo of me with a Van Halen belt buckle. And I wasn't into Van Halen. Now, the interesting part of the whole thing was that all the "cool" people who saw the picture loved my belt buckle. All the dorks laughed, because they knew it wasn't mine. And, for the first time in my life, I considered the concept of individuality. So, I'm grateful to all my dork buddies out there for helping me learn to just be myself, which is all I want to be now. Personally, I would've worn a JOURNEY buckle.

Tonight should prove to be interesting. Our company softball team has a game against my former employers. Grudge match!! Actually, we stand

201

about as much chance of winning as Marge Schott stands of winning Miss Congeniality in the Miss America pageant, but what the hell. It'll be good to see the guys I used to work with. Unfortunately, none of the people responsible for my untimely demise from that office will be there to meet with any well-timed bad hops. Not that I'm bitter.

So, I will end here. Have a good one and I'll talk to you soon.
Stupid questions suck, Journey rules. OUT!!

What?

Date: Jun 20
To: Duke
From: Jeff
Subject: Canciones de mi Belt Buckle.

Ya know, it's been approximately 15 years since I last pondered the Cool versus Superdork problem; and I think that you, you of the always-knowing-what-to-say, you of the incredible brilliance and insight, you have solved for me the biggest riddle of adolescence: Cool versus Dork. We all know that at the age of adolescence there is no middle ground between Cool and Dork. We were either one or the other. It wasn't until we had our own little group of Dork friends, who thought we were Kinda Cool, that we started to feel at least slightly comfortable in our pimply-faced, erections-at-all-times-of-the-day, not-ever-knowing-what-to-say-to-girls, uncomfortable bodies of ours. But I digress.

What I really want to say is that, in your latest batch of e-mail-wisdom, you mentioned something that really turned that little light bulb on in the far reaches of my brain. You mentioned that you did not tuck your Lightning Bolt shirts into your pants. And I finally realize, 15 years too late, that was why I was never ever ever Cool. Because I *did* tuck my Lightning Bolt shirts into my pants, and I did wear a belt, and it did have the word "Queen" on it. I never figured out that the Cool Kids were walking around campus with their Lightning Bolt shirts hanging out of their pants and, thus, were Cool. Now that I think about it, that was exactly the difference. Of course, I made up for my belt-wearing ways in later years. It is rumored that in my adult life (some would say I have not yet reached that stage) I didn't even own a belt (outside of a wear-to-work belt) until I met The Great One....

Lest you think, young man, that I was always the "weed of individuality," let me assure you this was not always the case. In high school, at least in junior year, I wanted more than anything to be Cool. Senior year, it didn't matter, because I was a senior and I was going to college and I quite frankly didn't give a shit what anybody thought; high school was now beneath me, because I was going to college, dammit! But junior year I would have killed to be Cool. So, I took my 1974 Ford Maverick (which I just recently had been given official government permission to drive), gave it a dandy new

202

dark-brown paint job, put some awesome orange and yellow pinstripes on it (all by myself!), bought some Cragar rims and some raised-white-letter tires, and hung out with a guy who had a similarly souped-up Vega. All the Cool Kids drove around in hot rod Mustangs and Bigfoot-type trucks; so I tried to take a '74 Ford Maverick and make it as Cool as a hot rod Mustang -- all 200 cubic inches of V-6 engine of it. I covered the little windows behind the driver's windows with all kinds of Lightning Bolt and Ocean Pacific stickers; I even had a sticker that said "I.B.", which, as you know, stood for Imperial Beach, the beach near my house at the time. I even tried to tint the windows of the car, but ended up with dark windows I couldn't see through because of all the air bubbles between the tint and the glass.

I now believe that the deadly combination of trying to make a '74 Ford Maverick Cool and hanging with a SuperDuperDork who tried to make a Chevy Vega Cool made for a very bad year for me. The Cool Kids wouldn't even look at me; in fact, they would drive by my house in their Mustangs, point and laugh and offer to race me. The Dorks thought I had completely sold out and, thus, avoided me like the plague. So, I was stuck hanging out with a guy who had a Red Vega that was raised three feet in the back to display his grotesquely oversized raised-white-letter tires. Ugh.

Of course, by the next year, I had realized the error of my ways and returned to being "Jeff the Superdork." I joined the newspaper staff as News Editor, removed all the tint and Lightning Bolt stickers from the Maverick, and blew off the Vega dork, who, as it turns out, later joined the army. He didn't show at the 10-year high school reunion, but I was ready to talk about our Superdorkdom and our attempt to transform ourselves into Cool Kids with him if he had.

You know what? The more I write about it, the more I completely understand why I never got laid in high school. What 16-year-old girl is going to go out with a pimply-faced, Maverick-driving Superdork who shows up at her door with his Lightning Bolt shirt tucked into his trousers and his "Queen" beltbuckle proudly displayed? Exactly.

Enough reminiscing for one day. Have a great weekend, won't you? I'll probably be working. The passing of Jimmy has left a huge hole in the office that has to filled mostly by one lucky Jeff Chacon, and we're still bringing work in the door. ~Sigh~ Whaddya gonna do?

Vega-s suck, The Weed of Individuality RULES!!!

-Dandelion

Date: Jun 21
To: Jeff
From: Anthony
Subject: The ball ain't soft

203

"Hey Lisa, who's that guy in the brown Maverick with the orange and yellow pinstripes?"

"Are you kidding, Candy? That's Jeff Chacon, and if you think his car is hot, wait'll he gets outta the car."

"Is that a Queen belt buckle?"

"Yeah, and ain't it cool that he tucks in his Lightning Bolt shirt so he can show it off?"

"I.B.? Does that mean he's from Imperial Beach?"

"Yeah, that really cool place three blocks from the border where all the FBI and narcotics agents hang out."

"God, Candy, he is getting me SOOOO hot!! Oooooh, OW!..."

"What happened?"

"I don't know. I think I'm sterile."

"Yeah, he has the same effect on me."

What a sad loss. Hello, I'm Roy McClure. You may remember me from such self-health films as, "Annoyed at Hemorrhoids" and "Take That, Gonorrhea!" Today, I'm here to address a particularly nasty problem among the teenage women of the population, "Spontaneous Sterilization." The cause of the problem? Cool Dudes. The only way to become immune to the powers of the Cool Dude is to know the warning signs and stay away. First, American cars with customized paint jobs adorned with citrus color pinstriping. Second, the "uptight look" created by tucking in casual shirts. Uncomfortable for him, hazardous for you. Third, fancy platter-sized belt-buckles. Nothing but badges for Satan's agents of evil. By recognizing these signs, you can avoid the Cool Dude and keep your womanhood intact.

I dunno, my man, I just can't see it. But don't despair, in some ways getting older is good, because it lets you rectify past image mistakes. Now, you are a confident young professional who doesn't base his entire image on having a really groovy car (or a Ford Maverick) and a really big...uh, belt buckle.

So, last night our company team went up against the company team I used to play for. We lost, but we managed to hold our own against their far superior team. I'd like to be able to report the score, but, unfortunately, we let one of our accountants be the scorekeeper. Never let an accountant handle numbers if there isn't a calculator or adding machine nearby. For one thing if you ask him/her, "What's the score?" he/she tells you something along the lines of, "We owe them five runs."

Today, at lunch I went to one of those fast-food Chinese joints. I particularly enjoyed the part where the Oriental girl behind the cash register yelled to the back, "Kung pao chicken, por favor." I always suspected that the ancient Chinese secret to cooking was, "Get some Mexican to do it." On the way back to work, I almost saw two Lincolns go head on. Can't you just imagine the argument that would've resulted? The cops show up and pull their guns on two eighty-year olds. "All right, put down the cane! And you, drop the walker. Oops, sorry."

I am ready for the weekend. Unfortunately, it's looking kinda dull. But what the hell, it beats working. You guys have a tremendous weekend and, if you go by any tuxedo shops, why not get measured? Check ya later.

Spontaneous sterilization sucks, Mexican Kung pao chicken rules. OUT!!

Antonio Chin

Chapter 20
Stair Diving

Date: Jun 23
To: Duke
From: Jeff
Subject: GET A HAIRCUT!!!!!

I'll get measured soon, I promise. In fact, it's on my "to do" list, so it will get done in the next couple of days. Should I just e-mail you with the results (which may be a little, umm, enhanced in certain areas, if you know what I mean), or do I have to regular mail you with the official stamped and signed copy of the official "Tux Measurers of America" results card?

And, yes, we are a mere four weeks away from your day of infamy. Still going through with it, I presume? Marriage is a good thing. It keeps you away from young female architects. It gives you a nice person (hopefully) to go home to after a long day of slaving over a hot desk, someone to steal the covers from on a cold winter's night, someone with whom to share your dreams, hopes, and desires; someone to drink beer with on Friday nights, even if she is a chick; and marriage keeps your house from becoming a quivering smelly pit of dirty underwear and bad decorating (women simply have a better eye for interior design). In short, marriage keeps a man sane.

It's funny how people treat you when they're under the impression, whether true or false, that you've got *dinero*. Take, for example, last Friday. I went to see a banker about possible loans for the Sanitarium Purchase. The banker woman obviously thought I was the man with the money, because I hadn't told her yet that I don't have any cash; I was merely stumping for the man with the cash. So, I showed up with my long hair (badly in need of a haircut) and my denim shirt (being Friday and all), sporting the "Country Club Yuppie Hunkamuffin With Long Hair" look, and this woman was treating me like I was The Shit. After all, we're talking about buying half-a-million bones worth of former Looney Bin here; I'll bet she gets some serious chump change and an "attaboy" from her boss if she reels me in So, I was getting the "Mr. Chacon, Sir" treatment, I was talking her out of all kinds of stupid fees, and I was getting the "we can probably negotiate with you on that" treatment all day long. It was all quite funny, because basically I was just practicing my limited acting skills.

The real hilarious thing was that after we concluded our business and were walking out of her office, in a great old mid-rise building downtown, I noticed a set of cool looking circular stairs leading down to somewhere and I said, "Say, Ms. Jones, where do those stairs lead?" Don't ask me why I asked; sometimes, I'm just curious. She replied, "I don't know, Lord Master Of My Universe. I've never been down there. Why don't we have a look?" "That would be great, Ms. Jones. Ladies first." So, she headed down the stairs, and I followed. Just as I neared the bottom step, I heard this "Budd-ud-ud-ummm." I looked over, and Ms. Jones had not noticed there were another couple of steps leading from the lower landing to the actual floor. She had fallen down the steps, and, at this moment, was lying on the floor, her papers all over the place, completely flustered, face red, the whole nine yards. I rushed over to make sure she was okay, and she brushed off the whole thing. "Uh, jeez, Mr. Chacon, I didn't watch where I was going....I'm leaving a bad impression on you, aren't I, Mr. Chacon?"

At that point, I remembered an incident from my childhood when I was riding down my hilly street on my bicycle and I noticed a cute young lass who I thought might want to be impressed with my prowess at handling the bicycle. I started to show off my prowess, only to run into a low fence in front of a house at the bottom of the hill, hurdling myself over the bike and fence and onto the lawn of the house with a sickening "thud." This was perhaps the most embarrassing moment of my life (at that time) and my first glimpse into just how much trouble women really are. Anyway, remembering this, I tried to calm Ms. Jones, but she would have none of it. "I'm really sorry, Mr. Chacon. I really made a bad impression on you." Jeez, it was like I was somebody important or something. Do all people with *dinero* get "the treatment" like this? I'm just a regular guy!!!

Anyway, there's a strong possibility that the Looney Bin project will move forward without me. I'm starting to think this may not be a good idea; because the reality is, it's a bit expensive and it would be hard to make rents from the beginning. How does $1,400 a month sound to live in a place where Jeffrey Dahmer probably belonged? Exactly.

How was your weekend? Yesterday both The Great One and I went to work; she to do *actual* work and me to clean up my office. I was starting to feel "I'm losing control" symptoms and felt that my office needed a good cleaning in order for me to feel comfortable heading into the hell that will be this summer. Bosses #1 and #2 were both there cleaning out Jimmy's office, which was kind of weird. In fact, I asked Boss #2, "Isn't this kind of weird?" and he replied, "No, because when I was in 'Nam, I had to pick up unidentified parts of bodies of unidentified people and put them all into a big freezer." This made me realize what an easy life I've had.

Well, have a great Monday. I might try a new sport this afternoon: Rollerblading. I've always wanted to try it, and Cindy (my new cellmate at work) does it, so we've tentatively scheduled to try it out today after work. I'll let you know how it goes in tomorrow's entry....

Bad decorating sucks, vacations RULE!!!

-Money Man

Date: Jun 24
To: Jeff
From: Anthony
Subject: Freedom of de-press

Yes, once you have your "measurements," just e-mail me and I'll handle them for you.

Well, hell, thanks for getting Monday off to such a gloomy start. Between Ms. Jones doing her stair diving (by the way, most people don't know this, but this sport actually was invented by our good buddy Randy the night of my 28th birthday), you and your handlebar hurdling, your boss and his *Apocalypse Now* mentality, and the thought of paying 1,400 bucks a month to share an apartment with the ghosts of lunatics past, the June gloom just became the June gloom-and-doom. Not to mention the fact that on this end, we lost our first softball game of the year Friday night (naturally, it was a playoff game; so, in order to win the championship, we have to sweep a triple-header next Friday). I had four beers on Saturday night and woke up Sunday feeling like hell.

Then the moving van with all of Alden's stuff showed up. The question of the ages has nothing to do with life's purpose, Stonehenge, extra-testicle beings, or whether Elvis is truly dead; no sir; the question of the ages is, how the hell did she manage to get all this shit in a one-bedroom apartment? Thanks to all the added weight, our second-floor apartment is now on the first floor, and our downstairs neighbors should arrive in China sometime tomorrow. Actually, it wasn't THAT bad, but the downstairs neighbors did come up to inquire about the strange bow in their ceiling. Yes, the little Packus Ratticus will be home today and I can't wait to sleep with...uh, see her.

I must disagree with one aspect of your "pros of marriage" list. Prior to Alden's arrival, my home was not a "quivering smelly pit of dirty underwear," but I'm guessing it will now become one within about, oh, two hours. You also forgot the best part about being married: it gives you someone to drink beer with on Fridays and you don't go home alone anymore.

Alden's moving-in this weekend allowed me the opportunity to meet a "real man." Now, I thought I had earned "real man" status when I went for a two-mile run just prior to my 90-minute FREE tennis lesson Saturday (one of the amenities to living at a place called "Racquet Club" heh heh heh), but, after Sunday morning, I realize that I'm nothing more than an uneaten cornflake left in a pool of milk all day. The moving guy showed up with all of Alden's stuff. Yes, one guy. There was only one because his partner got another job at the last minute. So, this one guy carried a full-sized bed, an oak desk, two dressers, a TV, a kitchen table, and at least forty boxes upstairs -- BY HIMSELF!! He wouldn't let me help him. Not only that, he did it in under two hours. This after he moved another guy that morning at 6:00 a.m.

So, I spent a pretty humble Sunday recovering from my four-beer hangover and questioning my manhood.

Rollerblading, huh? That's starting to catch on pretty big around here. In fact, the basketball courts we used to play basketball on at University City High School are now crowded with guys on Rollerblades playing roller hockey. So, I figure we'll give you about a week on the blades before you want a stick. I tried blading once, but it killed my ankles. Think I'll stick to tennis. The guy who gave me the lesson the other day reminded me an awful lot of that guy who does the painting on TV -- Bob Ross. "So, Anthony, what we want is to just meet the ball with a happy little volley. Just sort of get the racquet out in front of you and just tap it. We don't need a lot, just a little tap, tap, tap. See how nicely that works? And remember to breathe." This, of course, went over well until he said, "All right, Anthony, what we want to do now is to have you hit a couple of serves. Now, let's just take our time, think about the shot, and just ease it over the net...no, no, Anthony. Much too angry, much too angry. Happy little serves..." He did seem to help me with my backhand though, which is where I need the most help.

Right, guess I'll be toddling off. Have a great day and I'll talk at you *mañana*.

Happy little serves suck, having a Packus Ratticus for a pet rules. OUT!!

Soggy cornflake

Date: Jun 24
To: Duke
From: Jeff
Subject: Shadow Dancing

Sorry about the gloomy times you find yourself in. My e-mail was meant to cheer you up and make you laugh at the follies of humanity. Instead, you took it as "gloom and doom." Okay, let me try again. One of the funniest things I have ever experienced happened this evening as I was attempting to Rollerblade for the first time:

I'm whizzing around Washington Park at speed-of-light speeds in my shorts and University of California at Santa Cruz Banana Slugs T-shirt (in honor of Pookie's arrival, of course). After a lap or so around this gigantic park, I'm thinking that Mr. Happy needs to be drained. So, I'm looking around for a bathroom, looking around for a bathroom, looking around....aha!! There's one!! Oh, but wait, it's a porta-potty. Ugh. And there's a little plastic ramp leading up to it. Ugh. And I'm wearing Rollerblades. Shit. I climb my way to the top of this little ramp, open the door, and somehow climb into the porta-potty, thinking "Oh, if only Anthony could see me now." (This was perhaps the most precarious piss I've ever taken, save for that night long ago on the cliffs above Port San Luis, when you and I stood side by side, drunk as

209

bloody hell, draining ourselves, and that dude came towards us and disappeared into the hole we were peeing into.) Anyway, I'm in the porta-potty, Mr. Happy in hand, preparing for drainage, and I start to roll all around the thing. I grab the toilet paper dispenser, which is insecurely fastened to the wall of the thing. My darkest fears emerge: "Can you imagine? One wrong move right now, and I'm out in the park parking lot, on my back, Mr. Happy in hand, my head cracked open, one hundred billion people standing around laughing their heads off. How will I ever be able to face society again?" I'm hanging on for dear life, trying to finish the business at hand, trying even harder to not slip on the plastic floor. Jeez. Somehow, I finished up, rewrapped my package nice and neat, got out, and was able to return to my whizzing.

Hey, let your neighbors down below know they will probably need a structural engineer real soon to take care of that bowed ceiling. And, no, that floor was not designed to take the weight of all of Alden's stuff. By the way, your relationship with Alden sounds very similar to my relationship with The Great One, with one small catch: *I* am the slob in my relationship, and Alden is the slob in your relationship. Verrrrrrry interesting, no? We'll address that issue later, because I'm not quite ready to live up to the fact that I'm a slob.

I made a mistake today. The Great One lately has been calling me "Shaun" because my hair is long enough to qualify me for the "Andy Gibb/Shaun Cassidy Lookalike Contest" at the local retro-bar. Today, I accidentally told somebody at work. And guess what? Now, I'm "Shaun" at work as well. Shit. I have nicknames for everybody else at the office, but up until now I've avoided nicknames for myself except for the usual *El Jefe* or *Señor Almost Excelante.* Now, I'm "Shaun." Let this be a lesson to all you young 'uns out there. Keep the home nicknames at home, 'cuz once the vultures at work find an inch, they take a mile.

This gig thing is going to be more fun than farting in a bathtub full of beer. I'm looking forward to it immensely. One day, we'll tell our grandkids that "we had a band, made it big for a while (a couple of days), decided we couldn't stand each other (the drummer, anyway), broke up and went our separate ways -- then, when the worldwide demand could no longer be ignored, we reunited for a single solitary show that forever will be remembered (in our minds only)."

Well, it's time to do a little work, make a little love, get down tonight, get down tonight, baby. Enjoy this Tuesday, won't you?

Precarious Pissing sucks, Rollerblading RULES!!!

-No Shaun

Date: Jun 25
To: Jeff
From: Anthony
Subject: Period of adjustment

"Quick, quick, call an ambulance. Shaun Cassidy just Rollerbladed backward out of the porta-potty and broke his head open!"

"Is he all right?"

"I dunno, he just keeps mumbling 'Da Doo Ron Ron.'"

"Oh, my God, what's that in his hand?"

"Must be his Hardy Boy."

That's all I have to say about that. One question though: if you were "whizzing around Washington Park," why did you need a porta-potty (a.k.a. touring toilet)?

Yeah, Shaun, isn't it a bitch when people jump on a nickname and exploit it? Like, for instance, rumor got out that I call my woman "Pookie," which I do not, and now some people continue to use that name. Sucks, don't it, Shaun? Really stinks, don't it, Shaun? Makes you wish they'd fuckin' stop, don't it, Shaun? So, maybe we can work out some kind of a deal, eh, Shaun? Let me know if this works for you, okay, Shaun? By the way, I can't imagine your hair looking anything like Shaun Cassidy's, no matter how long it gets. I mean, when it was really long, you looked like the guy on Dutch Boy Paint. Could be worse though. When my hair got real long, people called me "Rick Springfield."

Sorry if I gave the impression I was gloomy yesterday. Nothing could be further from the truth. I just thought your e-mail addressed some gloomy topics. Actually, I was in a great mood yesterday, because Alden came home for good. Which means I finally got to utter the words I've longed to say for some time. I walked in the door and yelled, "Honey, I'm home." Now, I know you're an old pro at this, because you even had a cat named "Honey" while in college (clever boy that you are); but it was all terribly new for me and it felt wonderful to walk in the door and know she was there. Which is not to say that the whole transition is going to be a piece o' cake. Alden brings a lot of baggage into a relationship, literally. So she's going to be busy over the next few days putting stuff away.

I think we'll both need some time to get used to living with someone else. For instance, she's used to eating three well-balanced meals a day; whereas, I'm used to small breakfasts, huge lunches, and a snack for dinner. But the biggest problem we face is her tendency to hoard stuff, as opposed to my tendency to keep everything free of clutter. I think if we can work through this, everything will be fine. It's a very shocking transition to know that Alden's home and she's not going back. I'm so used to seeing her during weekends and vacations that it's very difficult to believe I actually had to work today instead of staying home with her. But the fact of the matter is that she's home now, and I now have a partner to help me battle life's little wars. I'm about as happy as I've ever been. Know that Alden will soon be my wife takes me into unexplored regions of The Happiness Wilderness.

We must never tell anyone we broke up the band because we hated each other. We must say "creative differences."

I shall draw Tuesday to a close now. I have a softball game tonight; but, afterwards, I will once again know the exhilaration of coming home to my woman. I think I could get used to this. Have a great day, buddy.

Horrific nicknames suck, exploring the Happiness Wilderness rules. OUT!!

Parker Stevenson

Date: Jun 26
To: Jeff
From: Anthony
Subject: Blue Dots and Buttheads

Ah, Wednesday. Having worked out Monday and played softball last night, tonight will be my night of leisure. Well, as much leisure as one can have when the house is wall-to-wall boxes. We were considering going shopping for a couch tonight, but the place is a mess and we need to restore some order. This is fine with me, because physically I'm a wreck. We had a game last night against the biggest bunch of anal-retentive softball Nazis I've ever encountered. We had the unfortunate luck of playing on an all-grass field, so the first thing they did was doctor it up by placing little cones everywhere to "designate the infield from the outfield." Then the game started and one of our guys fouled it over the fence and the pitcher asked us for a new ball. When our coach gave it to him, the guy looked at it and said, "Don't you have a Blue Dot?" "Uh, no, but sounds like you're kinda familiar with Red Square." Needless to say, this was not a fun game. We're not a very good team at all, but we do like to have fun, and these guys just weren't into it. They won, 18-8, but I overheard one of them complaining, "God, we didn't even score 20." So, if their basis for winning is scoring 20 runs, then I feel pretty good about the fact that we held them below that. My guess is that after the game they probably had to run laps, go to the batting cages, and succumb to more hypnotic propaganda and steroid injections to enhance their performance to ensure that they will no longer be humiliated and the pride will be returned to their glorious empire. As for me, I don't know what I did last night, but I have an awful pain in my side like I pulled an abdominal muscle or something. Oops, forgot, gotta have a muscle to pull it.

As stated, the apartment is SLOWLY taking shape. This morning was rather comical. I was trying to make my lunch and brew some coffee and, because Alden rearranged the kitchen, I couldn't find anything. So, I open up the fridge, get the honey-roasted turkey breast, and now I can't find the bread.

"Loo-see, where's da bread?"

"It's in the pantry, dear."

"Loo-see, where's de sanweech bags?"

"In the cupboard, dear."

"Whish cubbard?"

212

"The cupboard by the dishwasher."

"Where's de dishwasher?"

"Behind the brown box that says 'bedroom stuff.'"

"Aye, aye, aye. *Mira el pinche box que dice* 'Stuff de bedroom'." So, tonight, we're going to put stuff away. Afterwards, she's going to give me a tour of the place so I don't starve to death in search of food.

If you will check your calendar, dear boy, you will discover that today is June 26. Not a particularly significant day in the grand scheme of things, but it does fall precariously close to the first of July; and that is when the guys at the tuxedo shop have to have your measurements. Be forewarned, I am prepared to make up numbers in the event you don't provide me the info requested. And, by the time I get through with you, you'll look like a Shar-pei or whatever those dogs are called who have the wrinkly skin. Either that or we'll take the other route: we'll all be entertained as you pop the buttons off your tuxedo from the Michael J. Fox collection. I will say no more about the subject.

A potential problem has risen its ugly head. Alden's parents have both been really sick for a while so Alden's had to run errands for them. Last night, she starts complaining that she's not feeling well. Thus, following the logical order of things, if she gets sick, I can't be too far behind. I'm guessing it'll hit right around July 17 and be at its worst between the 18th and the 20th. After just starting to feel better, I'll get on a plane to Hawaii which will only re-aggravate the problem. This I totally can see happening.

So, I'm guessing your Provider is showing off its incompetence again. I'll stop here and, if I hear from you later, address your message if necessary. Take it easy.

Incompetent Providers suck, holding softball Nazis under 20 rules.

Desi

Date: Jun 25
To: Domestic Man
From: Jeff
Subject: Michelin man in black.

Honey, I'm home.

Rick, uh, Rick, this is Shaun. Hey, listen, I was thinking, maybe you and I could hit the tour circuit together this year. I mean, Boston and Cheap Trick, Alice Cooper and the Scorpions, they're all touring, why not us? We could call it the "Hair today, Rogaine tomorrow" tour. You could play "Jessie's Girl" and I'll play "Da Doo Ron Ron." Then you'll play....uh....another of your fabulous hits, then I'll play "Da Doo Ron Ron" again. Then you'll play....uh....another of your what I'm sure are many fabulous hits, then I'll play a Reggae version of "Da Doo Ron Ron." Then you can play an industrial/punk/metal version of "Jessie's Girl" and so on, and so on, and so on.....

Shit, dude, if you lived with me for all those years, sleeping on my couch nonetheless, you should have NO problem dealing with the hoarding tendencies of your little Latté of Love; because I am the King of Hoarding. You know what it is, don't you? It's because people like Alden and myself grew up on the poor side of the tracks; we never had a penny or a Rollerblade to our name. So now, whenever we get something, we hang on to it. You and Julie, well, you damn rich kids, you. Able to toss things out without even thinking about it, just like that. I mean, c'mon. Everybody knows that the 1988 issue of Rolling Stone with Duran Duran on the cover is going to be priceless someday, don't they?

I realized today, a day later, that a first-time 'blader (as the Cool Kids would have called it) looks remarkably like the Michelin Man, only in black. They gave me so many protective pads to wear that pretty soon I was hoping to have enough room to breath through. Black protective pads for wrists, knees, elbows, butt, Johnson, Swanson, etcetera etcetera. Yeah, I pretty much took to 'blading like yuppies take to Lattés.

I'm extremely happy to read of your current conjugal bliss. Yes, it is a beautiful thing to come home to a woman whom you consider to be your partner, even if she is a little cranky from time to time. This you will have to put up with; but she must also put up with your crankiness, which, if I recall correctly, you handle by going directly to the TV, do not pass go, do not collect $200, and watching a sporting event, whatever may be on, be it hockey, football, motocross, badminton, or bowling. Anyway, may you both enjoy these times together.

Right. So, another Tuesday is in the books. One day closer to retirement. Have a GREAT Wednesday, and tell Alden (notice I didn't call her "Pookie?") congratulations on graduating from college and having the foresight to secure her future and move in with you. It's a good move on her part. And yours, as well.

Reunion Tours Suck, Swanson RULES!!

-Mi Vida Mas Fina

Date: Jun 26
To: Domestic Man
From: Jeff
Subject: Looney Bin Euthanasia

.   Uh, yeah, I've got some blue dots, some red hearts, some green clovers, some yellow moons, and some new blue diamonds!! Blue Dots? Is that like, uh, a special kind of softball or something?

Here's Duke. Here's Duke Domesticated. Any questions?

Ya know, and don't think I'm into all of this holistic medicine crap or anything, but if you start to think NOW that you're going to be sick on July 18th or 20th, then you *will* be sick on those days. The power of positive thinking, my dear boy, must never be underestimated. Eat right, exercise, and take One A Day. Because you have a gig to play and a tennis match to lose, and I will not take any excuses for either. Oh, and, uh, there's a little event called a "weeding" or something that will also involve you around that time. So eat your Wheaties, young man, because the world needs you to be healthy.

I have eliminated two sources of minor headaches: I pulled the plug on the Looney Bin Lofts and I have a new Provider. As far as the Looney Bin Lofts go, my partners (The Great One and Boss #1) both agree that trying to get $1,400 a month out of a lunatic tenant would not be easy. Can you imagine?

"Look, man, can you see the colors?"

"Yeah, Charlie, do you have the rent?"

"Hey, man, The Great And Powerful Mizithra is here!! He's here!! And he's going to kill us all!!"

"Yeah, Charlie, mizithra, cheddar, monterey jack, whatever. Where's my rent?"

And I do have a new Provider, but since I have not had the chance to try it out and see if it's legit, I remain on the old screwed-up Provider for the time being. Look for a new address by Monday.

Look, man, my tux measurements are 30" waist, 14" (each) biceps, built like a hunkamuffin, and tall, dark and handsome. Whaddya expect? I'll get them to you by Monday, don't you worry. I wouldn't want to be the constant butt of the jokes at the wedding, because that's *your* role....

Hello again, and welcome to "Cooking with Anthony." Filling in for Anthony tonight is Mr. Jeff Chacon. "Hey, kids!! Tonight, we're gonna make some hamburgers. First, you get yourself a big ol' slab of ground up cow. Then you take whatever spices you like that you have in your kitchen there and you sprinkle them all over the cow. Then, you form little balls out of the cow, each about the size of a Blue Dot Softball. Then, you flatten them out and throw them on the grill which hopefully doesn't have any more burning human hair on it......"

Yeah, we made some of your burgers Monday night. Mmmmm good!!!! I've been making them that way ever since you and I were roommates so long ago, and people love 'em -- especially, The Great One. Thanks for showing me the burger light, dude; although admittedly I do put more condoms...uh, condiments on them than you. I seem to have gotten a handle on this barbecue thing. Propane + match = poof!! And, if it don't light, stand back about 20 feet, light the match, and fling it like a horseshoe right into the 'cue.

Well, it's time to go relax and prepare for another day. Tomorrow, we (the office) go to Jimmy's service in the afternoon. You know, we seem to be the Office of the Damned. First, our Office Manager's husband died, then

215

Jimmy, then our receptionist went home possibly for good because her MS is acting up. We're all wondering just when the good things are going to start. I've also noticed a bit of "Jimmy Syndrome" lately. First, Jimmy passed away, then out of the blue my other buddy Jimmy called me from San Diego; then we hired a temp named Jimmy to answer the phones, which is a bit creepy, especially when he answers the phones, "Hello, Engineers of Colorado, this is Jimmy." Finally, today, I went and got my haircut by Jimmy, my usual haircutter. Coincidence? I think not. And, yes, I no longer resemble Shaun Cassidy in any way. In fact, I pretty much resemble an intellectual Dolph Lundgren right now. You know, buff and tan, yet smart and sassy.

All right, all right. I'll knock it off. I know when it's time to quit, and it's time to quit right.....about......now. Have a great Thursday, won't you? And look for yesterday's message today, because I've already sent it out.

Predicting your own sickness sucks, yellow moons RULE!!!

-Silly Rabbit

Date: Jun 27
To: Jeff
From: Anthony
Subject: Chairman of the Hoard

I think the biggest difference between the kind of hoarding you and Alden do is that you hoard shit like records, games, goofy books, toys, etcetera. Alden hoards stuff like Jell-O molds, candles, fish bowls, CLOTHES, stuff that doesn't interest me in the least. Fish bowl? Where the hell did this come from and why? She didn't have fish in Santa Cruz. Although, I'm thinking that if we wash it out, give it a new layer of rocks, and stick one of those little deep-sea divers in, we can probably find some fool fish to pay $1,400 a month for the place. Can't you just see me shaking down some fish for rent?

"Uh, Mr. Fish, you're late on the rent again."

"Ya know, Mr. Reynoso, lately I've been hearing weird noises coming from the bottom of the bowl."

"Oh, that's probably just the ghost of some crazy fish who was incarcerated here when it was a looney bowl. Now, where's my rent?"

"Can I pay you tomorrow? I just lost my job."

"Yeah, what did you do?"

"I taught school." (Ba dum bum)

"Yeah well, if I don't get my money soon, you'll be sleeping with the humans." (Ba dum bum)

As to growing up poor, I would remind you that Alden grew up in Solana Beach, while I was raised in Santa Maria. 'Nuff said.

Yes, I was taken aback yesterday when I called you and heard "Engineers of Colorado, this is Jimmy." Kind of an eerie feeling, ya know.

Really sorry to hear about the misfortunes that have befallen your company of late. But don't YOU go and do yourself an injury. You have a gig to play and a tennis match to regret ever showing up for. See, if this were a boxing match, I could incorporate the latest boxing "head game" and say, "I like Jeff Chacon. He's so cute. I think after the match I'll let him come live with me and he can be my girl." Having seen no less than three boxers employ this tactic in recent months, I'm left to wonder who the hell came up with this stupid shit. Fortunately, the last guy who said it, Roberto Duran, got his ass waxed by Hector Camacho, so maybe this kind of rhetoric will stop. So stupid! Incidentally, what kind of perverse society do we live in where people actually arrange fights between senior citizens? Anyway, don't worry about me. I'll be raring to go for both the gig and the match and anything else you have in mind, Sweetie.

Mmm burgery. Yum, a nice plump piece of cooked bovine flesh sounds really decent about now. I can still remember the one time I cooked on a propane BBQ. It was actually in Denver. It had been a hard winter and none of us were working, so there was very little money. So, when we all got jobs, we decided to celebrate with steaks and the only way to eat celebratory steak is barbecued. Unfortunately, the day we were to BBQ it was snowing like hell. However, nothing, I mean NOTHING stops me when I want to barbecue. So there I was, up to my knees in snow, barbecuing in a blizzard. As a dumb Californian, this was just one of the reasons why the locals thought I was nuts. That and the fact that I was actually looking forward to the first time I could shovel the walk.

So, I is off. Have a splendid day, and I'll talk to you tomorrow. Once again, my regards to Jimmy and his family.

Unimaginative boxing smack sucks, barbecue rules. OUT!!

"Macho" Camacho

Chapter 21
Jeffstock

Date: Jun 27
To: Domestic Man
From: Jeff
Subject: Dancing Naked In The Rain

I can see into your future, young man, and it involves goldfish. Can't you see that Alden is setting you up for a future of fish as pets? That's why she's collecting fish bowls, duh. And, after that, she'll want a bunny.

Let's get one thing straight, just for the record: If for some stupid reason I ever have to graduate from this life into whatever Heaven the next one may bring, and if my friends and relatives choose to have a service to come to closure about the whole thing, *you're* in charge. I have one and only one demand for you: Do NOT hold my service in a church. Nossir. Religion has its place in life and all; but if I'm gone and you all are going to get together because of it, it better be a party of epic proportions. I mean, today's service for Jimmy was great, and I feel a good amount of closure, and I met some of his wonderful family and friends; but during the thing, I felt like it was a sales pitch for the Lord Above. All this talk about "Jimmy was great blahblahblah and you should all take Jesus into your lives." Yeah, yeah, yeah. We know. If I'm gone, you all better get together near an ocean, preferably the Pacific; or on a mountain top, preferably in the Rocky Mountain Range; or at Red Rocks, and have a whale of a good time. Tell stories about me, like the time I hit myself in the head with the guitar three or four times in a single setting; and get some great bands or singers. Live it up. Get yourself a keg of Railyard, or -- if possible -- some Jeffbrew, and get drunk. Take off all your clothes, dance around naked in the rain. It'll be "Jeffstock." That's how I want you to celebrate my graduation. Additionally, The Great One and I have recently had this discussion about what would be done with the body if either one of us bails out prematurely. She wants to be cremated. I would like to be cremated, too, and have my ashes incorporated into the veneer of a very nice guitar that you or somebody else would keep, cherish, and play on a daily basis. This would make me incredibly happy. I realize it's a morbid topic, but have you given much thought to what we would do if you were to knock off early?

It's Amazing What A Few Bones Can Do Department: Yesterday, Boss #1 calls me into his office to talk about something. Then, as I'm preparing to leave, he slips me an envelope, says the "for you" thing, and sits back. I'm thinking cash, cars, travel, prizes. Guess what? Cash!!! Real cash!! A bonus for being such an incredibly close-to-being-excellent engineer. I was a bit taken aback, naturally, because this kind of thing doesn't happen to me every day, or every month, or, come to think of it, every decade. Now, I've completely sold out to the company, dude. I feel responsibility again, I feel driven. I suck. I'm a Company Man again -- because of the money. Can you believe it? I gotta do something about this. Actually, it's a good place to work, and they let me take vacations whenever I want. Let's see, if only I could find a way to get those bonuses more frequently, say, weekly, then I truly could be happy, and I might make a salary that would be at least comparable to my wife's, which naturally would make me feel that much better about my manhood. Then I could get the "Pants of the Family" back from her and wear them myself.

All right, I'm out of steam and my imagination is snoozing away upstairs in the hidden rooms of my brain, where no one can seem to find it. Have a great weekend, won't you? Oh, and, uh, practice that serve. You're gonna need it.

Parakeets suck, Jeffstock Rules!!!

-Revenuer Man

Date: Jun 28
To: Jeff
From: Anthony
Subject: Bonus or Bone-us?

I saw Cher on some news thing last night. The woman is like 70-something and she still looks like she's 20. I swear, she's been made over more times than a hotel bed.

Bonus, huh? Congratulations, buddy, you deserve it. However, this DOES mean that you can be bought which, needless to say, makes me very proud of you. So, I guess all your e-mails for a while are going to be, "Can't e-mail. Working. Need bonus. OUT!!" Hoping against all hope, let me try to dissuade you from the evil darkside once again by reminding you that you make your money by dealing with architects. You remember architects, don't you? "Uh Jeff, look we know the drawings are due tomorrow, but do you think you could incorporate a three-story fountain that goes up through the middle of the building? Yeah, just cut a big cylindrical hole in all the floors. And, by the way, the drawings need to be in by 7:00 a.m. rather than close of business." Bonus or bone-us, you decide.

Apartment update: we are now able to see the floor in the front room and the dining room, and we project that we will regain control of the entire apartment by the weekend. The enemy still maintains a formidable stranglehold on the master bath, but its forces are now mostly concentrated in the guest bedroom. We attempted a full-frontal assault last night, but the battalion met with significant casualties. The nature of those casualties included stubbing a toe on the leg of the bed, which hurt like holy fuckin' hell, and a leg falling asleep so badly that it caused its owner to lose his balance and fall down go boom.

In a related event, our aquatic team met with some resistance last evening. Intelligence was correct in its assessment of the enemy's desire to acquire a fish, so a minor skirmish broke out, ending in our forces watching about fifteen minutes of the baseball game before resuming operations (very astute of you to notice that when I get cranky I reach for the TV). Again, we reiterate our desire to have the entire area secured by the weekend so that large equipment in the form of sofa, entertainment center, dresser, and coffee table can be brought in to complete the project.

Ya know, after that debacle with the 55-gallons of water on the floor of our Grover City house, I'm just not into having fish as pets. In my mind, the only good fish is one that's swimming in garlic-butter and lemon juice. However, if Alden wants to get a bunny, that's fine with me. Why not? Hell, I get one in the mail on a monthly basis.

Death and the consequences thereof. Hmm, admittedly I haven't given much thought to the subject of what they can do with my shell when I'm gone; but I'm also in favor of cremation. I'd really rather not have one of those "viewing" things, because I don't want the lasting image of me to be prostrate, eyes closed, with make-up on. Of course, I do find some sense of delight in putting my ashes in a beer bottle and having everyone file by to pay their last respects. Personally, I'm thinking that I'd like to divvy up the ashes between my parents, my brother, Alden, you, and my cousin Dave; then you can each sprinkle them somewhere you deem appropriate. It is unnecessary, however, to sprinkle them in the Ganges River or over Stonehenge or some weird place like that. Perhaps in the ocean at Port San Luis, or the backyard at my parents house. I think I'd find much peace in knowing that I came full circle and made it back to the beginning with each of the important people in my life. I promise you, I will do my best to organize an appropriate tribute to your memory; but, personally, I don't know that I'll be much in the partying mood. I will, however, guarantee you that I'll have at least a six-pack in your honor while listening to an old Calvin-and-the-Hip Monks cassette. Just do me a favor and don't die okay?

So this Sunday I will find out if I'm the best lead dramatic community theater actor in San Diego. Not counting on it, but the banquet should be a blast. You guys have fun and we'll talk to you soon.

Stubbing your toe sucks, Calvin and the Hip Monks rule. OUT!!

Hockey Deprived

Date: Jun 28
To: Jeff
From: Anthony
Subject: Never can say good-bye

Boy, can't believe we haven't harped on this yet. Have you heard that Sammy Hagar has left Van Halen? Why else? "Creative differences." The

220

best part of the whole thing is that they might replace him with, yes, David Lee Roth. Thomas Wolfe never considered the world of sports and entertainment when he said, "You can't go home again." Not only that, but apparently the door is a revolving one. Personally, I don't see the point in carrying on. I mean, jeez, how much money do these people need? Ya know, I'm really starting to respect (shudder) Larry Bird. I mean, the guy retired and we haven't heard peep one out of him since. But whatever. They're going to do it and make a serious killing off it. Then they'll talk shit about Sammy. Then Eddie will want to play kazoo on an album and Dave will get pissed and leave again. Re-enter Sammy, yadda yadda yadda. So, in honor of this occasion, I submit a rework of a very appropriate song, in the hopes that it will assist those who may follow. I call it, "Just a Geritol."

I'm just a Geritol
For those who have it all
But can't admit that it's all over
The one drug they can have
Just out of rehab
Ooh, clean and sober
There may come a day, when youth will pass away
But only if you doubt me
When Father Time gives you a call, then just take a Geritol
Life...can't go on without me
I'm just a Geritol
They say you're gonna fall
But that's a lot of bull manure
Extend apologies
Cut a new CD
Then go out on tour
And when the bank account
Has grown by vast amounts
Then we'll see who's dumber
Because then we'll call it quits
And we'll talk a lot of shit
Then reunite next summer...OUT!!

Date: Jun 30
To: The Groom!
From: Jeff
Subject: Soup Stories

Don't worry, buddy. I am not going anywhere. The way I see it, if life is a rock-n-roll show, I am still in sound check, and the concert that will follow will be epic.

I figure that right about now, some luscious young thang is presenting you with the award for "Best Dramatic Actor In A Play That Should Have Been A Disaster But For Some Reason Wasn't," and you are up there giving your li'l acceptance speech, thanking your mom, your dad, your co-stars, your light man, your makeup person, etcetera etcetera. Man, I wish I could be there.

Hike, Eat, Nap. These are the keys to a successful Saturday in Colorado. First, we hike up Twin Sisters Peak, a 12,000-foot mountain near Estes Park, eating trail mix and Granola bars and drinking water all the way. At the top, we rest our weary bones and enjoy the spectacular view; mountains to the north, south, and west, and the flatness of Colorado, Kansas, and beyond to the east. Being on top of a mountain with a 360-degree view is an exhilarating experience. When I am on top of a mountain, it makes me realize how mundane and trivial so many things in life are and also makes me think about what is really important, like love, liberty and happiness. The power of *Madre* Nature is unquantifiable, as far as I'm concerned. Then we hike down, beating up our already weary legs and realizing that we're going to be sore sore sore come tomorrow.

Once at the bottom, we head to one of our most favorite eating establishments, The Baldpate Inn, where we have reservations for a late lunch. This is quickly becoming a habit: Hike up Twin Sisters, eat at the Baldpate. Why is the Baldpate so wonderful, you may be asking right now? Well, at the end of a long hike, all I wanna do is gorge myself on yummy yet healthy food-type substance. And all they have at the Baldpate is *sopa y ensalada*. Yessir, the old soup and salad bar, wrapped up in the cutest little woodsy lodge you've ever seen. And the grub is damn good, all homemade. So I grab myself a Spinach Leaf and Garbanzo Bean and Ranch Dressing Salad -- the old standby -- and a bowl of Potato Leek Soup, which is quickly becoming my favorite soup, and some homemade bread. We scarf.

Three bowls of soup later, I am ready for a nap. Thanks to my clever "I'll drive there if you drive back, honey," maneuvering that morning, I am relieved from driving duties and are therefore able to nap in the back of the Saturn all the way from Estes Park to Denver. I can nap anywhere. Julie and her friend Jane sit in the front, and I nap in the back, all stretched out. Julie pops in her "Barbra Streisand Live" tape, which, as you can probably guess, is one of my all-time favorites. While I'm napping, I realize that Barbra really has a thing for soup. I mean, she's telling a story about her movie "Lentil," about a young lentil bean who dresses up as a kidney bean (in order to become part of the chili instead of the soup) and marries a pinto bean in order to be close to another pinto bean, whom she really loves. I'm halfway napping, halfway thinking "Man, this sounds complicated. No wonder I never rented that movie." Then Barbra launches into her song, "You Don't Bring Me Chowda" and I'm realizing that her affinity for soup has carried over into her songwriting.

How was the weekend? I'm hoping the Guest Bedroom Offensive went off without a hitch and without many casualties. I remember the skirmishes that The Great One and I went through when she got to Colorado and realized that (A) I am a complete and unqualified slob, (B) I didn't own a lick of furniture, save for two file cabinets and a couple of drafting tables, (C) my one bedroom apartment that I had set up so nicely for her arrival was really not even close to being set up nicely, and (D) said apartment was much too small for all of my guitars and all of her clothes. It's a slightly difficult time; but it's fun, too. We slept on a futon for a long while, which she really didn't like at all. But we were together, and therein lay the fun. I got to find out things I could have never find out without shackin' up with her. What time does she get in the shower in the morning? Which way does she hang the toilet paper, if she hangs the toilet paper at all (some people leave the empty roll on the holder and put a new roll of paper on the back of the toilet)? How does she handle crankiness (if Alden likes to watch, say, soap operas when she's cranky, look out; you two will be fighting over that remote)? What kind of pets does she want? Does she have any leftover fishbowls? What kind of stuffed animals does she have? The joys of cohabi...tio...shackin' up.

It is time for me to hit the ol' hay. Tomorrow, I get to drive down to Southern Colorado to boss some people around and answer all kinds o'questions like, "What were you thinking?" from the dudes who are building *mis escuelas*. There's a topic for tomorrow: Construction sites and the mentality therein. On the next "Jeffrey!"

Have a Marvelous Monday, won't you? And in three weeks, you'll be in HAWAII!!!!!!!!

Guest Bedroom Offensives suck, Potato Leeks RULE!!!

-Neil "Split Pea and Ham" Diamond

Date: Jul 1
To: Jeff
From: Anthony
Subject: Paparazzi pizza

"Ladies and gentlemen, we are outside the Mission Valley Marriott in San Diego where tonight the Associated Community Theaters are honoring their own by handing out the Aubrey Awards. The excitement is high (but that's nothing compared to the drink prices) as the stars make their way into the hotel. Who will walk away with the coveted...I mean converted softball trophies? And folks here comes talented, suave, deboner, and oh-so-hunky newcomer Anthony Reynoso with his lovely fiancé Alden. Anthony, what do you think of your chances tonight?"

"I dunno. I guess it depends on how much she drinks."

"No, I mean for the Aubrey."

223

"Oh, I consider it an honor just to be nominated. We're all winners here and to get the Aubrey would be the icing on the cake."

(Later that evening) "And the Aubrey goes to...somebody other than Anthony Reynoso."

(Much, much later to the point of being ridiculous) "Well Anthony, you didn't win, but congratulations on the nomination and a job well done."

"Fuck you! Fuck Casper Gomez and fuck de fuckin' Diaz brudders! I bury you cacaroaches!"

Yes, the Aubreys have been handed out, and I guess that space I was reserving on the mantle can now be used for Alden's snow globe after all. Interesting event. A lot like the Oscars in pomp and circumstance but without nearly the flesh. Also, quite similar to the Oscars in that the thing ran over its scheduled duration. I guess the theatrical community of San Diego doesn't maintain a regular job schedule, because the awards didn't finish until after 10:00. So, I'm a little sleepy today. I still feel really good about being nominated and it would've been nice to win, but we had a great time nonetheless. Who knows, maybe I'll get another shot at one at some point. I guess the better man won. He starred in a love story which required him to wear no make-up and use no accents (not to mention that he didn't have to age himself 40 years), but I'm sure it was really a true test of his acting abilities. But, like I say, let bygones be bygones and better luck next year. Maybe next year I can play the part of a 107-year old black woman who's blind, paralyzed, and speaks with a heavy Jamaican accent, then I can lose to some 24-year old who gets cast as Romeo. But, again, I was just happy to be there. Wish you could've been, too.

We are officially the Detroit Red Wings of softball. After going 10-0 during the regular season, we got beat in the finals. Boy, it was just one loss after another for me this weekend. We lost; but they won't soon forget me, because I made their lives a living hell. Actually, this was one of the better games I've ever played: four hits, three ribbies, and I made some really nice defensive plays requiring lots of diving, which meant I got to roll around in the dirt, which I love. Yet, despite my best efforts, we BLEW IT. Oh well, we had fun and the new season starts in a couple of weeks.

The crowning achievement of the weekend was buying furniture for the bedroom and living room. All told, we managed to get a dresser, headboard, mirror, two nightstands, sofa, recliner, coffee table, and end table for $2,200. Whether this is smart-shopping I don't know, but we're pretty happy with it. You would not believe the type of upholstery people will put on a sofa. We saw sofas with golfers, one with African animals, and one with clowns. There were prints, plaids, florals, and swooshy designs that made no sense at all. We finally wound up going with a sedate green-and-cream-striped couch and a forest green recliner, cuz we're into green. The whole process took a total of 10 hours and required us to shop at no less than seven different stores. We even managed to do it without any physical violence. So, while it was a productive weekend, it didn't leave much time for relaxing.

You, on the other hand, sound like you had a recreational weekend. Getting awfully enthusiastic about your soup these days, aren't ya? We went for seafood Saturday night and Alden ordered a whole lobster. I watched her literally tear this thing apart and eat it; barbaric, primitive, yet mildly arousing. She's busy of late trying to put the apartment in order. It's almost finished, save for a couple of boxes scattered hither and yon. Today, she starts sending out her first batch o' resumes, so hopefully this will be a relatively short period of unemployment.

That's Monday, and I am outta here! So, what are your plans for the 4th of July weekend? Let me know what up. Talk to you tomorrow.

Constantly coming in second sucks, rolling around in the dirt rules.

Pig-Pen

Date: Jul 2
To: The Groom!
From: Jeff
Subject: Aubrey Hepburn

What exactly is an "Aubrey?" Maybe Mister Theater meant to name the award after his wife Audrey but was a little drunk at the time. Sorry you didn't win (you're the only winner in my book) but at least you and your lovely fy-ants (just watched *Raising Arizona*) got to get all dressed up and go out and be celebrities and feel your fifteen seconds of fame, which basically means you've got 14 minutes and 45 seconds of fame left in this lifetime. How are you gonna use it?

You win. $2,200 for furniture? I never thought I'd see the day when little Anthony Reynoso would spend that much money on furniture. Nosirree. Come to think of it, I never thought I'd see the day when you had a bunch of furniture that matched. It does match, correct? Heck, for that price, you'd think they would have thrown in a house to put all that furniture in. Yeah, it's pretty amazing how expensive stuff like furniture can be. And it's good to know if times ever get tough around here, you have a couch that The Great One and I can come sleep on for a while until we get ourselves back on our feet.

Driving back from Southern Colorado yesterday, I saw the perfect place for the Branch Chaconian Compound, right there in the beautiful valley adjacent to Buena Vista. Plenty of mountains surrounding a happy little valley, just gorgeous. Yep, we'll build a big ol' compound with lots of space for you and me and our fifteen wives each and our servan...uh, I mean, our followers. We'll plant huge gardens of zucchinis, tomatoes, and green peppers. We'll live off the land. We'll live happily ever after. No guns or weapons, of course, because our Compound will be one of Peace and Love; besides, we don't want the government to have any reason to worry about us. I'll be the leader, naturally, because the thing is named after me, you know,

"Chacon," "Branch Chaconian." You can be my little buddy, my Gilligan, my Barney Rubble, my Tonto, my first lieuten...ant...mate. Yeah, that's it. Sound good? I'll start recruiting today in Middle America (Colorado), you start recruiting on the West Coast.

I am nominating myself for official "Granola Head" status. You see, I recently picked up a compost bin, for backyard composting; which, as you probably know, being the excellent worldly biologist that you are, is really just turning weeds and newspapers and leaves into fabulously nutritious dirt for the plants. Yessir. Last night, I built my first compost pile. I'm artificially speeding up the decomposition process, my friend. I'm playing God to the waste. To make the transition to "Granola Head" complete, I better head up to Boulder and spend $100 on the latest and greatest pair of Birkenstocks they have. And I better stop washing my hair, so in about six months, my hair will stink like a garbage dump but will have transformed into Granola Head Dreadlocks. I better volunteer for all kinds of environmental concerns, like Save The Ants. I better start my collection of tie-dyed T-shirts and Grateful Dead bootleg albums now, because I've got a lot of catching up to do. I better swap my truck for a 1972 Volvo. Then, and only then, will I have reached "Granola Head" status. But I am really on that road now, don't ya think?

Okee-dokey. It's time once again to head to *la oficina*. I'll call you today with my tux measurements, because you wanted them yesterday. That's pretty much my M.O., but I'm sure you know that. Have a Terrific Tuesday, won't you?

Matching furniture sucks, Branch Chaconians RULE!!

-Sunshine Chacon

Date: Jul 2
To: Jeff
From: Anthony
Subject: Branch Office Chaconians

Hey, I got a better idea. We'll open a branch office of the Branch Chaconians here on the west coast; that way I won't forever have to be Smithers to your Mr. Burns. We'll headquarter ourselves out beyond Pozo somewhere, and we'll grow grapes and make wine using the compost techniques taught by our divine head Jeff Chacon. We'll use the wine we make and the vegetables you grow to make the finest vegetarian spaghetti sauce in the world. We'll start off small. Each Thursday, we'll send a few of our more "personable" followers to the Farmer's Market in San Luis Obispo to spread the Chaconian doctrine and to sell spaghetti sauce. The legend will grow of a whacked-out cult in the hills of Pozo that makes the greatest spaghetti sauce in the world and, one day, little Moondust Reynoso will rush in and say, "Father...oops, you and Fantasy are busy. Anyway, there are some heathens at the gate wearing suits, bearing contracts, and carrying duffel bags of money. Shall I send them away and pray for their souls?" "No daughter, their desire to tempt us with sin requires that I speak to them in the absence of the Almighty." Shortly thereafter, we will inform our followers of our plans to begin marketing spaghetti sauce throughout the southwest. Naturally, each can of sauce will have the Chaconian doctrine on the label, thus spreading the good word. And you will make a personal visit to the west coast to answer questions regarding revenues, which will be used to save the world's deserts, and to purchase the palatial estates we now own. After you've convinced your followers we live in such places to appease "the pig capitalists," you will announce plans to build a new manufacturing facili...uh, compound in Chihuahua, Mexico, to further spread the word and capitalize on cheap labor. There will be much rejoicing and orgying into the night.

The next day, the workers will set off on foot, barefoot naturally even though they produce the new Chaconstock sandal. Unfortunately, the workers have no money to buy sandals. Many will die on their long pilgrimage to Chihuahua, but they will be happy because they finally will know peace; besides, they add that little extra "umph" to the compost. Once they arrive, we will be waiting for them with bread and water. We will eat with them, pray with them, then jump back on the corporate jet and return to Denver. Then one day, you'll announce plans to introduce a new line of spaghetti sauce with meat added and there'll be rioting in the compound, causing the *federales* to extort all our profits or threaten to seize compound. Penniless and disheartened, we will arrive at the compound with a huge vat of "special wine" and a lot of Dixie cups We will toast the fact that we just sold the movie rights for $100 million. And there will be much rejoicing and orgying into the night.

My friend, we have a BED you and The Great One can use if you ever need to. This, of course, under the conditions that you wash your hair and leave your Grateful Dead albums on top of the compost heap in Denver where they belong. The Great One can stay on the condition that she leaves the Babwa Stweisand albums on top of the Grateful Dead albums on top of the compost heap back in Denver where they all belong. Ya know, all this talk about potato-taking-a-leak soup, compost heaps, sandals, dreadlocks; you're either turning into some kind of swishy fruit or you're trying to get a rise out of me (you know the way to get a rise out of me is to emerge from the shower wearing nothing but a towel). Don't do this. You're too old and materialistic. Now, get out there and get a fast-food burger and a haircut.

Hey, forgot to tell you about this. Saturday, some higher plane of existence decided to jump into the Manchurian brown bear cage at the San Diego Zoo. Yeah, right in the middle of the afternoon, with a bunch of people standing around, this cerebral icon climbs a fence, swims a moat, and decides to visit Mr. and Mrs. Bruin. Naturally, the bears used this philosophical entity as a combination ping-pong ball and teething ring; he's now fortunate enough to just be in fair condition at a local hospital. His explanation? The bears were motioning him to come inside. Well, duh! Of course the bears are motioning you to come inside; they're motioning ALL OF US to come inside. But why would you trust a bear that you've thrown in a cage? Ya know, some things are just so naturally stupid that it's difficult to make fun of them. Case in point.

To answer your question, Aubrey is a gentleman here in San Diego who's very active in community theater. I believe his first name is John, but I can't be sure because I was ordering a drink when they introduced him. So between John and "Chardonnay," I'm guessing he's John.

Glad to hear I'll be getting tux measurements today. Actually, I'm not, because now I don't get to watch you squeeze into that 28-inch waist number I had all picked out. Thus I will wait with baited breath for your call. Have a good one.

Granola lifestyles suck, Manchurian brown bears rule (but ya can't trust 'em). OUT!!

Raindrop Reynoso

Date: Jul 2
To: The Groom!
From: Jeff
Subject: Silence Of The Fans

Speaking as a veteran of marriage, what with my tremendous one-year-plus of experience, it's pretty exciting to sense a young man's anticipation and excitement about his own pending matrimony. My friend, you are showing. Your last couple of e-mails have been fabulous; among your best, I must say. And methinks it's because of the recent arrival of your Little Love Thang and your anticipation and excitement about your pending trip to Hawaii...uh, I mean, wedding. This is truly a wonderful time in your life, make no mistake. Everybody is paying attention to you; relatives you don't even know you have are throwing you bones as if you are a ravenous dog; and behind locked doors your Love Thang is trying on a stunningly gorgeous dress that has one and only one purpose: To inspire you to rip it off of her after all the Friends/Relatives/Valuable Business Contacts have left the premises. Yessir, it's almost wedding time.

Hopefully, I can convince The Great One to rip my tuxedo off me after we have secured the premises (hotel room) and are alone as well. Which won't be hard, considering THEY MEASURED MY WAIST AND THE LYING-ASS-TAPE SAID 39 INCHES!!!! What is that? I might as well show up in a Hefty trash bag, it would fit better. I -- in no way, shape, or form -- have a 39 inch waist. Unless, of course, all of the pants I buy have been lying. Or I am weirdly dyslexic and have been reading the "39" on the waist as a "36." I'm gonna look like the thin Eddie Murphy in the Nutty Professor's outfit. I'll look like David Byrne singing, "...same as it ever was, same as it ever was..." in The Big Suit. I'll look like the kid at the end of *Big* when he turns from Tom Hanks back into himself but is still wearing the Tom Hanks-size suit. Well, at least I'll be comfortable. Oh, and, uh, are there any special suspenders I should be wearing to this thing? I'm gonna need some, that's for sure. Maybe I'll drive up to Boulder and trade my Birkenstocks for a pair of Mork From Ork rainbow-colored suspenders.

I climbed into a cage with a bear once; her name was Patty; 'nuff said. Oh, and, uh, that last remark in *no way, shape, or form*, reflects the actual opinions of The Branch Chaconians, and is in *no way, shape, or form*, intended to be libelous or slanderous or hurtful in any way, shape, or form. So, don't even think about suing us -- In *any way, shape, or form*.

I'M MELTING!!! I'M MELTING!!! Jeez, I can't stand this heat. I have firmly decided, at the tender age of 31 11/12, that I like cold sooooooo much better than heat. Hot weather makes me cranky and irritable (I wonder if heat and architects are related?). Today, it was Hhhhottttttttttttt!! The electronic bank sign that faithfully gives me the daily temperature on my drive home even read, "If you have to ask, you can't stand it." Which means 97 degrees. -- 97 degrees at 6:30 p.m. Nossir, I don't like it. And tomorrow it's going to be even hotter. At least when it's cold, I can pile on everything I own and feel O.K; I can heat up the truck nicely in about a half hour, too. In this heat, there are only so many clothes I can take off in public before being arrested; the truck has no air-conditioning, the house has no air-conditioning, my brain has no air-conditioning. Tennis is out of the question. Rollerblading is out of the question. Worst of all, there's no beach nearby where I can go and stick my head in the sand to cool off. L'Great One has a fan in our bedroom, which today is quite necessary; but the fan is LOUD. Yessir, and it bugs the shit out of me. I used to be able to sleep through a train wreck, but that was before I quit smoking and started playing tennis and loving The Great One. Now, this noise is mostly irritating. Maybe the Branch Chaconians need to branch out the operations and start producing a silent fan, because there's nothing like silence when a grown boy is attempting to get his beauty sleep.

All right, I admit it. I'm old. I'm materialistic. Make no mistake about it. And thanks for reminding me, dude. Living in Colorado makes a boy forget his roots and think that he, too, is an earthy Granola-Head type dude, which just ain't true. It's like if Los Lobos made a metal album. Some things just aren't meant to happen. Now, go make some more spaghetti sauce, would ya?

Tonight (Wednesday), we are going to Coors Field to watch the Skysox (a Rox farm team) play the Silver Bullets, a women's professional baseball team. It should be interesting. Girls playing baseball? Hmmm. I suppose it might be like if the Indigo Girls played Led Zeppelin songs. Which makes Joan Jett. Anyway, there'll be the whole patriotic fireworks display after the game, which I always dig. Fireworks are cool, as long as somebody else is setting them off. All around our neighborhood for the past couple of weeks, we've been hearing fireworks and firecrackers every night all night, which is annoying. Save it for the fourth, would ya? Are fireworks still illegal in California? One of the coolest fourth of Julys I ever spent involved you. It was that one when we rode around in the back of George's truck playing "Keep Your Hands To Yourself" on our acoustic guitars and we eventually ended up at Pismo Beach to watch the zillions of people play with sparklers and worms and shit. That was a cool fourth. That was a truly American fourth, as this one might be. First, the official Brother-In-Law and Girlfriend will be in town from *Tejas*. Second, we'll go watch some babes play baseball, and I'll be the fool in the left-field stands yelling "There's no crying in baseball!!!!" Third, on the actual fourth of July, we're going to repeat the Hike Eat Nap scenario, albeit with a different supporting cast, namely Bro-In-Law and Girlfriend from Tejas. And there'll be fireworks in Estes Park, so we'll probably hang around after the Eat, which inevitably will postpone my Nap and accompanying Soup Dreams. Hopefully, we'll get to see lots o'fireworks. All of a sudden, I'm feeling very patriotic. "My country, 'tis of thee. Sweet land of liberty, of thee I sing..." On Friday, I'll probably head into *la oficina*, where I'll be trying to appease some Architects From Hell; which, in this case, also is *Tejas*. If architects suck, can you imagine how badly architects from Texas suck? Exactly. So, I'll be e-mailing you on Thursday night with a wrap-up of the Hike Eat Preempted Nap day's events. You have a good one, and congratulations. Enjoy this time, *mijo*. It is a magical time.

Heat sucks, Hike Eat Nap RULES!!!!

-Uncle Sam Chacon

Chapter 22
The Home Stretch

Date: Jul 3
To: Jeff
From: Anthony
Subject: But it's a dry heat

Perhaps you are right. Perhaps my creative muscles have been re-energized lately by the arrival of my little woman and our subsequent marriage. I am certainly more happy than I've been in ages, but I'm wondering how much more happier I could be if I didn't have a few things on my mind. For one thing, I'm happy but, instead of basking in it, I find myself preparing for some impending disaster that I know can't be too far away. Sad, huh? I know this is a horrible, cynical way of looking at life but I just can't help it. I've always sort of admired you for your ability to enjoy things as they are. I know my life hasn't been any more difficult than yours, but at times I still feel like Somebody Up There is pushing the buttons and has it in for me. Truth be known, I'm a lot better than I used to be and I think a lot of that has come from hanging around with you. Perhaps I just need to learn to operate at a higher level of happiness and this point in time is my elevator to that level. I know things aren't always going to go my way, but I'd love to be able to enjoy happiness unconditionally. So how do *you* do it?

The other thing that continues to trouble me is the fact that I've been married before and it failed. Don't get me wrong, I'm really not worried about Alden and I, because I know we have something very special and I have undying faith that we have the tools needed to get through life together. It just worries me that I failed at something so important and, having only been married for 13 months, I almost feel like I made a mockery of it. What do you think? Any validity to this?

39 inches, huh? Don't worry, buddy, tuxedoes are cut notoriously small so they always add three inches to your measurements. Did some guy measure you? Cuz guys are known to add an extra three inches to most measurements. I wouldn't worry about it, you looked very trim in Vegas. But if this is the kind of thing that's going to cause you undo angst, try coming up with a recipe for Jeffbrew Light.

We are experiencing a heat wave ourselves here in San Diego, which means you're probably looking at more warm weather ahead. However, there seems to be a storm a' brewin' off the coast, because the clouds have moved in and produced ungodly humidity. Heat is one thing, heat and humidity is another beast entirely. I agree with you whole-heartedly about your preference for cold weather. I just find it hard to believe the sound of a fan keeps you awake. Perhaps when millions of them are clamoring outside the

231

hotel window, but one little fan in your bedroom? Besides, you know you shouldn't be bringing fans into your bedroom, it's bad publicity.

Yeah, I remember that Fourth of July when we were cruising Pismo in the back of the pick-up. I remember YOU GUYS were playing the song, I just kept strumming a D chord, because it was the only one I knew then. Still, it was a blast. I also remember when we mooned the camera for that one shot George wanted to put in the good ol' Mustang Daily. Ah, yes, back when stupidity was the order of the day. Mem--oo--rees!! Now that I'm all growed up, I want nothing to do with the insanity that is the beaches on Independence Day. Alden and I will be attending a neighborhood block party in Solana Beach, with all kinds of free burgers, hot doggies, and ice cold beer. Yes, all this is ours for the price of two of Alden's yogurt pies. I loves me some yogurt pie! It could be the most underrated dessert in the world. Very inexpensive, easy to make, clean, quick, *DELICIOSO*, and doesn't cause your waistline to go to 39 inches overnight. Unfortunately, I too have to work Friday, which sucks more than a prostitute with a head cold. Speaking of Independence Day, I'd like to see that movie so perhaps I'll make time for that this weekend.

Anyway, enjoy your day off as you Hike, Eat, and Nap to your little heart's content. I'll talk to you Friday. By the way, does The Great One know anyone in San Diego who's looking to hire a spunky, young intellectual with a Master's Degree in Psychology? There's a finder's fee of $2.83 in it for her. Happy 4th.

Humidity sucks, yogurt pie rules. OUT!!

Aunt Hillary Reynoso

Date: Jul 4
To: The Groom!
From: Jeff
Subject: Outside it's America.

Where else but in America can a boy experience the kind of freedom we experience here in the good ol' U. S. of A? The freedom to climb mountains, the freedom to scarf on yummy soup and salad as one pleases, the freedom to send wacky e-mail messages on a daily basis, the freedom to play the guitar as often as possible, the freedom to sing "Row Row Row Your Boat" at the top of our lungs as we hike back down a mountain, the freedom to purchase beltbuckles that scream "DORK" to the rest of the world, the freedom to hop on a plane to Vegas to be with our buddies, the freedom to live free. This is America, my country 'tis of thee, whatever that means. And, tonight, my neighborhood sounds like a warzone, as everybody and their brothers around here seem to have realized this freedom and decided in order to celebrate said freedom they have purchased a truckload of fireworks and are now setting them off. Jeez. Fireworks are fine, as long as they are legal and are being set off by professionals. But I keep expecting to look in my backyard and see some errant amateur fireworks fall from the sky and ignite the lawn, or the hair on my arms, eyebrows, and head. In which case, I might as well be barbecuing.

And as for you, my gloomy little friend. What the heck ever happened to you that was truly bad? Huh? Sure, you've had setbacks. A failed marriage makes you equal with approximately half of all Americans. What else? Nothing, right? Exactly. I live my life (mostly) with one "motto" in mind: *Don't sweat the little shit.* There are so many things that happen to us every day that we have absolutely no control over; things such as our bosses bitching at us, our clients bitching at us, the stupid drivers all over the place. It is completely useless and not worthwhile to worry about stupid shit like that. We've to go through life giving everything we've got to everything we are doing, then we can sit back and say, "I left it all on the court. Whatever happens now is completely beyond my control." I realize this is truly an ideal situation; there are many things that limit our ability to truly "leave it all on the court." But I strive for this, and you should too. Once you realize that so many things are beyond your control, you can be truly happy. Try it, you might like it.

Oh, and also: About the failed marriage thing? Shit happens, buddy. The best thing you can do when bad shit happens is learn something from it. This all became quite apparent to me when a certain young lady walked out of my life so many years ago to marry her boss. Nothing made me question everything about life more than that. It was literally months before I stopped bursting into tears at the stupidest things: certain songs, a smell, etcetera. But you know what did it for me? Acting. I started acting. Acting changed my life. All of a sudden, I was good at something, and, yes, people liked me. Of course, you still liked me; but you were too damn far away to hold me and tell me everything was going to be okay. Shortly after I got into acting and started making new friends and hanging out with a creative crowd, I realized I had learned a great deal from the Girlfriend-Marrying-Her-Boss-Incident and that I must never ever ever forget the lessons learned. I swore I would not repeat the mistakes ever. I also swore (I was doing a lot of swearing back in those days) I would never sweat the little shit and I would do my best to leave it on the court, to give my all to each and every day. I realized the Incident was a result of laziness -- a result of living life half-heartedly. If there is one thing that really irritates Jeff Chacon, it's making the same mistake twice. So I don't, and you shouldn't either. As we approach the time of your marriage, I suggest this to you: Think about the failed marriage. Open up your heart and let the blood flow. What went wrong? Why? What mistakes did you make? What mistakes did she make? Then make sure these things are available as reference material in your mind, because you will see them crop up in your relationship with Alden. When they do, you'd better be ready to deal with them in a healthy way. Do not make the same mistakes twice.

Does this all make sense? I don't quite know what the "disaster" that you refer to could be. You are a blessed person, my man. Respect that, admire that, be aware of that. You are healthy, you have all your limbs, you come from a middle-class background, which entitles you to so many things that so many people don't have; you went to the best college in America, you have more talent in your little finger than most humans have in their entire bodies, you are loved by friends and family; you have a good job, a sweet young lady, and an incredible muse. What's to worry about?! Enjoy life. Otherwise, what the hell are you still doing here?

All-righty then. Don't mean to be so serious, I just thought your e-mail and the "impending disaster" thing should be addressed. But, now, I gotta go, because the guests are wanting to go to bed in the guest room, which also is the computer room. So, you have a great weekend, and I'll talk you to you Monday.

Impending Disasters Suck, America RULES!!!!!

-MuseMan

Date: Jul 5
To: Jeff
From: Anthony
Subject: Co-dependence Day

Ah, yes, your stirring little speech this morning has aroused my patriotic tendencies and I concur with you that the U.S.A. is one pretty damn cool place to live. True, we have our problems, but it's good to know we have the freedom to bitch about those problems. This was probably the most uneventful 4th of July I've ever had. We attended the neighborhood block party, which was hardly a major social event, but it did sort of represent what the whole thing is about. The neighbors gathered around and brought food, kids played in the pool, adults commiserated, beer was consumed, and the menu weighed heavily on typical summer faire: burgers, dogs, chips, and deviled eggs. Yes, I believe this is the best way to celebrate our struggle for independence; by joining together and flaunting the fact that we ain't gotta do shit if we don't wanna. UNFORTUNATELY, the Powers That Be decided that today I should work, so I was one of maybe six people in my whole company who did. But that's okay, because in two weeks I'll be in Hawaii. That's another reason I love America. Who else would purposely annex an island paradise, except us fun-loving, vacation-worshipping Americans? God bless Us!!

Apparently I struck a nerve in you by bearing my soul. You are absolutely right in everything you said. I feel awful for giving the impression I'm feeling sorry for myself. I'm not really. I repeat again: I am as happy as I possibly can be, I'm just a little cautious about it. But, you're right, I may be the most blessed person I know. Plus, I have the added bonus of learning to cope with mild adversity, which is about all I've ever experienced in my life. In fact, I'm kind of ashamed for sounding so negative. Realistically, the things

I worry about are nothing more than ants at a picnic. But thanks for reminding me of all this. As you know, I'm not a negative person by nature; I've just discovered a new level of happiness, and I'm sort of easing into it to get the feel. Perhaps I need to adopt the Chaconian approach, which is to just cannonball right in. That's why we will be the Branch Chaconians and not the Branch Reynoso-ians (it helps that your name ends in a consonant); because you know how to best deal with all the happiness we strive to achieve. I've thought a lot about my past marriage and have realized that, at this point, there's nothing I can do but learn from it. Dwelling on it isn't fair to Alden or me. Perhaps now is the time when I should measure myself by my accomplishments rather than my failures. And so it will be. Thanks again for your wisdom; and, yes, I'm glad you took the "kick in the butt" approach rather than the "pat on the back" approach since that's what I needed more.

Well, I just got word yesterday that everyone's favorite French curmudgeon Chris LeBeau will be in attendance at the wedding, which means there will be an 80% reunion of the most popular boating excursion ever, next to *Gilligan's Island.* I speak, of course, of the 1987 Sacramento Delta Houseboating Voyage. I feel bad that Naked Idiot Man won't be there, but I haven't even seen the guy since college. Of course, one could argue that I saw quite enough of him on the Voyage to last me a lifetime; it cost me a few therapy sessions. Yes, once again, Captain George Smith (promoted to captain because he figured out how to maneuver us out of that skinny dock) will be joined by First Mate Jeff Chacon, Second Mate Anthony Reynoso, and Pri-Mate Chris LeBeau to pay homage to the S.S. Reynoso on his voyage into matrimony. It'll be great to see all you guys in the same place again.

Thus, I take leave of you at this time, to go enjoy what remains of the weekend. Revel and bask in the fact that you're an American, my friend, and that you not only have a choice of what beer to drink, you can even brew your own.

Picnic ants suck, America STILL rules!! OUT!!

Happy Boy

Date: Jul 7
To: The Groom!
From: Jeff
Subject: Polish Snausages

Wow. A reunion of the survivors (well, 4/5 of them) of the 1987 Sacramento Delta Houseboat Disaster. What a kick. That is still, without a doubt, the second best vacation I've ever had; second only to the honeymoon thing that The Great One and I did last year. There was something magical about The Houseboat Disaster, don't you agree? In fact, if I close my eyes and concentrate, I can still taste the Polish sausage, smell the stogies, and see the unshaven faces of the lads. Meeeee-mories. If only we had had beer on the boat. At least we had playing cards, a guitar, cigars, the "Joshua Tree" tape, a Walkman, and Chris LeBeau. One day, we'll have to do it again, just like last time -- five men on a little boat on a big river, with nothing to do but be bad and take off all of their clothes. Thus, Naked Idiot Man. I know where to find him, of course. Every time I go to San Luis Obispo, he's at Boo Boo Records trying to sell some naive young college student on the virtues of Tom Waits.

I tell you what -- I'll bring some cigars to the wedding, so that the Survivors can stand around smoking and mugging for the cameras. Better yet, I ll bring some Polish Snausages and we can stand around mugging for the cameras. Better yet still, we can all do our best impressions of Naked Idiot Man in his honor (since he won't be there), take off all of our clothes and stand around mugging for the camera. That's a wedding picture that most certainly would end up in your album, for sure.

Speaking of that, have you and your Yogurt Pie of Love made up the endless lists of photos you both want to get out of this thing? Certainly there's the "There's Anthony getting on a plane to Hawaii," and the "There's Anthony getting lai'ed in Hawaii." But seriously. Have you gone through this headache? You have bride and groom pictures, bride and groom and parents of the bride pictures, bride and groom and parents of the groom pictures, bride and groom and both sets of parents pictures, family photos, bride and groom and wedding parties, bride and groom and valuable business contacts, bride and groom and third cousins of each, bride and groom and The People Who Brought The Best Presents, bride and groom and The People Who Will Be Most Likely To Pass On Family Heirlooms, and so on, and so on, and so on. It's a little bit nuts. I've seen lists that go on forever. More often than not, you get to "Me and Grandpa Henry and Grandma Josephine and their dog Spot," then just say "FUCK IT" and give up on the rest.

Then there's the question, "when do we wanna take the pictures?" Most commonly between ceremony and reception; although this leaves open the strong possibility that by the time you and Alden get to the reception, everybody else will be on their fourth micro-brew and slurring Alden's name so that it sounds like "Allen." Of course, you could pull the "Julie and Jeff" routine and take the pictures prior to the ceremony, but this makes the day much longer than it already is going to be. Plus, you will have a hard time convincing the Important People Who Are Going To Be In The Pictures that, even though the wedding isn't until noon, they have to show up at 10 o'saka, which might make them cranky. Tip: If you go this route, make sure there are plenty o'donuts and coffee on hand to lessen the crankiness. Then there are the endless pictures at the reception of you and your bride and your friends, etcetera etcetera etcetera. In our wedding photos, you can see chrono...log..in order the crankiness of the groom. In the initial photos at the reception, where I'm newly married and loving the attention, my face says, "Hey! I got married!! Life couldn't be any better!! Please please please take more photos!!" By the last couple of photos, after I've been playing groom for five hours and am looking only for a nap, my face says, "If you don't get that

goddamn camera outta my face, I'm gonna go Sean Penn on your ass."
Because at the reception, everybody wants some; everybody wants the bride
and groom to spend time with them, hold them, tell them they too will one day
find a love as perfect as the one on display today. The photographer will
constantly be calling your name -- "Anthony!! Anthony!! Your third aunt
twice removed on your fathers side, whom you've never met, wants a picture
with you!!" At this point, you will need to find me, and, together, we will find
a nice quiet place at the bar where we can take a collective sigh of relief and a
collective respite from the maddening crowds, just like we did at my wedding.
That was a beautiful moment, my man. You and I kicking back at the bar,
drinking a Samuel Adams. Amidst all the hub-bub, that moment stands out as
one of the finest -- Until The Great One came in and said, "C'mon, we gotta
mingle." Right at that moment is when I transformed into the quivering mass
of "Yesdear" that I am today.

Needless to say, I am looking forward to your weeding immensely;
because if you are anything like our garden, you could use a good weeding.

Don't be ashamed about sounding negative. Hell, we all go through
it. In this land of the free, you should sound negative whenever you feel like
sounding negative. Wow. I'm scaring myself. Maybe I need to get a license
plate frame that says "I'm O.K., you're O.K." Or "Free to Be, You and Me."
Nah, because I don't own any Birkenstocks, and I think that in order to
purchase those license-plate frames, they ask to see your Birkenstocks.
Anyway, don't worry about it. You asked how I deal with life, and I told you.
Enjoy it. 'Nuff said. I know for a fact you aren't a paranoid delusional worlds-
gonna-end kind of guy. This is a time of transition for you; new wife, new
home ,and all. Transitional times are not always easy to enjoy. Last year, I
obtained a wife, a home, a "You're fired" and a new job, all within the span of
six months. Talk about *loco* times.

Julie and I have discovered we live in a haunted house. The other
night, The Great One and I and the Visitors From Tejas were sitting around
enjoying a nice beverage and an invigorating game of *Jenga* when the wreath
on the front wall of the living room literally lifted off the wall and "CRASH"
ended up five feet away on the floor. This defies the laws of physics as set
forth by the famous Smart Guy, Albert Einstein. Things fall down, not out, he
said. Actually, maybe it was Sir Isaac Newton who put the "down, not out"
theorem on paper. Whatever. Then last night The Great One and I were
enjoying our nightly respite when we both heard what sounded exactly like a
door opening. We jumped out of bed, grabbed our robes (in the heat of the
summer, we sleep naked) and carefully made our way downstairs. I figured
the wreath had once again jumped OUT from its place on the wall, but no. It
was still there. Slowly we turned on all the lights (I felt like I was a minor
character in a *Friday the 13th* movie, in which the audience knows the
character is going to get his eyeball impaled on a pitchfork if he opens that
door, but he does it anyway). We walked all through the house, but nothing.
Then this morning, I inspected the outside of the house, nothing. Then when

The Great One was napping earlier today, she heard what sounded like footsteps on the hardwood floors, but she didn't see anything. I think it's a ghost, dude. I think it's a ghost of a lunatic who was kicked out of the looney bin ghost home (to make room for the yuppie ghosts, no doubt) and found his/her way into our home. Or maybe it's the ghost of architects past, who are tired of my rantings and ravings about how much they suck. Or maybe it's the ghost of Adolf Coors come to scare me away from making more beer that eventually would run his company out of business. Now he/she wants to scare us out of here. Where is Scooby-Dooby-Doo when I need him? I'll solve this. And when I do, I'll get the standard "If it wasn't for you meddling kids..." line from the perpetrator of the ghostly haunting just before he or she is hauled off to Denver County Jail.

Well, time to go do some work. Yeah, I know. I've been working practically all weekend. Because when I get on that plane to San Diego next week, I want to leave it all behind. I will take no phone calls on vacation. In order to achieve this state of bliss, I need to be completely caught up by the time the plane leaves Denver International Airport. So, I'm working like a dog now. Sucks. To top it all off, the view from my office window is the pool and the lounge area of the upscale apartments across the street. So every time I check a beam or column location, my eyes wander and I start thinking maybe I should be the one sitting by the pool. Really inhibits the productivity of a young man, let me tell you.

Have a Magnanimous Monday, won't you?

Other people besides me lounging by a pool suck, Scooby-Doo RULES!!!

-Shaggy

Date: Jul 8
To: Jeff
From: Anthony
Subject: A little chat

Now HERE'S something to talk about. Apparently, Dr. Kevorkian has obtained a permit to carry a concealed weapon. Imagine the good doctor at the bedside of his latest "patient," thinking, "Jeez, this machine takes forever. I'm supposed to tee off in twenty minutes. Never make it, never ma...hmmm." I dunno, buddy. Isn't this sort of akin to giving Jack the Ripper a set of Chicago Cutlery?

Hope you had a great Independence Day weekend. Mine went pretty well. We had a BBQ for our Friday night softball team, and I got pretty hammered; which, ordinarily, is fine, except the next day Alden and I had an appointment to meet the minister and discuss the wedding ceremony. Mind you, it wasn't a bad hangover, but it was enough to make me very groggy and very anti-social. So, I spent a lot of the morning going, "Huh? Oh...yeah, whatever." This, of course, made me highly popular with the prospective missus. "Look, do you not wanna do this?" "Of course I wanna do this, I'm just tired." "You sure?" "Yes, I'm sure." "You positive?" The problem with this is the minister was up in San Marcos, which meant I was trapped in the car for about 20 minutes. Fortunately, fate intervened and I took full advantage. "Look honey, there's a mall," I said. "Why don't we go see if we can find that bikini you've been after?" Naturally, the idea of shopping didn't exactly thrill me, but it was a far better alternative than the current line of questioning. So, Alden got a bikini, I got to sit in a nice comfy chair, and everyone went home happy. Then I took a nap.

Are you familiar with a badger? Badgers are a cross between a wolverine and a halibut. They're very ferocious and they never quit. Thus, I am convinced that the most difficult object to handle on the face of the earth must be a mother badger. I love my Mom more than even I can believe, but yesterday she turned into a badger. Now, other people can be badgers too, but you can usually tell them to go to hell. I can't -- and won't -- tell my Mom to go to hell, so I had to put up with, "Listen honey, who's going to take the tuxes back after the wedding?" "Well Mom, I just assumed the party that wore them." "Well, your Father and I will be leaving early the next day and so is everyone else, so who'll be around to take them back?" "Gee Mom, I don't know. Let me work on it and I'll let you know." "Okay, but I need to know, so I can get them wherever they need to go." "Okay Mom, I'll work on it." "Okay, and let me know so I can tell everyone." "Yeah Mom, I got ya covered." "All right, I just want to make sure this gets done." "MOM, I'LL HANDLE IT!" Later on that evening, she called to ask whether or not we wanted to be in the name-drawing for Christmas. It just keeps coming.

ALERT: INCOMING MESSAGE. URGENT. And there it is, in big red letters: a message extolling the virtues of Polish sausage. Of course it's a good thing the CIA didn't get it, or they probably would've deciphered it to mean the Polish navy, aided by Cuba (stogies), the IRA (U2 reference), and the French (Chris LeBeau) is preparing to attack the Sacramento Delta in submarines. Since you bought it up, I will remind you now to set your alarm early for the morning of the wedding, because we will be taking the majority of the photos BEFORE the ceremony. So what'll it be, a buttermilk bar or an apple fritter? At least Alden and I agree neither of us wants to spend the day taking photos, so we'll probably take some at the reception site between rounds. I really hope there'll be time for a quiet beer and some commiserating with you and the other Survivors. It would be a real drag to get the crew of the S.S. Lead Weight together and not be able to reminisce about old times. Of course, we'd probably sit bored while Chris and George compare pictures of their kids.

This is all contingent upon whether or not Alden and I actually make it to the wedding day. During the last week, the bride-to-be has dropped a brass lamp on her toe, spilled hot lasagna on her leg, gotten a steam burn from microwaving peas, and last night she slid down the side of the wall while feigning fatigue and rolled over a large lamp plug which resulted in a nasty scrape on her hindquarters, which I guess is better than electrocution. Jeez, I feel like I'm marrying Inspector Clouseau.

Ya know, I was worried about this: If there's one thing in this world (or any other world, for that matter) that ghosts hate, it's being dissed. So when you pulled out of the Goofy Gardens Apartments project, it probably wrinkled some spook's sheet and now he's declared haunting season on Chacons and Great Ones. Just don't be too surprised if Julie's sewing stuff is missing; for, with ghosts, as with people, "As ye sew so shall ye wreath." Perhaps your wreath is possessed by the ghost of wide-receivers past, which would explain the tendency to go "down and out." I once shot a ghost in my pajamas...oops, I forgot you sleep nekkid, so that won't work for you. Ha Ha!! Boy, these ghost jokes get funnier and funnier, don't they? Actually, early Sunday morning, Alden and I both thought we heard someone running past our bed. You don't suppose a certain restaurant-owner (from the Vanilla Stew days) got hit by a bus do you, or a certain droomer died after the weight of his ego snapped his neck while he was napping? At least The Great One went with you to check things out. Alden stayed in the room, reasoning, "Someone has to be ready to call for help."

All right, I'm outta here. Got some songs to work on. Have a fab Tuesday, and I'll talk at ya later.

Drummers with heavy necks suck, Inspector Clouseau rules. OUT!!

Dreyfus

Date: Jul 9
To: The Groom!
From: Jeff
Subject: E-mail revival

Whoo-Hoo!!!! We are back on the e-mail circuit, finally!!!! I finally figured out how to set up my *nuevo* e-mail account; it is now up and running. We have moved out of the stoned age (which my last Provider must have been) and are now firmly entrenched in the '90s. I feel whole again. I sent about 10 e-mails to everybody on my "nickname" list just a few minutes ago, and it was faster than a speeding houseboat on the Sacramento Delta, able to leap tall compost piles in a single bound, more powerful than a propane-fueled flash fire; in a word, fast. I could not believe it. I'm gonna call my other stoned Provider tomorrow and tell them to "take a hike." In fact, last night I had to go to one of these "cyber-cafes" to send my e-mail to you, because my e-mail was completely down. Ever been to one of these cyber-cafes? An interesting concept. A place with coffee and e-mail. The e-mails probably look something like this: *Sohowsitgoingandhowareyouandi'vebeensitting heredrinkinglattésforthepasthourandnowi'mliketotallywiredandmyheartisraci ngexplodingcan'thandletheheatcan'tstoptwitching*..........What if there was a place with beer and e-mail? It'd look something like this: *heyblotha, hooz i goin? i drikin all ight lon./ i noooo dru`nkkkk. honext, ocifer. BURP!!!!* Or maybe a place that offers foreplay and e-mail: *Hey baby, you're looking pretty fine tonight. Why you don't you come on over to my e-box and I'll show you a good time. That's right. Let's slip into something more comfortable. Hmm, I like that lacy little thing you got on now....*

Let's settle this right now: I'll take the penguin outfits back to the penguin outfit place for you, okay? It's the least I can do for a man who has to endure the grueling task of getting on a plane to Hawaii that Sunday morning. Actually, I can help with any aspect of this weeding that you need me to. Is there anything else I can do for you, oh Hawaii-bound one?

So, I suppose sometime in the near future our e-mails will start addressing the "kid" thing, seeing as how we're both gonna be married and both of our wives are going to hear the "biological clock" as loudly as a bomb ticking in their heads. Eventually, they're gonna wanna talk children, which is fine with me. We'll have some, someday. As far as names go, I recently heard a VERY cool name for a kid; naturally, I'll share it with you. My friend Mike Smith recently had a son, and do you know what he named his son? Miles Davis Smith. It's funny at first, but I think it's actually very very cool. I mean, what a way to honor your heroes. I can see it now: John Elway Reynoso. Stevie Ray Chacon. Steve Perry Kidd. Chris Duarte Chacon. Patrick Roy Chacon. That's a way to ruin a kid's life. "Hey, whimp, did I hear that your middle name is "Wah?" As in "wah wah, I'm a little baby? Get him, boys." Something to think about, no?

I am so ready for a vacation. And for the wedding, of course. I've practiced my guitar, I've practiced my tennis (to avoid a total blowout), I'm ready to go. I even prepared a batch of beer for your bad self, but it may not work out. You don't wanna know the gory details; suffice to say it's been so hot lately the fermenting has revealed some funny smells that aren't typical to the normal brewing process. I asked the guy at the "Make Your Own Beer" place, a.k.a. the North Denver Cellar, if a "dirty underwear and socks" smell is normal. He said it might just be the heat messing with the beer. He said to scrape the nasty stuff off the top (Reminds me of college dorm food: rice peel-off was when you peeled off the nasty stuff to eat the rice) and give it a whirl. So I scraped off the weird shit, tasted it, and it didn't taste too funny. I mean, no matter what happens, it's still better than mass-produced beer. So, I bottled it. I'll check it again before the Big Day and let you know if I'm bringing any. No guarantees; and, if I can't bring any, I'll ship a case of the yummy stuff to you after you return from Hawaii; because once domestic life settles in, you may be looking for a good beer every now and again, especially when all you hear is "You sure? You positive? You absolutely certain-lidly scrump-didly total-idly positive?" This gets annoying. I've resorted to letting The Great One check out situations herself, which always reveals that yes, I am sure, and I am right.

241

Whenever I wear any of my California State Polytechnic University at San Luis Obispo gear, there's always some joker (or five) who comes up to me and asks, "Did you go to Cal Poly?" To which I respond, "Yes, did you?" Then I get the answer, "No, but my fourth cousin on my stepdad's side did. His name is Joe-Bob Smith. Did you know him?" At this point I ask, "What was his major and when was he there?" "Uh, I think he majored in animal husbandry (now there's a major I could NEVER understand) in 1985." You know, there were 16,000 students at Poly every year, and I basically knew 48 of 'em, my lab buddies. How the HELL am I supposed to know some needle in a haystack guy out of nowhere? This always happens to me. If I knew everybody who ever went to Cal Poly, I'd be God. I need to come up with a smarter response than "Well, it's a big school, blahblahblah...." Got any ideas?

"...last night she slid down the side of the wall while feigning fatigue and rolled over a large lamp plug...." Huh? I don't get it. Do you live in a crooked apartment? And if I'm going to show up early for the Pictures d'Weeding, will there be coffee? Good coffee? Starbucks coffee? Excellent.

Ya know, maybe a certain restaurant owner did get hit by a bus. Or maybe he got accidentally buried by a big ol' pile of polyester shirts in his house. Or maybe he leered at somebody's wife one too many times and became a victim of domestic violence. I could see him here haunting our house. He's probably still pulling his "James Bond" routine and checking to see if I have any of the things I "borrowed" from Vanilla Stew. I better go and hide those cereal bowls. Can you believe it? Ten years later and I still have a bunch of bowls from that place -- along with my apron, souvenir T-shirt, a couple of plates, table and chairs....

Well, my friend, it's time once again to head to the Kathy Lee Gifford memorial sweatshop. I can't believe someone as wholesome as Kathy Lee would actually use sweatshops to produce her products. Why don't they ever raise a ruckus about "These drawings were prepared by severely overworked and grotesquely underpaid engineers and nobody should use these drawings to build anything until conditions are brought up to 1950s levels?" Maybe it just became my job to inform the public of this National Crisis, huh? In the meantime, have a Topflight Tuesday, won't you?

Certain Restaurant Owners suck, vacation anticipation RULES!!!!

-Forrest Gump Chacon

Chapter 23
The Beast Called Marriage

Date: Jul 9
To: Jeff
From: Anthony
Subject: Addition to the family

Can you imagine a combination opium den and Internet Cafe? "I hear you talking, but I can't see you. Can you see me? If I sent myself a message would I disappear?"

Very, very kind of you to offer to take back the tuxedoes, but I think we're all going to try and return them right after the wedding. The place closes at 6:30 and the reception is over at 4:00, so we'll have plenty of time to run them over. It might be worth bringing a change of clothes so you can do the same. You can just come over to the hotel with us afterwards, change, and we'll take the tuxedoes back. This is all contingent, of course, upon someone being able to drive. Perhaps I'll keep your generous offer in mind; but I hate to stick you with all the hassle. Since we're on the subject, Alden and I are currently taking orders for the Rehearsal Dinner. The Event will be held at Papachino's. You and The Great One have a choice of the following: lasagna, tortellini (with cream sauce or marinara), or chicken parmigiana. No big rush to decide, but I need to know by the 18th. So what are you guys going to do that Saturday night?

Way ahead of you on the subject of naming kids after heroes buddy. I've tossed the idea of little John Elway Reynoso around before, but Alden's ex-boyfriend's name is John, so forget it. However, we continue to refer to our future child as little Luc Robitaille Reynoso, in honor of my favorite hockey player. This one actually has kinda stuck, because now we're thinking Luc (or Luke) wouldn't be a bad middle name. Then, of course, there's always little Nicolas Cage Reynoso, little Helen Hunt Reynoso, and little Jeffrey Chacon Reynoso (he's the one who hates bagels, spills hot chocolate, brews his own formula, and constantly whacks himself in the head with his toy guitar).

Yes, I get the Cal Poly line of questioning, too. But you can't really blame these poor infidels, can you? We are, after all, members of a highly select group, and it's only natural that people want to know more about this wondrous kingdom within the enchanted city of San Luis Obispo. Cal Poly always sort of reminded me of Oz; people have heard that such a place exists, but they're not quite sure what it is. In California, Cal Poly gets some serious respect. Outside, however, people are kinda clueless, and I think it's best they remain so. The people I met when I lived in Colorado thought Cal Poly was the state parrot. Naturally, I get the "Hey, did you know blah, blah, blah...," but the other day, someone asked me about someone and, damned if I didn't know them after all. But the majority of the time, when I don't know the person in question, I just say, "Nah, don't know them. What was their major? Fish wifery? Oh, well, those guys were way over on the other side of campus."

Guess I didn't explain clearly: Lean with your back against a wall, bend your knees, and allow your back to slide down the wall until you're in a seated position on the floor. Now, do it again; only this time, find a wall outlet with something plugged into it and run your ass over the plug as you slide down the wall, this producing a thick red scrape on your butt. I never said this was the most intelligent thing she's ever done.

If I were a ghost and I really wanted to haunt you, I'd take the form of a big rat and I'd sit on top of your refrigerator at night, eating your Cheetos. Don't know what made me think of that rat, but I can still remember watching him grub those Cheetos while you stood there with that look of terror on your face.

My friend, I am afraid it is time for this wedding to commence, so that it will end. This "thing" we found one day, when it was just a cute little idea, has grown into an unclean entity that sucks the life out of everything it gets its evil claws into. Now I fear I must ride headlong into the belly of the beast and destroy it from within. Sure, I'll probably lose my life in the process, but I now have a new appreciation for the movie *Braveheart*. At the end when Mel's all tied down and they're skipping rope with his innards, he looks to the heavens and yells, "Freedom!" Powerful stuff. I know now that sacrifices must be made to escape the tyranny of an oppressing force. Therefore, I am now more than ready to relinquish the freedom I once cherished as a single male, in a country filled with beautiful women, for the opportunity to rid myself of this wedding. And don't kid yourself for one minute, I love Alden with every ounce of my existence; but I hate the wedding more. Again, I remind you, I'm saying "wedding" and not "marriage."

Boy, do I feel better. Sorry for the medieval epilogue, but I just had to rid myself of some steam. Now, however, the terrible wedding beast knows I hate it, and it will seek to make my life even more miserable. Do your best, unclean beast, for I am now numb to your power. You cannot hurt me anymore, because I have come to terms with my sacrifice. Man, does it feel good to be free. Oh yeah, like you didn't get a little punchy just before the big day. Anyway, have a good one and we'll talk again.

Evil wedding beasts suck, Cheetos rule. OUT!!

Sir Oinksalot

Date: Jul 9
To: The Groom!
From: Jeff
Subject: Attitude Adjustment Hour.

I get home from work, and fire up my computer as usual. At my new e-mail station, there are 6 messages waiting, perhaps a new record for a single day. So, I'm a little excited -- because an e-mail from you is always cause for celebration; it is one of the top reasons to go on living. And I expect that at least one of the six e-mails is from you. BUT NO. Four of them are from the new server Provider people; one is from Carol O'lsen, telling me she's gonna get hold of a P.A. for the gig; one from a friend of Julie's from Seattle. Let's see, that's six e-mails received, none from you. Disappointed, I head to the Sacred Couch to drown my sorrows in a rerun of *"The Simpsons"* and a hour-and-a-half nap, because I've been feeling extremely burned out all day. I awake to find The Great One finally coming home from her long day, and decide to check with the e-mail once again. Still nothing. Not a damn thing. Where is my e-mail? Where is my reason for living? I feel lost, angry, even a little worried. Then I wonder if maybe you forgot to change the address for "Jeffrey C. Chacon" on your computer! So, I spend a good while resetting my computer to go to the old stoned Provider and finally I am able to check the stoned e-mail. Sure enough, there you are. Now, I have to change again all of the settings on my computer to use the new e-mail service. This is a pain in me ass, my friend. So pleasepleaseplease CHANGE THE ADDRESS FOR "JEFFREY C. CHACON" ON YOUR COMPUTER!!!! Thanks. Don't mean to be harsh, but it really is a pain in me ass to have to check two different e-mail spots.

Taking back penguin costumes AFTER your wedding is not a good idea, trust me. Nossir, I don't like it. First of all, all you're gonna wanna do after the wedding, contrary to your own popular belief, is take a long nap. Second of all, all I'm gonna wanna do after the wedding, contrary to my own popular belief, is take a long nap. So, please, spare yourself the loathsome idea of having anything to do besides napping after the wedding, and allow me the luxury of returning the penguin suits to the igloo on Sunday. This will be MUCH easier than trying to coordinate the thing after the wedding Saturday, trust me. And l'Great One and I both will have the tortellini with cream sauce, your liver with some farva beans, and a nice Chianti, thanks for asking.

Ya know, it's true that Cal Poly does command some serious respect within the state of California. However, I have noticed, since moving to Colorado, that the entire state of California commands nil respect outside of itself. For example, our friend Tina thinks the entire state of California is packed wall-to-wall with people who are incredibly vain about what kind of cars they drive, how much they paid for their houses, how big their fake boobies are, and how white, I mean blonde, their hair is. I try and try and try to tell her "no, that's only Los Angeles," but since she's only seen Los Angeles and not San Luis Obispo or Northern California, she's not buying it. This attitude exists everywhere, and I really can't fight it; so I don't. Besides, if everybody knew how lovable and quaint and pristine and peaceful the Central Coast is, they'd all move there and turn it into Los Angeles North, which would ruin it for you and me. So, I don't bother fighting the myopia.

You had to bring up the rat, didn't you? You had to do it. I had almost forgotten about the monster rat, who was as big as a poodle. I had almost forgotten how I lay there at night, listening to him run back and forth across the living room carpet like he was in some kind of a rat road race; realizing I was glad it was you sleeping on the couch out in the living room and not me. I had almost forgotten how we tried to catch him with mousetraps that got bigger and bigger, until we realized it would take a mousetrap not invented yet to catch him, because he was just too damn brilliant for us. I had almost forgotten how we tried all kinds of different foods on the mousetraps, from peanut butter to cheese, all to no avail. I had almost forgotten how we finally resorted to filling up his entry hole behind the sink with an entire box of S.O.S. pads and sealed off the hole with spackle in order to never see him again. I had almost forgotten all of these things, but no. You had to bring it up. That rat ruled our lives for a good month or so, didn't he?

Okay, I'm almost done for today, but I have one more thing to throw out for you. I think you're going about this weeding thing all wrong, buddy. The only way to truly live the good life and enjoy this thing is to rise above it. While the wedding beast sucks the lifeblood out of everybody around you, it is your responsibility to not let this happen to *you*. Rise above, and enjoy yourself! Don't let everybody else's attitudes and perceptions color your view of the thing. Basically, it's just a party for your friends and family, so they may bring gifts (by the way, where are you registered?) and schlep down lots of food and beverage, all the while congratulating you on your decision to take the plunge and get hitched. It has very little to do with you. These are the things I explained to Julie last April, shortly before our own weeding. She took them to heart, and by May 6th, we were both loose and laughing and truly enjoying ourselves. No sacrifice of freedom here, nossir; and you shouldn't have to sacrifice either. Just because everybody else is being sucked dry by the evil wedding beast doesn't mean you have to be, does it? And, ya know, we scheduled the gig to help take your mind off the wedding. That worked tremendously well for me last year; I hope it's helping you. Concentrate on the song and dance, and the wedding will fall right into place. Rise up and slay the wedding beast; for its only desire is to make you miserable, and miserable you shall not be!

Have a well-groomed Wednesday, won't you?

Rats suck, new e-mail rules!!!

-Ben

Date: Jul 11
To: Jeff
From: Duke
Subject: Well EXCUUUUUUUSE me...

Yes, a mere nine days before my wedding and here I am getting yelled at and being made to feel guilty, even though I THOUGHT I HAD CHANGED THE FUCKIN' ADDRESS!! Look, I'm at a very emotional time right now, and if you can't see that, then maybe we need to rethink this little e-mail relationship of ours. I've got wedding responsibilities to dodge, honeymoons to plan, and I have to find out whether or not everyone wants a fuckin' dinner salad with their *pinche* chicken parmigiana. I am SORRY if you had to wake up from your nap and rewire your circuits so I could pop up on the screen and amuse you. And, because my computer took a big dump yesterday, I guess now you're really pissed because I didn't e-mail you. A piece o' meat, that's all I am to you!!. Just take me out of the fridge, shove a spit up my ass, and throw me on the fuckin' BBQ whenever you need satisfaction (although I can take heart in the fact that I'll probably cause you to burn more hair off your arms). Well, Mr. Jeffrey Chacon, may I remind you that I am not some sort of court jester at your majesty's beck and call. I am a human being and, as such, I have feelings and (sniff!) right now they're just a little pained. You...you...big BUTTHEAD!!

Boy, do I feel better. Look, sorry I got the wrong address on my last correspondence, but I really did think I had changed it. So, today, I've recopied your name in my address book with the new address; I'm hoping this solves the problem. If not, well I still seem to have a little bit of ass left, so you and Alden can split it. Also, as you can see, I am on-line again. I think my computer got a virus or something, because it was sicker than a dog yesterday.

Concur on your observations regarding outsiders' perceptions of California. When I was in Sacramento, Nebraska (population. 5, I shit you not) visiting some relatives of the ex, we were the subjects of conversation that night as people sat awestruck by the fact that we were from California. People seem to have the impressions that all Californians live a block from the beach, that all Californians surf, that we're all dope fiends, that we all go to Disneyland every weekend, and that there's an 8.3 earthquake every ten seconds. In fact, this is the only thing that keeps the entire United States of America from becoming the United Peoples of California -- the fact that they're scared to death of earthquakes. Never mind the fact that everyone else endures twenty tornadoes annually that rip the roofs off the barns.

WEDDING PARAGRAPH: Okay, I'll bear in mind that you can return the tuxes if need be. Thanks for your help. I have you guys down for two tortellinis with cream sauce, but I forgot to ask if you'd like a dinner salad. If so, what kind of dressing? Here is a list of jobs I do not wish to have: structural engineer, architect, biologist, lawyer, any job where I'd have to work in Los Angeles, and wedding coordinator. I'm slowly finding out that, to be a coordinator, I'd have to be a childcare specialist, psychologist, mathematician, engineer, communications expert, home economics major, secretary, lawyer, hit man, actor, guru, and caterer -- all at once. Yes, I can see the wisdom in your thinking, and I usually can ignore the roar of the great wedding beast, but sometimes it just gets difficult. I just hope it all turns out reasonably well, so Alden will be able to relax and enjoy the honeymoon. She's definitely the kind that dwells on anything that is anything less than perfect. So, I'm putting a lot of pressure on myself to make it right, but I think it'll be fine.

Since time is such a precious commodity these days, allow me a few moments to thank you for everything you've done and everything you will do in the future. This goes far beyond the scope of the wedding. From the most menial requests to the most imposing favors, you are one of the very few people I've ever known who's always answered the bell, without question or reservation; and you're the only one who's kept me laughing through it all. Believe me, that's meant a helluva lot at times. I mean realistically, a person can live life without friends like you, but why in the world would anyone want to? Without you, I would've missed about half the fun I've ever had in life. So thanks, Jeff. You're a great friend.

Thus, I shall bring this Thursday to a close. A little heavy on the sentiment, but I was afraid if I waited until I was drunk to say that, I'd cry, then I'd puke, then you'd be slapping me on the head while I stood over a sink, again. Not pretty. Anyway, enjoy the rest of the day, and tomorrow is Friday; and Fridays are good.

Anything less than perfect sucks, Jeff Chacon rules. OUT!!

Ardent admirer

Date: Jul 11
To: The Groom!
From: Jeff
Subject: Dangerously low levels of testosterone

In an ironic bit of poetic something or other, a spider (the one creature that causes The Great One to go into a girlish "killitkillitkillit" whine) just fell from the ceiling right into The Great One's broccoli, rendering the broccoli unfit for The Great One's consumption and sending her screaming out into the streets of the West Highlands neighborhood.

Dinner salad, *sí*. Emotions running wild, no. What up with you? A little too much hanging around the mother of the bride-to-be, I imagine. She's messing with your mind, bro. You remind me of a couple of my former girlfriends, when they were in a drunken rage: "Jeff, I love you. I HATE YOU!! I really really really love you. I FUCKING HATE YOUR GUTS, YOU PIECE OF SHIT ANTI-CHRIST!! Oh, Jeff, will you marry me? Tomorrow? YOU SPINELESS, GUTLESS, CLUELESS PIECE OF HUMAN REFUSE, WHAT THE HELL DID I EVER SEE IN YOU?" And so on and so on. How did I keep ending up with those kinds of women? Thank goodness for The Great One. Remember, dude, on July 21, none of the napkin colors, none of the dinner salads, none of the songs will matter. You'll be *married*, and the wedding beast will be far far away, chewing on some other poor soul's gristle. (Wow. There's a word.)

Your "friendly" words are too kind. It takes two to tango, brother. Believe me, there are a heck of a lot of people on this earth, and a heck of a lot of people who eventually cross the desk of my life. But there are very few who are actually worth hanging on to as lifelong friends, and you are him. I wouldn't be a great friend if you weren't such *un amigo que bueno tambien*. (That's a great example of the inherent difficulty of being a male in this society and expressing true feelings; instead of saying it straight out, I hid it behind a foreign language.) And because true friends are so few and far between, they mean a lot to me. Thus, I will go to the corners of the earth to help them in any way I can. So, can I take the tuxes back, or what?

You know, our relationship wouldn't have lasted as long as it has if it weren't for the humor. You are the only person I know (well, The Great One is quickly catching on) who understands and appreciates my humor -- virtually all of the time. And I completely and overwhelmingly enjoy your humor as well. When we started this e-mail thing, I thought to myself, "Self, this will be great. Anthony has always written the best letters, and now you can maybe get him to write more often on his computer." Never ever ever did I think we would do this just about every day. And never in my wildest dreams did I think it would come to mean so much in my life. E-mail as brought a new outlook on life. It's made me look for the humor in everyday mundane things -- like architecture, barbecuing, tennis, broccoli. Now that I think about it, that's the greatest value of this. The fact that I am looking for humor (and taking notes) in virtually every situation I encounter. Makes me feel alive. I sit at home every night (except Fridays and Saturdays, of course) writing my observations and thoughts and responding to your observations and thoughts. Man, it makes me feel alive! You are like the brother I always wished I had, a brother who understands me, thinks like me, and inspires me to take up acting (if only for a short while). For all of these things, I thank you, dude. And you know what? I'm gonna miss you the next couple of weeks. I realize you'll be in Hawaii and I'll be somewhere in California sitting on a beach -- but I'll miss you. Maybe I'll take lots of notes of lots of ideas and be completely ready to start it all back up when you return. Although maybe now it'll have to be "A Couple Of Married Guys Sitting Around Talking," which is okay., because we'll be A Couple Of Married *Smartass* Guys if anything.

Enough of the mushy crap. I need to go watch a hockey game or something. I feel the testosterone oozing out of my body as I speak; I'm going to need to replenish it soon or else, tomorrow at work, Jeff, the Nice Structural Engineer, will be saying things like, "Hey, boss, I love you, man. Mister Architect, I know we've had our differences, but I love you, man." SOMEBODY GET ME SOME TESTOSTERONE!!!!

With all of that said, I must depart -- to go and do some more work. Not to bore you with the gory details, but every time Boss #2 walks into my cubicle, he says, "Oh, we got another project for you to do, Jeff." This is getting more and more ridiculous by the minute; but we'll talk about that in a couple of weeks, after we've all sat on a beach for a week or four. Have a great weekend, my brother (WHERE'S THAT TESTOSTERONE, GODDAMMIT!!!!) and I'll see you Thursday. Oh, wait, some details: Ranch dressing for myself, Italian for The Great One; plane lands Wednesday night late; staying at l'Parents d'Great One; no plans Thursday except to rest for the gig; all yours Friday; all yours Saturday; everything else is up in the air, except I know it involves a LOT of relaxing.

But first, I would like to offer up my predictions for the future: Wednesday, your body will begin to sweat and shake from the Stage Fright Zoo. Thursday, you will break into tremors and accidentally hit your obnoxious co-worker in the head with a beaker, sending him to the hospital. Thursday night, the gig will go down as the Greatest Rock-n-Roll Show in San Diego history, and six or seven hundred members of the listening audience will ask you for your autograph, which will make Arturo extremely happy and Alden extremely jealous; at which point, she will "ground" you, even though at one point in that same evening she will autograph at least one buttcheek of an 18-year-old nearly-naked hunk, while holding four single dollar bills in her mouth, to be retrieved by the 19-year-old nearly-naked hunk standing over her. Friday, I will organize a raid on your apartment, in order to rescue you from the "grounding," at which point we will head to your local tennis court to begin Grudge Match 2. I will take the first set, 6-4; you will take the second set 6-4; and we will get to 4-4 in the third set, before realizing that war is good for nothing, lay down our racquets, and declare a draw. (PLEEEEEEEEEEEEAAAAAAAAAAASSSSEEEEEEEEEE GET ME SOME TESTOSTERONE!!!!!!!!!!!!) We then will head down to the Chicken Pie Shop, where we will scarf on yummy chicken pot pies, mashed taters, and vegetables d'jour. With our bellys full, we will head to a park or beach, where we will sit and contemplate life and all of its travails. (AAARRRGGGGGGGGGGHHHHHH!!!!! WHERE THE HELL IS THAT TESTOSTERONNNNNNEEEEE!!!!!!) That night, we all will partake of dinner salads and Italian food, all the while feeling the energy and the buzz of the room as everybody is a little giddy about the next day's events. Friday night, you won't get much sleep, if any. The excitement, the anticipation, the nerves will be too much. You will lay there all night, thinking about what you are about to do. Thinking that it will be good. Thinking that nothing could be more right. Saturday, the pictures will be taken, the donuts will be eaten, the coffee (Starbucks or nothing, pal) will be drunken, and the guests will be showin' upin. "Do you, Anth, take this Pookie, to be your....." You will pull off a Jeff move and try to get off of the stage as soon as possible, forgetting to kiss your bride. You will get tired of saying, "Thanks for coming." You will get tired of saying, "A thousand dollars? For me? Thanks!!!" We all will head to the reception, where much food and beverage will be consumed; although none of it by you, because you'll be much too busy "mingling" to partake of any of it -- until I come to your rescue and insist to your New Bride that your biological genius, and only yours, is needed in the bar or else the whole place will have to be shut down, because of some biological malfunction that only you can fix. And only I can be there to assist you in the solving of the biological malfunction. You and I will sit alone at the bar, drinking a beer, reflecting on our relationship and your wedding, saying things like "I love you, man." (OOHHHH SHITTTT!!!! HE'S REALLY LOSING IT NOW!!!!!!!! PLEASEPLEASEPLEASE GET THAT BOY SOME TESTOSTERONE!!!!!!!!) Soon, The Missus will come in, we all will hug, (AAAARRRRRGHHHHH!!), and you will have to go, out into the party and into the world, leaving me alone with just The Great One. I will be sad, if only for a moment. (SOMEBODY GET THAT BOY SOME GODDAMN TESTOSTERONE!!!! HE'S BREAKING UP!!! HE'S BREAKING UP!!!!) Then, my shipment of testosterone will arrive at the reception and I will return to normal. There will be much partying and orgying on into the night. The next day, you and Alden will begin your splendid life together by getting on a plane to Hawaii; and The Great One and I will head to Morro Bay to re-live our own honeymoon. We all will live happily ever after.

The end.

Date: Jul 12
To: Jeff
From: Duke
Subject: Noche de los Mexicans

Look, I'll hook you up an IV to my own testicles IF YOU'LL JUST SHUT UP!! No more kind words for you. You turn into this spineless mass of oozing, festering, floral compost. Look, should you happen to luck out and take one set 6-4, then the boat rights itself and I take the next one 6-4, there will be no 4-4 in the third. 6-0 buddy! I'm gonna make you my girlfriend. Then we will eat Chicken Pie Shop because it's the cure-all, perfect for celebrating a victory and soothing the feet...I mean DEFEAT. Truth be known, there's really only one thing I'm nervous about to this point -- the gig. I guess I really shouldn't be nervous about it, because I know it's gonna be a lot of fun, but the problem is you guys sounded great last year and I'm just hoping I don't bring you down. Practice, practice, practice!!

I happen to be extremely exhausted this morning and I attribute this to *tres pinche* guys who decided to sit in their car and drink *muchas cervezas* at *tres* o'saka *en la mañana*. *Problema* with this is that the car was parked on the street just outside my window and *los tres pinche* guys got real *stupido* and were making more noise than a *mariachi* band at Cinco de Mayo. Naturally, I didn't want to call *la policía* on *los tres pinche* guys, so I tried to sleep through it; then, just as I reached the point where I was ready to call the cops, they dispersed. All the while, my *gringa mujer* was going, "Your people. Your people." Yeah well, at least "my people" are being honored at *El Stadium de los Dodgers* on Sunday night. *Sí sí,* Sunday night is Hispanic Family Night at Dodger Stadium. (An aside here. I wonder if e-mail is starting to rule my life, because after Vin Scully made the announcement, the first thing I did was laugh; the second one was think, "Hey, e-mail tomorrow!") Imagine this, if you will. "Buenos tardes everyone, this is Vicente Scully and tonight it's the Los Angeles Dodgers versus los Grandes de San Francisco. Tonight's game is being sponsored by Farmer Juan, maker of 'los perros de Dodgers' and by Jack en la Box. Para los Dodgers. Pitching, Ramon Martinez. Catching, Mike Pinata. First base, Eric Churros..." Hispanic Family Night? Aye, aye, aye.

I applaud The Great One's courage. If a spider fell into my broccoli, I think I'd die on the spot. At least she had the stones to get up and go screaming into the night. It's a good thing it was a rat on the fridge that night and not a tarantula, or you would've been sharing your bed with one frightened patron of Hispanic Family Night. I fuckin' hate spiders. This I, actually attribute to my grandmother. Now, don't get me wrong, my grandmother is a beautiful, wonderful woman, but sometimes she just says the wrong thing, like the night when I was six and had the hiccups really bad. My aunt was doing everything she could to get rid of the hiccups but nothing was working, so my grandmother yells in a blood-curdling voice, "Mijo, there's a big spider on your back!" The resultant hysteria was comparable to a European soccer match. I mean she's my grandmother, right? She wouldn't bullshit me. And judging by the shrillness of her voice, I estimated the spider to be around 25 pounds. So, I screamed bloody murder, blasted out of the house, dived to the ground, and started rolling in the dirt -- like Jeff on BBQ night. Got rid of the hiccups, but to this day I hate spiders. And I don't necessarily believe everything my grandmother says either.

I didn't realize this will be the last correspondence for a while and my last one as a single guy. As such, perhaps I should mark this occasion with some singular words of wisdom. Nah, it's not necessary. Perhaps some things in my life will now change (I'm guessing for the better), but I don't expect anything drastic. I'm going to miss the opportunity to engage in witty dialogue with you over the next couple of weeks, but it'll be here when I get back. Perhaps it'll be good to get away from the daily task of trying to match your entertaining, provocative, and hilarious messages. For me, it's always a challenge to try and hang with your creativity and absurdity; I think it helps me keep a necessary edge on life. I'm also reminded to look for the humor in life and, when I can't find it, make it up. This may not be on the same level as oxygen, but it keeps me alive in a different way and I suspect it will become more important in later years. So, I'm going to recharge my battery now, and when I return, I will be ready to be the Hobbes to your Calvin, the Moe to your Curly, and the Felix to your Oscar. Thanks for the opportunity to spar with you on a daily basis. See you soon.

Spiders suck, e-mail rules. OUT!!

The Groom